How George Washington Fleeced the Nation

HOW GEORGE WASHINGTON FLEECED THE NATION

... and other little secrets airbrushed from history

Phil Mason

A HERMAN GRAF BOOK
SKYHORSE PUBLISHING

Skyhorse Publishing books may be purchased in bulk at special discounts for sales promotion, corporate gifts, fund-raising, or educational purposes. Special editions can also be created to specifications. For details, contact the Special Sales Department, Skyhorse Publishing, 555 Eighth Avenue, Suite 903, New York, NY 10018 or info@skyhorsepublishing.com.

www.skyhorsepublishing.com

10 9 8 7 6 5 4 3 2 1

Library of Congress Cataloging-in-Publication Data

Mason, Phil, 1958-
  How George Washington fleeced the nation : and other little secrets airbrushed from history / Phil Mason.
      p. cm.
  "A Herman Graf Book."
  Includes index.
  ISBN 978-1-61608-075-4 (hardcover : alk. paper)
  1. History--Errors, inventions, etc. 2. Common fallacies. 3. History--Anecdotes. 4. History--Miscellanea. 5. Civilization--Miscellanea.
I. Title.
  D10.M384 2010
  902--dc22

                                    2010020529

Printed in the United States of America

Contents

For Phillip – who finds history difficult enough already.
Here's some unlearning to do. Sorry, son.

Introduction

This book is about the history you are not meant to know. Contained within these covers is some of the grit that has been systematically removed from the wheels of history to ensure that the telling of our past runs smoothly.

In *How George Washington Fleeced the Nation* you will discover a side of history that is not the one your teacher taught you at school, not the one that forms the common construct of history that you are likely to recognise. It is history, but not as you know it.

There will be revelations. Things you never knew you never knew about some of the greatest figures (and a few events) of history. Characters (and characteristics) that have been cemented in time – by omission, commission or cover up – turn out to have unexpected sides. By the end, and forever more, you will look upon some of the most familiar staples of history with a very different eye.

Some of the most renowned reputations take on an entirely new hue in these pages, as – if we were to give any time to think about the matter – they naturally should. For what is history? It is, literally, a story – a collection of facts woven together to create a meaningful account of events before our own time. Not any old facts thrown together in any old weave. The facts are threaded to tell a deliberate story.

But facts are awkward things. Some flow in the direction we want, but some do not, especially with people. The people who stand out in our telling of history do so because of their own achievements and, sometimes too, because they encapsulate by their existence a wider meaning of a past period. Down the ages, we extol these famous forebears, endowing them with importance, holding them in our collective memory as embodiments of sentiments we cherish as a culture and perhaps want current and future generations to emulate – bravery, selflessness, leadership, integrity, duty, wisdom, innovation . . . and endless others.

So when the facts pull in different directions, it presents a problem to neat and compelling storytelling. Our historical icons *were* real people, with all the foibles of humanity. They had secrets, dark sides, aspects that aren't quite a 'fit' for the position we want to place them. So what happens?

Simple. The elements that support the narrative we need tend to be kept, enhanced (sometimes even invented) and the less helpful, contrary ones, get lost, buried, smothered. In that way, the picture of history that we get taught as children and which we hand down from generation to generation is clear and straightforward, easy to understand – and all too often also an artifice: rarely wholly untrue, but mostly not the whole truth either.

Just like the uneven stones tumbling around in a gem polisher's machine, or the first rough shot at the mercy of the photographer's airbrush, the unsuitable edges get smoothed away. Over time, the 'image' gets created – the refined, uncomplicated picture that we all agree upon, the one our society, through its teachers, bequeaths on to future generations. Down the years, decades, centuries, the agreed image becomes reality. The story makes sense. History can be told.

'Fixing' history, in both senses of the word – settling on an agreed version and its frequent manipulation – is a timeworn process. It is rarely a deliberate act by malevolent historians out to distort the truth. It's a lot more subtle and anonymous than that. The practice usually unfolds unconsciously as a shared enterprise of a whole society, surreptitiously creating for itself an account of the past that it feels comfortable with, that serves some present or subconsciously perceived deeper need.

How George Washington Fleeced the Nation puts back the bits that history has taken away. It rattles the skeletons that have been hidden in the cupboard, and ruffles the smooth, neatly pressed images our standard history hands down.

The tale is indeed grittier, with shocks and surprises, secrets and subterfuges that will change forever the way you think about those you had been taught to know so well. How George Washington, America's 'father of the nation' was far from the selfless servant he is now portrayed; how Admiral Nelson was literally a self-made hero, and a bit of a fraudster too; how Julius Caesar may have been less the victim history has made him out to be; and how the modern Olympic Games were reinvented for very different sentiments to the ones the movement would now have us believe.

We will show how the lives of British Prime Ministers and American Presidents have had their hidden sides, largely now unknown today, and certainly hidden from the electors at the time: the premier who, in three months, wrote 151 love letters while he was meant to be chairing the Cabinet; the PM who spent almost all his premiership hiding away at home in a state of psychotic depression; the PM who started life as a financial fraudster, and the PM who was a serial adulterer, even while in office; the one who was an aficionado of the paranormal, and the one who was so forgetful of faces that he failed to recognise one of his Cabinet members who had been serving him for 10 years.

Then there is the President who preferred to conduct business while sitting on the toilet; Abraham Lincoln, renowned as 'the Great Emancipator', who was actually an open and articulate advocate of slavery; and the President who authored the Declaration of Independence ('all men are created equal') who was himself an owner of 83 slaves. We see how the wartime encounter which allowed John F. Kennedy to save his patrol boat crew – and cast for himself lasting folk hero status – was largely due to his own folly. And how, in the darkest days of the Cold War, as he led America's response to the Cuban Missile Crisis, he was dosed up by a quack medical adviser with a daily cocktail of eight drugs, some of them strongly hallucinogenic.

We range widely through the worlds of art, music and poetry, and see how many of the finest talents history has produced became so largely through the ill-fortune of mental and physical disorders. How some of the best regarded painters in history used a clever but simple cheat to create their masterpieces. How Enid Blyton, Walt Disney and Charlie Chaplin, pioneers of some of the most innocent and beloved literary and film creations, had deeply unpleasant sides to their characters that have been dutifully swept aside. We show how war, how we fight it and how we remember it, throws up all sorts of opportunities for historical amnesia and manoeuvring.

If, like most, you thought that history was something that was somehow 'out there', separated from our reach, objective, a given, in the past and therefore by definition unchanging and unchangeable, *How George Washington Fleeced the Nation* will help to convince you otherwise. It challenges the simple (but admittedly sometimes comforting) view that the history we believe in is always the truth. Not so. We've moulded it and shaped it ourselves, often for a purpose.

Mark Twain called history 'fluid prejudice', and Napoleon thought it 'a set of lies agreed upon'. They both knew well the power of words and history – and of humanity's capacity, and need, to distort them. They challenged accepted norms. So do we.

Whatever you thought you knew – prepare to think again. And then wonder further at what else in the past you thought was true that now may not be.

Phil Mason

1

History's Heroes – Hits or Myths?

History has granted some individuals heroic status for their achievements and influence on the world. The characters that have been passed down to us by our forebears are, however, not quite what they seem. This chapter looks at some of our most revered figures, but from a perspective that your teacher is unlikely to have told you about.

SANTA CLAUS – THE REAL THING?

While **Father Christmas**, the Western world's most iconic figure of childhood, has a genuine religious pedigree, the image we carry today of the yuletide deliverer has a darker and less saintly origin: Coca-Cola. The archetypal Santa Claus that epitomises Christmas for us is, in fact, the invention of an advertising campaign. And still more unexpectedly, it was as recent as 1931.

The patron saint of children, 4th-century martyr St Nicholas became associated with gift giving as long ago as the 12th century. His feast day – 6 December – gradually superseded the traditional pagan practice of exchanging presents at the year's end festival of Saturnalia. So far, so good. But for all the generations of children who have ever wished for Santa's call, it is only the last three or four who have conjured up the visage of the rotund, bearded old man clad in a red tunic, trimmed with fur and topped off with a bobble-tailed hood.

Very Different Beginnings

Until the mid-Victorians, the image of Santa was very different. The figure was not universally portrayed in red. His suit was more often green, or simply entirely comprising animal furs. In an American depiction of 1858, he does not even have a beard. There was no association with a reindeer-driven sleigh. It was America that was to mould the image towards our present one. Its penchant, first for PR and then for commercial exploitation, brought the image into modern focus, starting with the Civil War.

The earliest modern depiction of Father Christmas, by illustrator Thomas Nast, appeared in the January 1863 edition of *Harper's Weekly* ('A Journal of Civilization') showing a patriotic Santa clad in the Stars and Stripes, perched on a sleigh pulled by reindeers and dispensing gifts to Union soldiers.

By the 1880s, commercial US greetings cards were standardising the full, round figure clad in red. But the polished image of today – jolly, red-cheeked face, flowing white beard, bright red suit, black belt and boots and the fur-edged nightcap hat – finally appeared in Coca-Cola's 1931 campaign to promote its soft drink. It was painted by a 32-year-old advertising artist and immigrant from Sweden, Haddon Sundblom, who had been on the Coca-Cola account since 1924. By the 1940s, he alone was producing half of the company's entire advertising art. Sundblom fixed on the red and white scheme simply because it was already Coke's house colours.

Commerce Dictates Design

The 1931 campaign, which has left its indelible cultural impact, was motivated by two very down-to-earth considerations. First, the reason for having a campaign at all was to try for a gear change in people's perception of the drink, to persuade consumers to drink Coke all year round and not just in summer. Hence the campaign being launched at the height of winter, an advertising pitch that must have seemed rather off key to a company marketing a cooling beverage. Second, they picked the Santa character because the campaign was unashamedly targeted at increasing sales to children – and at the time it was actually illegal to show children themselves drinking the stuff because of the cocaine derivatives which used to be part of the drink's recipe.

So from these two very practical and self-interested commercial motivations, our modern view of Santa Claus derives. In view of the commercialisation of Christmas itself over the last decades, it might seem all too appropriate to discover these less than pious origins to the figure that is the very personification of it all.

ROBIN HOOD – YOUNGER THAN YOU THINK

Another example of a cultural icon commonly believed to have a far longer pedigree than in fact they enjoy is **Robin Hood**. Unravelling his true history has exercised the talents of a steady stream of historians down the centuries. Modern research over the last 30 years has shown that almost every facet of the story that we think we are familiar with turns out to have been added after the tale first appeared, and sometimes surprisingly recently.

The earliest written reference to the existence of Robin Hood comes from William Langland's *Piers Plowman*, which is thought to have been completed around 1387. It is simply a passing mention and appears to be referring to already well-known stories about the character. The first piece of false memory is our traditional view that Robin Hood takes up his fight in the 1190s against authority in the shape of John, governing England while his brother Richard I, the Lionheart, is away at the Crusades. The earliest stories of Robin Hood in fact place him no earlier than the reigns of the early Edwards, between 1272 and 1377, around a hundred years later.

Late Additions

According to what has come to be regarded as the definitive work on Robin Hood, published in 1982 by James Holt, Professor of Medieval History at Cambridge, the first reference to Robin being 'a good man' does not come for another half century after *Piers Plowman*, by a sheriff clerk writing in 1432. The idea that Robin Hood was a nobleman (supposedly the rightful Earl of Huntingdon) temporarily down on his fortunes did not appear until the first half of the next century, and Maid Marian did not join the tale until after 1500.

Perhaps the most unexpected discovery relates to the bit about Robin Hood that we are likely to think we know the best. Surprisingly, in the early telling of the tales Robin Hood's fame comes from his bravado in flouting authority, not his acts of banditry. That he stole from the rich to give to the poor only starts to feature in the 16th and 17th centuries, and the perfection of the formula as Robin's defining purpose, believe it or not, was inserted in Victorian times.

AN INVENTED CRIMINAL HERO

'Gentleman highwayman' **Dick Turpin** enjoyed a reputation not dissimilar to Robin Hood's for much of the 18th and 19th centuries. Romanticised by legend and music-hall ballads, his claim to fame came from his daring 15-hour ride from London to York on Black Bess to give himself an alibi against a crime for which he risked arrest. Harrison Ainsworth, long forgotten now but a hugely successful Victorian author, is largely responsible for cementing this image of Turpin into the popular mind through a successful novel published in 1834. The trouble was that he attributed to Turpin the antics of someone else.

Historians are now satisfied that the ride to York was completed by a Pontefract highwayman, John Nevison, who lived 50 years before Turpin. It is far from clear how Ainsworth came to do this, whether by accident or literary licence to embellish his story. The bit about

Black Bess dying exhausted having delivered her master to his destination was entirely made up by Ainsworth.

Turpin, who did end his days in York, being hanged there in 1739, is more accurately described as 'a squalid little horse thief'.

King Arthur – a Welsh Nationalist PR Operation?

Academic research in the 1990s into the emergence of **King Arthur** as a historical figure presented a radical new twist on the origins of the Camelot legend. Whether he and his associates ever actually existed has always been a source of controversy. Few pieces of evidence have been found that could substantiate any facts. But that has always been put down to the simple passage of time. The new findings of medieval historian John Gillingham in 1992 put a different, and more earthly, complexion on the tale. He maintained the evidence showed that King Arthur was largely invented as a Welsh heroic figure to serve as a public relations boost to the nation at a time when the Celtic margins of Britain were coming to be seen as barbarians by 12th century English Kings. Far from Arthur being a historical character simply suffering from poor provenance, or a fantasy figure like Robin Hood born of centuries of word-of-mouth storytelling, he was more a deliberate fabrication for a clear political purpose.

Arthur Emerges in Troubled Times

Although there are sparse references to the name of Arthur in earlier Welsh chronicles, the dating of Arthur's first detailed appearance, in Geoffrey de Monmouth's *History of the Kings of Britain* in 1139, is held to be significant. The politics of the day, Gillingham asserted, were moving inexorably against the fortunes of the Scots, Welsh and Irish. English monarchs had long tended to regard their border populations as equals in religious, cultural and social terms. That changed with the Norman invasion in 1066, and as the reach of new regime spread, impressions changed. From 1125 onwards, the record shows a distinct antipathy growing for the Welsh for the first time. They were increasingly portrayed as uncultured outcasts.

The work of Geoffrey de Monmouth, a Welshman, was, in Gillingham's contention, a response to this development. It presented Arthur as a refined descendant of an eminent royal lineage tracing its roots back to the founders of Rome. It showed him as King of all Britain (and Ireland, Norway, Iceland and parts of Gaul) successfully uniting the country and defeating the Saxons in the 6th century. The chivalric exploits of his Round Table and his own wise leadership were intended to show there were civilising threads running through the Welsh nation.

Emerging on the back of the Welsh success in the 'great revolt' of 1136–8, which had seen the Welsh defeat English armies twice and recover large tracts of land, the existence of Arthur as an historical anchor for the Welsh could be seen as a timely bolstering of the Welsh image. It was canny politics, if questionable history – and we have been befuddled by it ever since.

A Nation's Defining Moment – a Scottish Spin Story

Scotland's **Robert the Bruce** undoubtedly existed, and his defeat of the English at Bannockburn in 1314 is one of the central icons of Scottish nationhood. His inspiration, which schoolchildren have learned for generations as a spur to determination – the struggling spider which tried, tried, and tried again, before climbing up its web – emerged in 1996 to have been a historical spin story, woven by that 18th century purveyor of 'good stories', Sir Walter Scott.

It had always troubled historians of Bruce's exploits that such a pivotal moment in his fortunes had never been mentioned in near contemporary accounts of his life. The first, an epic poem written by John Barbour around 1375, less than 50 years after Bruce's death, did not refer to it, nor did John Fordun writing in 1383 in what is regarded as the first complete chronicle of Scotland's history.

Real Origins Discovered

The document that was publicly displayed for the first time at the Scottish Record Office in June 1996 showed that the spider story, which first entered the public psyche in Scott's *Tales of a Grandfather* series published between 1827 and 1829, was actually based on a family history of Bruce's general, Sir James Douglas, written 200 years earlier by one Hume of Godscroft. According to this, it was Sir James who told Bruce of having witnessed the spider's travails, using the story to encourage his flagging chief to action. In the version told by Sir James, he saw the spider succeed only on its 13th attempt. He is recorded as urging his King, 'My advise is to follow the example of the spider, to poush forward your Majestie's fortune once more, and hazard yet our persones the thirteen tyme.' (Whether Sir James actually saw an event of this kind or whether it was invented to stiffen the backbone of an indecisive leader will forever remain unclear.)

Scott picked up the anecdote and transferred it to Bruce himself, and a popular and inspiring image from history was forged. Historians commented that at the time Scott was writing, in the midst of the Romantic movement, there was a strong impetus in literature, of which Scott was perhaps the greatest exponent, for creating a heroic picture of Scotland's past 'to help them flourish in the Union as proud partner rather than sullen satellite'. An academic expert on Bruce observed that 'the Victorians weren't troubled about whether Scott attributed his sources. It is a bit like Hollywood scriptwriters today.'

THE GREATEST DECEPTION IN HISTORY
THAT BECAME THE GREATEST OWN GOAL

Christopher Columbus is, in equal measure, renowned or reviled depending on one's view of the consequences of his opening up of the New World to European discovery. Leaving aside the age-old disputes about whether he actually was the first to truly 'discover' America (there are claims for at least a dozen others from the Phoenicians, Romans and Chinese through the Vikings to Poles, Scots, Welsh and Irish adventurers), the supposed reasoning behind Columbus's endeavour has been pretty well accepted – that he was hired by the Spanish royal court to advance the worldwide interests of the Spanish Empire. That story is the standard narrative of 15th century exploration. Until recently, that is.

In 1991, a Portuguese scholar suggested an intriguing alternative explanation to Columbus's mission, and indeed his personal origins. Augusto Mascarenhas Barreto set out a case for believing that, far from being the offspring of a humble Genoan wool weaver, Columbus was in fact the illegitimate son of a Portuguese prince, and was sent to Spain as the secret weapon of the King of Portugal.

A Mission to Distract

Barreto had spent 20 years researching the genealogies of the Portuguese royal family. He claimed also to have uncovered documents signed by Columbus implicating himself in the plot. Under Barreto's theory, Columbus was the son of Prince Fernando, nephew of the Portuguese King John II. Having undergone navigation training at the famous school established by Portuguese hero, Henry the Navigator, he was despatched to Spain in a classic deception operation to drive a stake at the heart of Portugal's greatest rival.

Columbus's mission was to divert the Spanish court's attention away from what was surmised to be the only viable sea route to the Indies, around the southern tip of Africa. The Portuguese King had commissioned an expedition to explore the route in 1486 and Bartholomew Diaz duly confirmed it in 1488, just four years before Columbus's famous voyage to the Americas. They were intent on keeping this route, and the fabulous wealth that was known to be at the far end of it, secret as long as possible.

Added weight was lent to the theory, Barreto claimed, by looking at the dates of the two enterprises. Columbus had his first audience before the Spanish court in May 1486, just a few months before the Diaz mission set off. Countless historians' bafflement about how a supposedly humble and unconnected commoner so readily gained access to a royal court is now more easily understood. Columbus would have been carefully insinuated into the royal circle with the help of Portugal's diplomatic representatives.

The devious ruse was intended to persuade Spain to waste its time, money and energies looking in the wrong direction for a way to the Indies. It did not, of course, quite turn out that way. In the ultimate of historical ironies, the Spanish discovery of the New World and the even greater material wealth returned by the Conquistadors, propelled Spain into becoming the world's first true global power which, within a century, had eclipsed its neighbour to such an extent that Philip II of Spain had invaded and occupied Portugal and taken over the crown for himself.

If Barreto's claims are true, the Portuguese deception plan would rank as one of history's greatest own goals. And Columbus's reputation would look very different to the one with which we have always been familiar.

POLO MINCED

Exploration in the other direction has also suffered a recent dent. In 1995, the Head of the Chinese section of the august British Library published her conclusions that **Marco Polo**, famed as the 13th-century European discoverer of China, probably never actually made the trip.

Polo's write-up of his 22-year journey published in 1298 became an instant best-seller. It told how he and his father journeyed across central Asia and spent 17 years in the previously unknown civilisation as ambassador at the court of Kublai Khan. His descriptions of life in China convinced Europeans he had discovered a new world. Dr

Frances Wood's researches into Chinese archives raised another prospect: that Polo made it all up from other travellers' tales.

Dubious Origins

Polo's book is already known to have been ghost-written (Polo only wrote it when he found himself in jail in Genoa and happened to have as a cell mate a writer of romances who persuaded him to dictate his story). Wood's evidence – or rather absence of evidence that ought to have been there – strongly suggests that Polo's amanuensis took some literary liberties in embellishing the story, probably by plagiarising existing Arabian and Persian guidebooks.

Wood pointed out that despite supposedly being in China for nearly two decades, Polo never mentions the Great Wall of China, an astonishing omission for an enquiring traveller. Although he recorded visits to tea-growing areas, he provided no accounts of the elaborate tea-drinking ceremonies for which Chinese custom is famed. He mentions nothing about the language being in pictogram form, or the strange custom of foot binding for women, which was a cultural anomaly that no long-term visitor could reasonably have failed to notice or pass comment on.

The Chinese archives are replete with references to the many visits by named foreigners at the Khan court, but none in fact mention Polo. Indeed, there are no records of any visit by Italians.

Couple these mystifying lapses with knowledge of the origins of the writing of the book, and a rather more earthly image emerges. Urged on by a cell mate who could spot a commercial opportunity, what may have been a sojourn to the well-trod margins of the known world – Dr Wood suspects Polo himself never made it further than Persia – was turned into a successful travelogue built on the second-hand reports from the 'front line'.

A MAN FAR FROM TRUE TO HIS WORD

Thomas Jefferson is rightly remembered by history as the man who put into words the sentiments that drove the 13 colonies of North America to break their bonds with Britain and establish themselves as a separate nation, basing their self-Government on certain (and 'self-evident') principles, chief among these being that 'all men are created equal'. Author of the Declaration of Independence in 1776, and third President between 1801 and 1809, Jefferson's clarion call for equality was the thread that ran through the separation with Britain and the founding of the new republic. But despite the elegant prose and stirring phraseology of Jefferson the communicator, Jefferson the man was a rather lesser commodity.

A SECRET LIFE

Even at the time he was writing the Declaration with its glowing phrases about human equality, he was himself a slave owner – he owned 83 on his Monticello estate in Virginia – while maintaining his public posture against slavery.

When his beloved wife Martha died at the early age of 33, worn out after giving Jefferson six children in the 10 years of their married life, Jefferson took up a relationship with one of his mulatto slaves, Sally Hemings (in fact a half-sister to Martha, the product of an illicit affair between Martha's father and one of his slaves).

Hemings also bore six children, two of whom died in infancy. Visitors to Monticello are said to have remarked that the resemblance between Jefferson and one of his slaves was so strong that it was impossible to tell them apart from a distance. The relationship was denied throughout his life (rumours were published in the papers while Jefferson was President which damaged him politically) and, while suspicions remained, were officially unfounded for more than 170 years after his death.

Modern Confirmations

In 1998, with the advent of modern DNA technology, historians began to test descendants of Jefferson and Hemings to try to settle the matter. In January 2000, the President of the Jefferson Memorial Foundation announced that a panel of distinguished historians brought together the weigh up all the evidence – DNA, original documents, oral accounts and statistical data – had concluded that Jefferson was almost certainly the father of one of the Hemings children, and conceded that he may have been the father of all six. As well as the DNA results, one of the most important pieces of the jigsaw was the fact that the dates of conception of all six children coincided with times that Jefferson was known to be at Monticello.

Jefferson maintained the relationship with Sally Hemings for the rest of his life until his death, nearly 40 years after their liaison began.

Reality and the Legend at Odds

In later life, Jefferson did come to view slavery as doomed, but his conversion to the spirit of his Declaration was never substantial. In his *Notes on Virginia*, written in 1785, he made clear his attitude to Negroes: 'They secrete less by the kidneys and more by the glands of the skin, which gives them a very strong and disagreeable odour . . . They are more ardent after their female, but love seems to them to be more an eager desire than a tender delicate mixture of sentiment and sensation.' They had 'a disposition to sleep when abstracted from their diversions and unemployed in labour . . . Comparing them by their faculties of memory, reason and imagination, it appears to me that, in memory they are equal to whites; in reason, much inferior . . . and in imagination they are dull, tasteless.'

He prophesied that Negroes, after emancipation, would not be able to live alongside whites in America and demanded that they all be returned to Africa. If any emancipated slaves remained in Jefferson's Virginia, they would, in his words, be 'brought under restraint'. One of Jefferson's biographers has gone so far as to suggest that the Ku Klux Klan can been seen to be ideologically descended from his standpoint.

WHEN EQUALITY MEANT
THREE-FIFTHS

It is not, however, fair to single Jefferson out. The **American Founding Fathers** were all of similar mind. The writing of the Constitution, the purpose of which was to set out in legal and organisational terms the meaning of the Declaration of Independence's aspirations, also bumped up against the reality of the times. Despite the sentiment underpinning the Declaration ('these truths to be self-evident') that 'all men are created equal,' for the first 80 years of the Republic, the Constitution contained a provision that was manifestly in contradiction. Moreover, it was not an accidental outcome, the result of some unrecognised cultural blind spot, but a premeditated measure inserted only after prolonged consideration.

Article 1, Section 2, Clause 3 specified how representation of the states in the House of Representatives was to be calculated. The number of delegates for each state would be based on population. However, in calculating the 'true' population of a state, the section set out the method of calculation: it would be determined 'by adding to the whole number of free persons . . . three-fifths of all other persons'. These 'other persons' were the Negro slaves. The valuing of a slave as three-fifths of a free person had already been adopted by an earlier act of Congress for levying taxes on people, so the Constitutional Convention saw no difficulty in replicating the rule here. Few seemed to see how it drove a stake through the high-minded principles they had enunciated earlier.

The provision remained part of the Constitution until the post-Civil War 14th Amendment was adopted in 1868, establishing constitutional civil rights for ex-slaves.

AMERICA'S DECLARATION OF INDEPENDENCE – IT'S NOT WHAT YOU THINK AT ALL

For a new nation, the importance of the 'creation story' is paramount. It is the narrative from which citizens of a new country and their descendants take their identity. It defines the society that emerges. Nothing better illustrates how history gets bent and moulded to ensure that the story is uncomplicated – even if inaccurate – than America's **Declaration of Independence**.

All Americans will recite the central tenets of their creation document. In its own words, it purports to be the 'unanimous Declaration of the thirteen united States of America', done 'In Congress, 4 July 1776'. In actuality, the vote for independence had been taken two days earlier, on 2 July. At the time, John Adams, who would later be the second President, wrote that 2 July would ever more be celebrated as the birth of the nation. The only significance the Fourth of July had was for being the day Congress formally adopted the text of Jefferson's declaration.

So already the story was muddled. It got worse. There never was a vote for independence that was unanimous. When the decision was first taken, on 1 July, only nine voted in favour (the four New England states, along with Georgia, Maryland, New Jersey, North Carolina and Virginia). One delegation, Delaware, was split, and the New York delegation abstained. It was operating under 12-month-old instructions from its state assembly to do nothing to impede reconciliation with the mother country. Two states – South Carolina and Pennsylvania – actually opposed independence. Business leaders recommended they delay their 'final decision' until the next day to try to get unanimity.

On the Second, states in favour had risen to 12. South Carolina switched its vote; the split in Delaware was broken by the arrival overnight of an extra delegate; and Pennsylvania switched from 4–3 against to 3–2 in favour. But it remained only 12 out the 13 who formally declared independence on 2 July, despite the words of the Declaration. New York did not decide until a week later to join, and only registered their decision in Congress on 15 July. It was only on

19 July that Congress ordered the Declaration to be signed. Delegates did not get round to doing that until 2 August, when most did, but some had already left Philadelphia. One did not append his signature until 1781, five years after the event. Some members who had taken part never did at all, and some who had never even been there, did – confused?

Further Unravellings of the Tale

On closer inspection, other elements of America's 'founding story' are also not quite as clear cut as our teachers led us to believe. The original break with the mother country is laid at the feet of the British, whose policy of **extortionate taxation** viciously pushed the reasonable colonists too far. In fact, all the taxes raised in America stayed in America and were to be used for ensuring the military defence of the colonists themselves. They always intentionally aimed only to recover a small proportion of actual costs, the rest having to be met by British taxpayers.

The infamous Townshend duties, imposed by the British Chancellor of the Exchequer in 1767 on a range of household goods, including glass, paper and, notoriously, imported tea, and which history portrays as being responsible for igniting the American Revolution, were planned to raise in their first year a mere £43,000 (from two and a half million colonists) to contribute towards defence costs estimated at £406,000. The individual scale of the demand was minimal. At the time, the average American paid sixpence a year in tax (about £2.60 in modern values). By comparison, their British counterpart was stumping up 25 shillings, 50 times more.

Strange Bedfellows

Even **Benjamin Franklin** could see some potential merit, writing in a pamphlet in 1764, 'It is very possible that the Crown may think it necessary to keep troops in America to . . . defend the colonies; and that Parliament may establish some revenue arising out of the American trade to be applied towards supporting those troops. It is possible, too, that we may, after a few years' experience, be generally very well satisfied with that measure, from the steady protection it will afford us . . .'

He would change his position as headier forces overwhelmed rational debate. Deeper trends were at play. A maturing society was casting off its perceived shackles. It meant rejecting bonds that had existed for a century and a half without there being much good reason, beyond a youthful nation's growing pains, for doing so. There was no doubt guilt about this, and to help with that, the story needed an enemy. Inconvenient details ended up getting buried under an easier and more compelling narrative, of a parent country unreasonably bleeding its offshoot colonies dry. It became the explanation for the breach. And most Americans still believe it in their heart of hearts.

The Famous Cry That Was Never Heard

Nor was anybody going around shouting slogans about '**no taxation without representation**'. There is no contemporary record of the man credited with the phrase, a member of the Massachusetts House of Representatives, James Otis, actually saying the catchphrase. He was first cited as coining it by his biographer who published a lustrous account of Otis's contribution 61 years after he had protested about relations between Britain and the colonies in 1762. The tag, therefore, entered American mythology long after the Revolution itself was over and 40 years after Otis himself had died. While the sentiment clearly underlay much of the discontent around at the time, it was never the simple rallying call on the lips of Americans that our history makes us think it was.

Otis was an odd choice to ascribe the sentiment to in any case. He wrote one of the most famous pamphlets of the pre-Revolutionary period in 1764, but in it declared very clearly that there was no escape from obedience to Parliament, even if it was wrong. He maintained that the King had 'the most pure and perfect intentions' and that 'a most perfect and ready obedience is to be yielded to it while it remains in force . . . There would be an end of all Government if one or a number of subjects or subordinate provinces should take upon them so far to judge the justice of an act of Parliament as to refuse obedience to

16

it . . . Therefore let Parliament lay what burdens they please on us, we must, it us our duty to, submit and patiently bear them till they will be pleased to relieve us.'

Otis repeatedly emphasised the supremacy of Parliament over the colonies, otherwise the colonies would be independent 'which none but rebels, fools or madmen will contend for'. He certainly disagreed with how Parliament was taxing America, but he is far from the separatist that American folklorists now portray him, on account of a single – but undeniably catchy – phrase invented 60 years after the event.

Furthermore, the sentiment was an extremely hollow one to rest on. Most colonists were unrepresented in their *own* assemblies due to the rules on qualifying for the vote, usually relating to ownership of a certain amount of land. Thus, fewer than six per cent of adult Virginians had the vote at the time of the Revolution. Only 16 per cent qualified in Massachusetts, and in Pennsylvania it was only two per cent.

CREATING A LEGEND FROM A PUB BRAWL

Totemic episodes turn out to be not quite the cataclysmic events history now projects. The so-called '**Boston Massacre**' in 1770 was actually a drunken skirmish in which just five people lost their lives when two dozen British soldiers opened fire after heavy provocation from a much larger, intoxicated and out-of-control mob. Future President, John Adams, defended the accused in court, and secured acquittals for all but two. It was more radical rabble-rousers who spun the historical portrayal of the event into a national assault and 'massacre' of the innocents.

The Smugglers' Mutiny That Became a Heroic Revolt
The **Boston Tea Party** in 1773, the iconic rebuffing of excessive British taxes, was in fact nothing of the sort. The measures being protested were injurious all right, but not for the reasons history asks us to remember.

The attack on the tea shipments in Boston harbour was in reaction to the introduction of the Tea Act, by which Britain was seeking to increase tea imports into America to help save the ailing East India Company from bankruptcy. The Act in fact *reduced* taxes on tea. That was the problem for American traders, who had profited enormously from smuggling the stuff in and undercutting the official market where tea sold very expensively because of the customs taxes levied. The Governor of Massachusetts estimated at the time that five-sixths of all tea consumed in the colony was smuggled. There was so much of the illicit trade going on, and few prosecutions, that engaging in it was regarded less as a serious crime and more as a commercial gamble. So reducing the tax threatened to undermine the lucrative smuggling trade with mountains of cheap legitimate tea. That was the problem the Bostonians had. And that was why they revolted. Post-Revolution, the story took on a far different and more uplifting patrioticly shade.

The Invention of History

Paul Revere's legendary midnight ride from Boston to Lexington and Concord in 1775 to warn of the imminent arrival of British troops was primarily that – legend. He was actually one of three riders that night, and was himself arrested before he got to Concord. The story only became part of the Revolutionary iconography when Longfellow wrote his famous poem about it – taking many liberties with reality – in 1863, 90 years after the event. It thrust Revere from unremembered nonentity to hero of the revolution. He immediately entered the prestigious *Dictionary of American Biography* when before he had failed to be listed in any previous catalogue of national worthies.

And the idea that news of the Declaration of Independence was announced in Philadelphia by the ringing of the **Liberty Bell** was simply made up in 1847, 70 years later, by a hagiographic local author George Lippard in a book appropriately entitled *Legends of the American Revolution*. Although the bell was certainly there at the time, it had had no connection with the Independence movement and was not known as the Liberty Bell (the city had actually tried to sell it for scrap in 1828). That name was coined only in 1839, and not for anything to do with America's founding, but by anti-slavery activists who noticed the wording on the bell was a slogan convenient for their own cause. It remained unremarkable, and certainly no national symbol, until Lippard came along.

THE VARNISHING OF A REPUTATION

The best example of historical airbrushing is **Benjamin Franklin**, who enjoys a gilded reputation in the pantheon of American heroes. A true polymath, he was one of the Founding Fathers of the American Republic, being a pivotal figure in both the Philadelphia Convention that drew up the Declaration of Independence in 1776 – he was one of the five members of the committee responsible for producing the draft – and in the Congresses of the 1780s that wrote the Constitution. He is revered as the only person to have signed the four key documents which gave birth to the United States – the Declaration of Independence, the Constitution and the treaties with France during the War of Independence that provided the ally crucial to victory and the peace treaty with England at the end which confirmed the break with the mother country.

He was one of early America's first printers and produced one of the first newspapers in the colonies. He served as diplomat representing the colonists in London in the years leading up to the break with England, and in Paris during the war securing Revolutionary France's support for the American cause. He was a pioneering scientist, famed for his experiments into understanding lightning and electricity, inventor – he invented the first bifocal glasses because of lifelong poor eyesight, a curious musical instrument called the armonica which comprised revolving glass bowls that are made to hum by touching their rims, and he even investigated how to make flatulence less odorous.

But the modern uncomplicated image of a dyed-in-the wool

19

patriot hides a less clear-cut reality. His virtues are rather less unvarnished than the historical image that comes to us would suggest in the story of the founding of America.

To start with, he wasn't there most of the time. He spent almost all of the two febrile decades before the War of Independence in London. Apart from a two-year break from 1762 to 1764, he was in England between 1757 and 1775, the key years of growing ferment on the other side of the Atlantic. And his activities were quite different to what might have been expected. Most of the time was dedicated to trying to win a *royal* charter for the Pennsylvania colony to replace the proprietary rule of the Penn family who had founded the settlement. This itself represented a change of loyalties that was quite astonishing.

Biting the Hand and Revelling in the Mother Country
He had been given his start in life by the Penns when, at the age of 17, he secured a post in the colony's administration from which he rose to the deputy postmastership by 21. Yet when he was elected as member of the Pennsylvania Assembly a generation later, his loyalties were found to be fluid. He turned against his patrons and accepted a mission from the Assembly to go to England to try to break their rule.

In London, lauded in cultured society for his talents and refinement, he actually became more and more a royalist and advocate of the British Empire. Biographers struggle with this period in his life as it contradicts so markedly his later role as the iconic figurehead of the birth of an independent America. In reality, Franklin was a very late convert to independence, and only reluctantly shed his identity as a Briton. His vision tended towards strengthening, not severing, the ties and to building a transatlantic common trading community.

Having failed in his first attempt in London to get a better deal from the Penn proprietors, he returned to Pennsylvania in 1762 and argued there for royalist Government. This was against the trend of the times, made him deeply unpopular, and he was quickly re-despatched to London in 1764 to continue the struggle against the Penns and for instituting royal Government. His empathy to Britain's attempts to control the increasingly rebellious colonies was evident. Although he tried in London to oppose the notorious Stamp Act of 1765 which, for the first time, imposed direct taxes on the American colonies, after it was passed he recommended a friend for the post of stamp distributor in Pennsylvania which appalled his erstwhile colleagues and hardly added to his credentials of standing up for his fellow Americans.

Rupture

What led him personally towards the final break with Britain is far from clear. By 1768 he was writing of a vision of the colonies becoming separate in regard to the ability of Parliament to make specific laws for them, but still fundamentally connected by owing loyalty to the British monarch – an early concept of devolution. 'The question', he wrote, 'is whether a union like that . . . would or would not be advantageous to the whole. I should have no doubt of the affirmative.'

As late as 1774, he was still highly esteemed in British society. He was present that year in 10 Downing Street to witness Prime Minister Lord North installed as Chancellor of Oxford University. But his time in England now started to unravel when, also in 1774, a collection of 13 official letters between the Governor's office in Massachusetts and the Treasury in London, which put British policy in an unfavourable light, and which Franklin had mysteriously (some say corruptly or illegally) acquired and passed in confidence to contacts in America, were published by Boston independence activists. Franklin stood accused of duplicity and underhand dealing. His character besmirched, he was pilloried in the English press as a political chameleon and fraud. It may well have been the last straw that caused him to cut his losses in his endeavours to keep the Royalist Empire in North America alive. What was certain was that he left England under a cloud, and under threat of prosecution, in March 1775.

By the time he was back in America, the war was under way and, once the smoke and dust had settled, Franklin's unsullied reputation as a Father of the Nation was already solidifying for history.

One Idea That Didn't Make It

Franklin's less than adept antennae for what the people wanted found expression also in his contribution to the debate on the choice of America's national symbols. He opposed the eagle, reasoning that it was 'a bird of bad moral character' as it lived by 'sharping and robbing'. Instead, he proposed – bizarrely – the turkey. Fortunately for posterity, he lost the argument.

AMERICA'S SULLIED FOUNDING FATHER

George Washington, 'father of the nation' is, according to the custodians of the first President's museum home and final resting place, best remembered by Americans for four virtues: self-denial, sacrifice, patriotism and disinterestedness. History shows, however, that in reality he also made the very best of the cards that were dealt to him. Although esteemed for his service to the new republic, he did handsomely out of it too. By the time of his retirement after an almost unbroken 48 years of public service, which included eight as the first President, he eased himself back into life in his Virginia home at Mount Vernon, just south of the new capital named after him, as the most revered man in America, and the richest too.

Owner of the Nation

In practice, Washington denied himself little. Over the years, he had developed Mount Vernon into an 8,000-acre estate. At his death, it comprised the main 22-room house, five separate working farms and quarters extensive enough to house 300 slaves. It was just one asset among many. By the end, he had accumulated through land specu- lation a further 15,000 acres in Virginia, 5,000 in Kentucky, 3,000 in the yet-to-be developed 'northwest territory' (modern Ohio, Illinois and the Great Lakes region), 1,000 apiece in Maryland and New York and just over 200 in Pennsylvania. American biographer Douglas Freeman has conceded that Washington's 'ambition for wealth made him acquisitive and sometimes contentious'. When in office, he would insist upon the exact payment of every farthing due to him. He was determined, according to Freeman, 'to get everything that he honestly could'. And sometimes dishonestly too. He has been described as an 'inveterate land-grabber', and in his youth he illegally had a surveyor stake out some lucrative territory in an area that had been decreed off limits to settlers.

Fleecing His Nation

An oft-quoted illustration of Washington's dedication to the service of his country is the decision he made, when asked to take command of the Continental Army at the start of the War of Independence, to gallantly agree to forego a salary. He merely asked to be paid his expenses. It was a canny choice. Had he taken the pay (at $500 a month) he would have garnered $48,000 for his pains in his eight-year war service. By opting for expenses, his account at the end amounted to an eye-watering $447,220 (by the smallest estimate), in the order of $9 million in today's values. He even managed to include in the bill the cost of a new carriage and imported wines for his headquarters.

When Washington became America's first President in 1789, he again offered to work 'just for expenses'. A wiser Congress this time insisted on paying him a salary. At $25,000, it was the equivalent in modern values of over $600,000. (The official salary of the President today is only $400,000.)

Slaves Too

Like Jefferson, Washington was also a slave owner. At the time of his death in 1799, he owned 123 and had another 193 so-called 'dower' slaves on the Mount Vernon estate (ones he did not have legal ownership of but whom he had inherited through his marriage). Although he frequently agonised over the rights and wrongs of slavery, he managed to resist exercising his legal right to free the ones he could right up until his death. He eventually did so in his will, but even then only indirectly — the will specified that they were to be freed as soon as his wife, Martha, died. (She actually released them two

23

years later while she was still healthily alive. One explanation has it that she feared her own demise might come unnaturally sooner in the delicate circumstances.)

During Washington's presidency, the country's capital was moved from New York to Philadelphia. He was so disappointed with the quality of food there that he brought his slave cook Hercules up from Mount Vernon. As, under Pennsylvania law, slaves were automatically freed after six months' residence in the state, Washington would regularly send him back to Virginia just before the period was up, have him stay home for a few days, and then return.

Refusing to Lay a Rumour to Rest

Washington had no known offspring. In 1998, an Illinois woman claimed that she was a descendant of Washington by an illicit child born from a liaison with a slave from Washington's brother's plantation. Linda Allen Bryant, who published a book on the claim six years later, asserted that Washington had had the child with Venus, one of John Augustine Washington's slaves around 1784, when he would have been 52. The boy was said to have later moved to Washington's Mount Vernon estate. The modern trustees of the estate confirmed that there were records of Ms Allen's slave ancestors playing an important part in Washington's family. However, they refused the family's request to provide DNA samples that would prove or disprove the claim. Oddly, they continue to refuse to this day, despite the precedent set in 2000 by the Jefferson case.

Odd, because most historians believe Washington was sterile, at least in later life. Supposed to have never produced any children, it would seem an easy one to clear up . . . unless there is something the trustees know that would alter our settled picture.

Fighting for a Reputation

Another picture that needs re-touching is Washington's military prowess. It seems that he was actually not a terribly good fighting commander. From the heroic figure that comes down in the American national memory, one would be forgiven for believing Washington to

24

be the master strategist who led his young country to salvation. Even in his own time, his peers had their doubts. Jefferson felt he was 'not a great tactician'. John Adams, who would follow Washington as second President, called him 'an old muttonhead'. When appointed Commander-in-Chief of the Continental Army, he confidently predicted the war would be 'an exertion of a few weeks'. It took seven years, and Washington would lose more pitched battles than he won.

Standing on Ceremony

Despite his near hero status from his war exploits and as first President, Washington appears to have irritated as many as he impressed. He had an abiding envy of pomp and ritual – one of the reasons cited for his deep-rooted anti-British sentiment at the start of the revolutionary war was his rejection by the snobbish British military elite that he yearned to be part of. When he had the trappings of office, he made the most of them. Although head of a democratic republic, he required strict observation of the dignity of his position. He insisted on everyone bowing to him, instead of greeting with a handshake. More than one witness described how as the President performed his dignified bow 'his hands were so disposed as to indicate that the salutation was not to be accompanied with shaking hands'. On ceremonial occasions, he had every chair removed from the room so that no guest could take a seat in his presence.

GREAT EMANCIPATOR? – GREAT ILLUSIONIST

Abraham Lincoln has hero status too – as the President who ended slavery. He certainly pronounced the Emancipation Proclamation halfway through the Civil War in 1863, but history has tended to airbrush out the uncomfortable realities of Lincoln's personal views on race that were far more complex than the simplicities that history portrays. He never believed in the equality of races. Campaigning for the Senate in 1858, he made his views crystal clear:

'I will say then that I am not, nor ever have been in favour of bringing about in any way the social and political equality of the white and black races . . . There is a physical difference between the white and black races which I believe will for ever forbid the two races living together on terms of social and political equality. And inasmuch as they cannot so live, while they do remain together there must be the position of superior and inferior, and I as much as any other man am in favour of having the superior position assigned to the white race.'

As President, speaking in a White House meeting in 1862 with freed black leaders, he told them to their faces:

'Even when you cease to be slaves, you are yet far removed from being placed on an equality with the white race. You are cut off from many of the advantages which the other race enjoys. It is better for us both to be separated.'

According to biographer Jan Morris, in all 175 speeches that Lincoln made between 1854 and 1860, he always insisted that it would be unconstitutional to abolish slavery.

A Hand Forced and Freedom Tempered

The move for which history places him on the highest pedestal – his Emancipation Proclamation in 1863 – was only taken for the most politically expedient of reasons – it aimed to reduce the risk of foreign intervention against the North which had been growing significantly, and would heal a split in his Party about the running of the war which was, according to one historian of the conflict, 'rapidly getting out of hand'. Moreover, as barely anyone now likes to remember, it freed slaves only in the rebel Confederacy (over which he did not actually have any pretence of control), not in the states that had remained loyal, and of which he was legally President, nor even in the Confederate territories then occupied by the Union. All of these were expressly excluded. In fact, only 200,000 of the estimated three and a half million slave population were freed during the war as a result of the proclamation. One cynic observed that Lincoln 'freed all the slaves except the ones he could free'.

Lincoln never contemplated that the results of his actions would be that Negroes would become proper, equal citizens of the United States. He actually favoured colonisation as the solution of the 'problem'. Research published in 2000 showed that in two State of the Union addresses he called for the deportation of black people. Shortly before the end of the Civil War in 1865, he said,' I believe it would be better to export them all to some fertile country with a good climate which they could have to themselves.'

According to author Lerone Bennett, who had spent seven years delving into White House records, it revealed the extent of the myth that had been allowed to grow up around Lincoln as the icon of post-Civil War reconciliation, perhaps essential for the nation to have, but far from a historically accurate rendering of the reality. It is 'one of the most extraordinary efforts I know to hide a whole man and a whole history.'

Domestic Troubles

The chief skeleton in the White House cupboard of Abraham Lincoln was his wife Mary. Always a highly strung character, she would explode in furious tantrums at her husband, and once chased him out of the house wielding a kitchen knife. It didn't help that she was often irked by Lincoln's lifelong habit of morosely retreating into long periods of unbroken silence. Research published only in 1995 suggested that he had married her only because she had been pregnant and her father, a prominent banker in Kentucky, forced the pairing. According to the testimony of a friend, Lincoln went to the nuptials with the look of 'a beast going to the slaughter'. Their first son arrived three days before his parents' nine-month anniversary.

She came to the verge of a nervous breakdown when their second son Edward died a month short of his fourth birthday in 1850. Lincoln himself was then still recovering from his defeat after a single two-year term as an Illinois member in the House of Representatives in Washington. Worse came when they reached the

27

White House in 1861. Mary's attempts to fit in with the Washington social scene ended in disaster. Unknown to Lincoln, she ran up a clothes bill of $27,000 (over $500,000 in modern values). She bought over 300 pairs of gloves in four months. She shocked society at the inaugural ball four years later at the start of Lincoln's second term, with the country still deep in the morass of the Civil War, when she appeared in a new silk dress which cost the modern equivalent of $28,000. A vicious poem was published by a leading Washington playwright entitled *The Queen Must Dance*. After years of instability following Lincoln's assassination in 1865, she was formally committed to an asylum for a period in 1875, and died seven years later still never fully recovered.

A Cause to Fight for?

Lincoln was not alone in his ambiguity. **Ulysses S. Grant**, who led the abolitionist Union Army in the American Civil War that was fought to end slavery, actually owned four slaves himself.

Manufacturing a National Hero

One of the most enduring of America's 'foundation' heroes, **Davy Crockett**, whom conventional wisdom has meeting his end fighting to the last in the defence of the Alamo, turns out to be rather more complicated than the memorial history has given him.

Crockett, a Tennessee-born firebrand, tagged by the 1950s Disney television production, the 'King of the Wild Frontier', secured his fame in the chaotic early days of the American West by volunteering for the revolutionaries of Texas, not then part of the United States but a province of Mexico, in its six-month rebellion against the Mexican state which began in the autumn of 1835. It ended famously in the 11-day siege of the Alamo, a former hospice at San Antonio now converted into a makeshift fort, in March 1836. Around a hundred Texans faced 3,000 Mexican Government troops. According to the account that long filled patriotic Americans' schoolbooks, Crockett died a hero defiantly swinging the butt of his rifle, Old Betsy, at oncoming Mexicans after running out of ammunition.

A Different Story Surfaces

In 1975, a previously untranslated diary written by José Enrique de la Peña, senior Mexican officer at the battle, revealed that Crockett and six other survivors had actually surrendered. According to this account, they were executed shortly afterwards. The revelation did not come without controversy. Historians still dispute whether the diary is genuine, pointing to the unclear circumstances of its emergence in the mid-1950s in Mexico, just at the height of Disney's fictionalisation of Crockett's story across the border in the United States. Advocates cite a supporting pamphlet that was lodged in the archives of Yale University long before the Crockett fad began, which they suggest point to the diary being genuine. A crude Mexican attempt at Party pooping? Or bursting the bubble of a fabled tale? The truth may never be known, but the episode once more demonstrates Oscar Wilde's observation of the truth being rarely pure and never simple.

Furnishing a Myth

How his end became to be portrayed by his countrymen seems rather typical of Crockett's entire life. Much of his Wild West character – famed for fighting Indians, even killing a bear at the age of three – had been a complete invention by his political agent to help get him elected to Congress in 1833. The strategy worked, and it was soon bolstered by a stage play *The Lion of the West*, which introduced Crockett wearing the coonskin hat that became the motif by which he was remembered. (Modern researchers now believe he probably never actually wore one in real life – no account had ever been found of him doing so – the play is the only source.) He lost his seat at the next election in 1835, left the Eastern states embittered by his rejection, and went searching out west for others who could satisfy his lust for action and acceptance.

29

FOILED BY FOOLISHNESS NOT FATE

The imagery of **Robert Falcon Scott**, 'Scott of the Antarctic', entered our folklore in well-defined terms after his expedition's demise, aided by the pitiful circumstances of his and his Party's end. Sacrifice, honour, unyielding determination to the bitter end – for an Imperial power at its apogee of global reach, it was a most fitting scene. This small tragedy in the farthest flung part of the world has been etched ever since in the national psyche as a typically English story to stir the heart: valiant and heroic failure.

Longer perspectives have drawn a more critical picture. The first British arrivals at the South Pole were beaten by the better equipped and more rational-thinking Norwegian Party led by Amundsen. The comforting explanation of plain bad luck began to evaporate when historians started to take an unemotional look at Scott's decision-making. Failings were far more avoidable, it seems. Against the previous experience of Arctic explorers, Scott made it clear he would not use dogs as his main method of haulage. Instead, he determined to rely on ponies and men, both of whom were far less suited to the conditions. (Amundsen succeeded with a dog strategy.) He also insisted on experimenting with mechanical tractors. It would have been an innovative strategy even in a benign location, but was hopelessly unrealistic in the Antarctic. Both broke down within days, having covered fewer than 50 of the 1,600 miles of the journey.

The ponies gave out earlier than expected too, leaving the bulk of the trek to be done by manpower. Scott's fateful decision to take four men with him on the final leg to the Pole instead of three meant that on the return their rations were depleted more quickly. When they died, they were famously just 11 miles short of a food station.

Freezing the Image
The public imagination, peeved at being bested by little Norway and mortified by the heroic circumstances of Scott's death, was very effectively honed by the graphic and stirring diary entries that Scott made sure he kept up right to the end. These guaranteed an iconic

status for him and his faithful men: 'Had we lived, I should have had a tale to tell of the hardihood, endurance and courage of my companions which would have stirred the heart of every Englishman. These rough notes and our dead bodies must tell the tale . . . ' They also ensured that any critical questions about Scott's management and leadership would seem like churlish and unpatriotic nit-picking.

SWISS MYTH

National stories need simplicity – even if they turn out to be historically inaccurate. Switzerland's 13th-century folklore icon **William Tell** suffered a setback in 1986, when research by Fritz Mathys Weist, a Swiss expert in arms and armoury, demonstrated that the tale of Tell being forced, on pain of execution, to shoot an apple off the head of his son with a crossbow could not have happened, as the crossbow had not reached Switzerland at the time.

The legend first appears around 1475, a century and a half after the supposed events in Uri canton in 1307. Weist published his uncomfortable findings to mark the country's National Day, demonstrating that crossbows were never mentioned in any military records of the period. He had examined contemporary drawings of all Swiss military encounters up to 1388. Not a single one showed the use of the weapon.

Crossbows are not even Swiss, as is commonly thought. They have long been known to have been invented in China around 500BC.

NELSON – BENEFITS TRICKSTER

The quintessential British hero, **Admiral Nelson** comes down through the pages of history renowned for his selfless devotion to duty, sacrifice and, despite disabilities that would have laid low any

31

other man, an indefatigable thirst for carrying on. Recent studies have cast a different light on this image.

The Royal Society of Medicine's *Journal of Medical Biography* published research in 1998 that suggested that Nelson had played up the significance of his famous eye injury in order to win a military pension. The wound to his right eye, gained at the siege of Calvi in Corsica in 1794, did not end in blindness at all. (It is a myth that he subsequently wore a patch over the eye as depicted in so many representations.) Caused by rock and soil debris from an exploding cannonball, the effects were apparently temporary. A few days later, Nelson is recorded as telling his commander, Admiral Hood, that his eye was 'much better', and by 1804, he was being quoted by *The Times* as saying he could see well with both eyes.

However, recently unearthed Admiralty records showed that in 1795, a year after the incident, he submitted a claim to his masters saying he was effectively blind in the eye and that he should have a £200 annual pension (worth in the order of £15,000 in modern values). He claimed 'the loss of an eye in [the King's] service'. He claimed that his eye 'is now grown worse and is almost total darkness'.

The Admiralty were clearly dubious, as it took them three years to consider the request. Intervening events might have persuaded them. By the time they decided to grant it, Nelson had gone one better in a more readily observable way and lost his right arm at Tenerife in 1797, for which the Admiralty had no excuse not to award him a pension. So, in 1798, it awarded him a certificate accepting his eye claim, treating the loss as equivalent in financial terms to his lost arm. To Nelson's dismay, however, no additional cash came with it for the second injury.

The author of the journal article suggested that Nelson overstated his case for compensation for his eye, until it was clear he was not going to succeed in extracting any response from his employers. The loss of his arm secured his pension, so he no longer needed to play up the eye. Hence, on the eve of Trafalgar, he was cheerfully denying any problems with his eyesight at all.

The Self-Made Hero – Literally

The dubious circumstance of his eye is not the only shadow to have fallen on Nelson's reputation in recent years. In 2002, researchers at the National Maritime Museum produced a less than flattering portrait of Nelson's publicity tactics, showing he had a distinctly modern sense of spinning his achievements to his seniors and the press.

Over a thousand letters newly discovered in archives have added a new perspective by showing how he organised carefully timed leaks to newspapers exaggerating his bravado. After battles, he would compose his own account, and his own role in it – often claiming to have done alone what in fact others had helped him do – and send it to a close confidant in England, Captain William Locker, under whom Nelson had served as a lieutenant. Locker would pass the reports to the press. They would appear under the Delphic byline 'by an officer'. It is far from certain that the Admiralty ever firmly knew it was Nelson producing the very material that turned him into a national icon.

The research also uncovered correspondence to printmakers and painters giving specific instructions that depictions of him be replaced to make him appear much fitter. 'He made himself into a hero for the masses. It was very sophisticated,' commented the National Maritime Museum's leading expert on Nelson who un-covered the new evidence. 'He was a naval genius who made Britain safe from the French for decades afterwards, but he was also a philanderer and PR smoothie who upset the British establishment.'

An Unbefitting End

Some inkling of the feathers Nelson ruffled can be gained from the fact that 18 of the admirals invited to his funeral declined to attend. His commanding officer, Earl St Vincent, wrote after Nelson's death that 'animal courage' was his sole merit, 'his private character [being] most disgraceful, in every sense of the word'.

No Sex Please, You're British

Inspirer of the professionalisation of nursing, **Florence Nightingale** has a solidly cast image of the 'up against it' reformer – the weak female entering an alien world and taking on the two crustiest – and male – pillars of the establishment: Victorian politicians and the military; the 'lady with the lamp' lighting the way for change. All this is true, but there was a shadier side that rarely gets the light.

Her pioneering work in the Crimean War, which launched her path to historical fame, was indeed perilous and fraught with obstacles – not least from the men she was trying to save. The legendary image of her patrolling the wards with her lamp, showing a light of hope amidst the darkness, and of solace to her suffering men, was not quite what history would have us believe. She patrolled because she had discovered, on arrival, that most of her nurses at night were providing other comforts and services to their charges. Describing them as mostly drunks and whores, she instituted a strict regime that had the soldiers just as discomfited as her nurses. No one was allowed in the wards after 8pm except herself, and she made her rounds with her lamp to make sure there was no illicit sex going on. She may have never left the bedside of a dying man, as the story goes, but the men themselves are not likely to have found the attention wholly rewarding.

Bed Operations

When Florence returned to England in 1856, aged just 36, her great works really took off, badgering the military to change a system that had not reformed since the Napoleonic Wars half a century before. But she did it almost entirely from her bed. She physically collapsed shortly after her return from the hell that was the Crimea (where of Britain's 22,000 war dead, 75 per cent died from disease rather than battle), and took to her bed to convalesce. She basically stayed there for the rest of her life, which stretched for another 55 years.

She ran her campaign from bed, issuing strict orders to followers. Medical historians do not doubt she suffered an affliction from her time in the Crimea, but most conclude that it then became psychosomatic. Some regard her as the best textbook case of crippling hypochondria. It was noticed that she would suddenly have alarming attacks of breathlessness, palpitations, giddiness and anxiety whenever there was an event or person she did not want to deal with. The timeliness of her 'illnesses' allowed her to complete work uninterrupted by giving her excuses to rebuff the visitors who set siege to her after her return, except the ones she wanted to see. It also entrenched the sympathy that she had won in the public imagination. And sympathy for her meant sympathy for her causes. Accustomed by now to working the political system, her post-Crimea life may well have been a carefully concocted stratagem to achieve her goals.

Historians note a pattern that started in her early life. She had battled with her mother over her choice of vocation, and her rejection of two highly desirable marriage proposals which her mother never forgave her for turning down. The arguments prompted the same health problems that would appear later, and she retired to her bed in consequence. Going to the Crimea was as much an act of defiance to her family as anything else. While she was there, the symptoms ceased and she never had another attack – until she returned to England. During her service in the Crimea, she had been a virtual dictator of her world, without obstacles to her plans. Back home, the frustrations began to hem her in again, and she reacted as she had done before.

A Woman's Wiles

Florence spent most of the half century that followed her extra-ordinary rise to national fame as a bedridden recluse in the home her father had bought her in Mayfair. It did not stop her achieving enormous progress, for which she is duly remembered. Her *Dictionary of National Biography* entry observes that she 'astutely exploited the isolation provided by her illness to further – mostly by remorseless use of correspondence – reforms in the Army, the promotion of sanitary science, the collection of statistics, the design of hospitals, and the reform of nursing and midwifery services: no Victorian, except perhaps the Queen, made more effective use of attrition by letter! Not for her were the waiting in the corridors of power and the attending of committees; people came to her and by appointment.'

A great achiever – but also perhaps not a small deceiver?

A CRIMINAL LAUNCH PAD TO FAME

James Watt, the 18th-century 'father of steam', appears to have bankrolled his early experiments by indulging in forgery, according to evidence discovered in 2002 in London's Science Museum. Curators announced that they had found among his personal effects stored there a fake identity stamp of a master musical instrument maker. It bore the name of French flute maker Thomas Lot, whose Paris workshop produced the most sought-after flutes in the mid-18th century. He was widely known as the Stradivarius of flutes.

Watt is known to have been a flute maker too in his youth to scratch out a living. He was poverty-stricken, and from 1759 onwards, when just 23, he was becoming more and more obsessed with experimenting with steam machines, which was clearly an expensive undertaking. Watt made his flutes out of cheap boxwood and sold them around Glasgow. Now found among his possessions was a crude lead stamp with four letters, 'T LOT', the trademark of the Lot workshop.

The evidence was suggestive that Watt stamped his low-quality output with the most illustrious brand name then available, and passed them off to unwitting local amateur musicians as the work of the world master – because his abode was conveniently far distant in those days, the chances of discovery were greatly reduced. To a trained ear, the difference between a Lot flute and a fake, like a Stradivarius and an ordinary violin, would have been clear. The theory goes that there were plenty of amateurs around who would readily have been taken in.

A clue that the tale appeared all too true came with the revelation from musical historians of evidence that Lot's work was known to have been faked. In the 1890s, a musical expert was once given a supposed Lot flute and quickly concluded from playing it that it was not the real thing, describing the workmanship and musical tone as 'execrable'.

America's Greatest Industrialist – and a Forgotten Reputation

Henry Ford was one of the world's most influential men in the first decades of the 20th century. His invention of mass production for motor vehicles (and eventually a whole mass of other consumer goods) probably changed the lives of more people more fundamentally than anyone else in those years. His Model T motor car gave undreamt of mobility to the average citizen, and opened up new opportunities for a modern progressive world. He achieved his aim of 'democratising' the car. 'When I'm through everybody will be able to afford one and [just] about everybody will have one.' And he lived up to his word. Starting in 1908, he had produced his 500,000th car by 1914; by 1930, his 20 millionth. One in every five Americans owned a car by then, and Ford had produced the vast majority of them. There were more cars in the United States than in the rest of the world put together. He was truly the great democratiser of technology and history remembers him for it.

But a darker side of Ford, well known at the time, has gradually dropped out of sight. He was a notorious anti-Jewish agitator, who used his vast resources to promote one of the most systematic anti-Semitic campaigns in American history. Largely forgotten today, it prompted Hitler to keep a portrait of Ford on the wall next to his desk in his Munich headquarters, to include favourable references to Ford's ideas in *Mein Kampf* and, on Ford's 75th birthday in 1938, to award him a medal, the Grand Service Cross of the Supreme Order of the German Eagle.

Crusade Against the Jews

Ford's efforts began in 1918 when he bought a local weekly Michigan newspaper, the *Dearborn Independent*, which Ford dealers were set quotas for selling alongside the cars. Starting in May 1920, he published a series of 91 successive articles on the theme 'The International Jew: The World's Problem.' It was classic anti-Semitic propaganda, ploughing the well-worn furrows of fear and hatred that Jews were engaged in a global conspiracy to dominate the world. Hitler would develop the same theme in his tract four years later.

By 1923, the *Independent* had a circulation of a quarter of a million; in the next four years it increased to half a million, despite vociferous objections from leading mainstream politicians in America calling on Ford to stop his gutter journalism.

The articles were later collected in book form and were particularly successful in the volatile Germany of the late twenties and early thirties. Its effect in Germany was chilling. At the end of the war, Baldur von Schirach, leader of the Hitler Youth movement, told the Nuremburg War Crimes Tribunal of the impact of Ford's writings. 'You have no idea what a great influence this book had on the thinking of German youth,' he said. 'The younger generation looked with envy to the symbols of success and prosperity like Henry Ford, and if he said the Jews were to blame, why naturally we believed him.' By the end of 1933, it had gone through 29 editions. On Hitler's coming to power, the book became a staple of the Nazi education system.

Some authors have pointed to the great similarity between Ford's book version of his articles and Hitler's *Mein Kampf*. Some passages are so identical that it has been suggested that Hitler copied large chunks directly from Ford.

Financier of Hitler

There is evidence that Ford also contributed financially to Hitler's nascent movement in Germany. There were both ideological and commercial reasons for this. In 1921, Ford had tried to set up production in Germany, but the restrictions being imposed by the Versailles Treaty that ended the First World War made it impossible.

That year, Ford is said to have sold just three cars and six tractors in Germany. He saw in Hitler an ally in unlocking the German car market – and an ideological soul mate.

Given Hitler's unseemly views, secrecy was politic for Ford. The Nazis, too, wanted to be discreet to avoid being tarnished as agents of a foreign power. Although documentary evidence is believed to have existed at one time – there are statements by usually reliable officials of the Bavarian Parliament to this effect in the early 1920s – none has been found today. It is likely that any incriminating material was destroyed when the Nazis achieved power in 1933.

However, there is circumstantial evidence aplenty. Ford hired Boris Brasol, a White Russian émigré, as a writer on the anti-Jewish articles in the *Independent*. He made frequent trips to Germany to consult with the Nazis in the 1920s. According to a 1978 investigation by American author James Pool in *Who Financed Hitler,* up to half a million gold marks are thought to have been provided by Ford, through Brasol, to the Nazis in 1922 and 1923 alone. In 1924, a special Nazi representative, Kurt Lüdecke, actually visited Ford at his estate in Michigan. He was on an American tour specifically for the purpose of raising funds from the German émigré communities. He had been introduced to Ford by ardent Nazi backer and close friend of Hitler, Winifred Wagner, daughter-in-law of the famous composer.

Although, again, no current proof exists of any deals, Wagner herself admitted in an interview in the 1970s that Ford had told her personally that he had provided funding to the Nazis. Another source claimed Ford had given in the order of $300,000 (about $3 million in modern values). A Congressional enquiry in 1933, after Hitler came to power, however failed to find conclusive proof.

As in all shady dealings, it is extremely rare to find written proof. But the circumstantial evidence appears strong. Ford did not hide his sympathies, and it does not seem a step too far to link the probability of financial support during Hitler's crucial early days with the Führer's subsequent lauding of Ford, both in *Mein Kampf* – the only American mentioned in the tract – and, all those years later, by awarding him the highest honour possible for a non-German.

LIVING THE HIGH LIFE –
TO DEPRIVE OTHERS OF IT

Hero to millions in the 20th century, the reputation of **Karl Marx** dived somewhat after the collapse of communism in the 1990s. The once presumed infallible seer was left washed up on the beach of ideas as the tides of world opinion changed. Had folk known a little bit more about Karl Marx the man, he may have found it rather harder to win their convictions to begin with. For a political theorist whose world view centred on the iniquities of capitalism and big business, it was one of the biggest contradictions in Marx's life that he relied so heavily for financial support on Friedrich Engels, the wealthy son of a Manchester cotton manufacturer.

By the time the 49-year-old Marx published his magnus opus, *Das Kapital,* in 1867, he had known Engels for 25 years. Engels had first come into Marx's orbit as a contributor to the Cologne newspaper that Marx edited. The pair met again two years later when Marx was living in Paris in 1844, and after 10 days of intense philosophical debate, fuelled apparently by copious amounts of red wine, the duo pledged everlasting friendship.

Engels was true to his word. He became the poverty-stricken Marx's financial life support. He himself was then engaged in a magisterial survey of working class conditions in England. The two complemented each other perfectly – Engels garnered a mass of real world experience of capitalism at work; Marx had the conceptual brains to work out the system that appeared to make it function. But few at the time ever really knew how reliant Marx was on the rich son of a capitalist for his survival, and how he really savoured the indolent life of a kept man.

A Contradictory Life

His lifestyle at the time of this watershed event was, for a married man with a daughter under a year old and another on the way (he had four children in five years between 1844 and 1849), bohemian to say the least. He spent long mornings in cafés and, according to one biographer, 'even longer nights of card playing and tipsy conversation'. When Marx moved to London in 1849, Engels quickly followed. Although he and his family were destitute, Marx refused to dirty himself by taking up a trade like many of his other fellow exiles (he dismissively referred to 'vile commerce'), but rested on the small handouts that Engels regularly sent him. Engels was enjoying an allowance from his father of £200 a year (which is equivalent to earnings of around £150,000 today), had two houses, one in town and one in the country. He wrote to Marx that the family firm was twice as profitable now as it was a decade earlier, so 'it goes without saying that I shan't be needlessly scrupulous'. With friends like that . . .

Marx took Engels for all he could. Even in his parlous state, he employed a secretary, not because he really needed one but because a person of his stature and purpose in life should keep up appearances. (Marx once said he refused to live a 'sub-proletarian' life.) At the same time, the local baker was refusing to deliver any more bread to the house until Marx settled his bill. Engels always responded generously. Biographer Francis Wheen estimates that around this time in a good year he received £150 from his backer, 'a sum on which a lower middle class family could live with some comfort'.

Marx still hardly produced any writings and drifted for years in endless 'research' in the British Library. He notoriously kept up the dissolute lifestyle. One night in the 1850s he and two revolutionary colleagues undertook a celebrated pub crawl along London's Tottenham Court Road, near Marx's dwellings. They determined to have a pint in every pub on the street – there were 18 of them – and they succeeded. At the end, at 2am, they started smashing street lights – Marx claimed five – before being chased by police.

Things hit rock bottom in 1863 when the family was again penniless, Marx threatening to Engels that he would be forced to move them all into a refuge for the destitute. Engels, himself financially straitened because of a collapse of the cotton market, ended up stealing a cheque for £100 from his father's accounts department and made it payable to Marx. When in 1864 Marx inherited a windfall of £820 from the will of a political activist he had worked with on the

Continent 20 years earlier, instead of holding on to this rare fortune, he completely redecorated his new house (he had moved upscale just two months before, even though he knew the upkeep would be beyond his means), and, remarkably for the supposed arch-enemy of capitalism, played the stock market to some success.

Failure to the Very End

Even after Marx had completed the first volume of *Kapital,* success was elusive. It certainly did not bring him financial returns – even Marx himself famously remarked that it would not even pay for the cigars he smoked while writing it – and politically it had little immediate effect as its literary style was dense, convoluted and extra-ordinarily hard to understand. It took four years for the first print run of 1,000 copies to be sold. Most of the reviews that appeared were actually written by the indefatigable Engels. Marx was despondent about the tepid reception. He hugely regretted that he never saw in his lifetime his dream of an English translation.

To the end of his days, Marx relied on dear old Engels. Three years after *Kapital* was published, Engels sold out his partnership in the family business. His first deed was to arrange for Marx to have a pension of £350 per year for the rest of his life. So the guru whose thoughts would eventually challenge the capitalist way of life, shamelessly eked out his existence on the benevolence of a capitalist. Gratitude, he certainly had. Whether he ever paused to reflect upon the irony, history does not reveal.

'DO AS I SAY . . .'

In the world of child care, American **Benjamin Spock** achieved global fame as the 20th century's most celebrated guru on how to raise children. His seminal 1946 manual, *The Common Sense Book of Baby and Child Care,* framed the way a large proportion of the Western world's post-war babies were raised. It has sold more than 50 million copies worldwide – often claimed to be the second best-selling non-fiction book, after the Bible. It transformed mothers' approach to child rearing, shifting from the strict pre-war disciplinarian attitudes (where, in the words of one Spock advocate, raising a child was seen more as an exercise in 'training and taming') to a theory based around providing love for the child. It caught the wave of post-war permissiveness, made Spock a household name and a £15 million fortune, although by the time he died in 1998 aged 94, long illness had consumed it all and he ended his life penniless.

The sad impoverishment of his latter years was not, as it turned out, the hardest knock the Spock phenomenon was to take. Shortly before his death, his two sons went public with a less than flattering portrayal of their father. If Spock the expert had encouraged parents around the world to kiss and cuddle their babies ('Every time you pick your baby up . . . smile at him'), at home Spock the father ignored completely all the rules that he had set for others.

Different Strokes

The Spock sons, by then 52 and 63, described their father as a cold and undemonstrative figurehead who presided over a deeply unhappy family. They claimed that they received no physical affection. John Spock told journalists that 'all through my growing up, if we got together after we had been apart, he would shake hands. We didn't hug and he wouldn't kiss me'. His brother, Mike, described a childhood where 'we remember my father not being capable of that kind of warmth'.

It was conspicuously different to the sugary injunctions he offered to the wider world: 'We know for a fact that the natural loving care that kindly parents give their children is a hundred times more valuable than their knowing how to pin a diaper on just right or how to make a formula expertly.'

For the guru who supposedly had the secret of homely perfection, Spock's own family bordered on the dysfunctional. His wife broke under the strain, suffered from manic depression and alcoholism, and eventually became paranoid. Although the marriage lasted a remarkable 49 years, it was clearly much of a sham. Spock divorced her in 1976. He married his second wife later the very same year. She was a 30-year-old. He was 73.

Experts Getting It Wrong

Ellen Fein, author of America's best-selling manuals on building relationships, *Rules – Time-tested Secrets for Capturing the Heart of Mr Right*, announced in 2001 that she was divorcing her husband of 16 years. She did so just three months before the publication of her third volume in the phenomenally successful series: *Rules III – Time-tested Secrets for Making Your Marriage Work*. Hundreds of advance copies had already been distributed.

She was not the first 'expert' to trip. The 1960s pioneers of sexual behaviour research, American academics William Masters and Virginia Johnson, announced their separation in 1992. **Masters and Johnson** had become worldwide names for their studies on how couples could ensure happy sex lives and stable married relationships. They had been married for 21 years.

Fakir or Faker?

Mahatma Gandhi, the 'half-naked fakir' (in Churchill's less than endearing words) continues to enjoy an image burnished with its inspiring mix of purity, pacifism, simplicity of life and personal sacrifice. Beneath that well-honed surface, however, the truth is a little more blurred than most would think. The Mahatma's austere lifestyle captured India's and the world's imagination. It was, though, supreme political spin long before the term had ever been dreamed up. The poverty of his commune was spectacular PR, and tellingly faux. An aide famously once bemoaned, 'It costs a great deal of money to keep Gandhi in poverty.'

The power of his image has always been well nigh impenetrable. Revelations of his predilection for 'allowing' teenage girls from the community of followers he gathered around him at his ashram to sleep naked with him (and thousands hysterically vied for the privilege) were put down to Gandhi 'testing' his vow of chastity. He is also recorded as enduring for his cause nude massages for an hour each day by the same retinue of girls. They gave him a daily salt and water enema too.

He is reported by close associates to have been an extremely difficult man to work with. He dictated every movement of his followers, including what they should eat and when they would eat it. Compromise was not a word in Gandhi's dictionary. He told a meeting of the Indian National Congress in 1920, 'So long as you choose to keep me as your leader, you must accept my conditions, you must accept dictatorship and the discipline of martial law.'

Enthusiast for the Empire

Gandhi's pacifism was a late arrival in his philosophy. In his formative years in South Africa, he eagerly volunteered to raise an Indian brigade for the British Army in the Boer War. The authorities were not convinced of the value of the men and eventually trained them as stretcher bearers only because, in the words of one biographer, of the 'relentless importuning' of Gandhi. As a sergeant-major, he won medals in both the Boer War and the Zulu War four years later. When he launched his non-cooperation movement in India in 1920, he ceremonially returned them to the Viceroy, 'not without a pang', he admitted.

Even in the latter days of the anti-British campaign in India itself, he approved of conflict. He endorsed vicious rioting in Calcutta on the grounds that it was 'using violence in a moral cause'. He gave his blessing to a princely ruler, the Nawab of Malerkotla, who issued orders to shoot 10 Muslims for every Hindu killed in his territory, and in a prayer meeting in June 1947, a few months before his death, he told his audience, 'If we had the atom bomb, we would have used it against the British.'

Fast . . . and Loose

Gandhi pioneered the tactic of fasting as a political protest. He later used it to effect against the British, but his first use, in 1932, was for distinctly unappealing reasons. As a higher caste Hindu, he was opposing a proposal by the British authorities to grant the 'untouchables', the lowest caste in society, a separate electorate to enable their interests to be better represented. It was declared to be a fast to the death. It lasted five days, after Hindu leaders put pressure on the Untouchables' leader to reject the British reforms.

Notes taken of British Cabinet conversations at the time, which were discovered only in 2008, have Churchill dismissively rejecting the threats of another of Gandhi's fasts. 'We should be rid of a bad man and an enemy of the Empire if he died.' The Cabinet was told that Gandhi was receiving glucose in his orange juice, and having oil rubbed into his body that was nutritious. Churchill observed, 'It is apparently not a fast, merely a change of diet.'

Gandhi's poverty, and opposition to all things modern, was the backbone of his philosophy. He declared his hatred of modern industry and communications, deplored the invention of the telegraph, radio and telephone, yet later broadcast extensively on national radio during his high-profile fasts, as his campaign for independence reached its crescendo.

His professed ideal world was the simplicity of the spinning wheel and the bullock plough. He advocated a lifestyle, in the words of biographer Judith Brown, 'based frankly and consciously on poverty'. He rejected modern medicine, and refused to allow his wife to have a penicillin injection when she contracted pneumonia. She died as a result. (Although he himself found it acceptable to take quinine later on to cure his own malaria.)

A Cultured Image

His historical image now is as the man suffering on behalf of humanity and living by the unselfish deed, a leap beyond the mean and sullied world of politics. In reality, he was also the arch manipulator, a maestro of the modern arts of persuasion and appearance, years before the dark arts of image management became the driving force of modern politics. It was often remarked that Gandhi was a man out of his time. They didn't know how truly they spoke.

DEATH BY SUICIDE?

Another for whom image now appears literally to have been a matter of life and death is **Julius Caesar**. According to new studies in 2003, one of the earliest and certainly one of the most famous assassinations in history may have been an engineered suicide by a politician more intent with preserving his image to history than with his earthly fate.

Historians have long puzzled over the series of curious lapses in security and judgment that surround the events of Caesar's stabbing in the Roman Senate on 15 March in 44BC. He famously ignored the warnings of the soothsayer to beware the Ides of March. The night before the assassination, at dinner with friends, he engaged in a morbid conversation on the subject of 'What is the best death?' His own answer was, 'A sudden one.' On the day, his wife urged him not to go out as she had dreamed of him lying dead in her arms. He ignored the plea and even dismissed his bodyguards for the walk to the Senate. He also did not read a note thrust into his hand by a friend as he arrived which outlined the whole plot. Moreover, the apparent scale of the conspiracy – up to 60 are thought to have been involved – has always left a question mark over how Caesar, by all accounts the sharpest politician of his time, could have remained unaware of such an extensive move against him.

The work of a modern Italian forensic policeman suggests that perhaps Caesar actually knew very well what was about to befall him, but that it suited him for it to unfold. The assassination, far from a shock, was the opportunity for Caesar to gain his perpetual legacy in history.

In March 2003, Colonel Luciano Garafano, a *carabinieri* forensic

47

investigator, claimed that evidence assessed by him and by one of the world's leading forensic psychologists from the Harvard Medical School, pointed to a scenario that allowed these apparently odd circumstances to all make sense. He claimed that the pieces added up to a contrived suicide which achieved Caesar's ultimate ambition – an immortal unstained image.

Caesar's Seizures

The motivation Garafano gives is Caesar's declining health. At 56, he was already long in the tooth for a Roman. There is evidence from near contemporary accounts, particularly from historians Suetonius and Plutarch, that Caesar had developed a form of epilepsy – judged by Harvard experts to be temporal-lobe epilepsy – that involves sufferers losing bodily control, especially the bowels and to suffer from diarrhoea. The other side-effect is a psychological tendency towards rashness and grandiose thoughts.

In a politician who was supremely concerned about how history would view him, this combination, Garafano suggests, was enough to prompt Caesar to a decision. He faced either a prospect of years of decline, dominated by the likelihood of increasing episodes of losing self-control, or he could choose to go out in a blaze of glory and cement his reputation forever.

Garafano maintains that Caesar allowed events to take their course and did nothing to disrupt the plot. He even suggests there was political calculation too. By perpetrating the killing in the Senate, the conspirators had broken Roman law by taking weapons into the meeting house. This swept away any chance for them claiming legitimacy afterwards, and thus denied the plotters the grounds to assume power themselves.

In their place, the only viable successor now was Octavian, Caesar's 19-year-old nephew whom he had nominated only a few months earlier when he had tellingly changed his will. By this change, and his death at this time, Caesar magisterially achieved his ambition to create a personal dynasty against the increasing demands for a republic that were coming from the plotters. In an ultimate irony, an assassination that was ostensibly carried out precisely because of fears that Caesar was planning to create a personal fiefdom, ended up securing for Caesar exactly that.

Securing the Legacy

There is more evidence in Caesar's will that it was all a cleverly contrived masterstroke. Read out at his funeral, it cannily left most of his possessions to the people – one account says it was enough for each Roman family to live for up to three months at his expense. The public reaction naturally swung in the deceased's favour, and by nightfall mobs were torching the houses of the assassins and forcing them to flee for their lives.

As Garafano points out, Caesar's reputation was, thereby, solidly secured. He went out at the top, reputation unblemished, even enhanced – the ambition of any politician, if achieved by so few. Until now, it has been seen as an accident of fate. It may, however, have been a supremely cunning political act.

2

Politics – Dark Arts
Getting Darker

If you thought politics couldn't get muckier, read on. For good or bad, our history books have managed to erase from the record some dubious attributes of history's leaders.

Our Prime Ministers come down to us through the history books enrobed in the reputations they earned through their tenure of office. Mention Winston Churchill, and the mental pen-picture instantly appears in our minds of 'the man of the hour', 'the nation's saviour' in the Second World War. Likewise with William Pitt (who became Prime Minister at 24) – the precocious swotty upstart; Gladstone, the 'Grand Old Man' and the height of Victorian propriety; Disraeli, the amusing and agreeable fop.

But each had another, less well-known side. We start by shedding a different light on some famous historical reputations that will make us think again about the image we commonly have.

LEADER OF THE PACK

Our first recognised Prime Minister, **Robert Walpole**, whose term spanned 21 years from 1721 to 1742, still the longest on record, had a conviction for corruption while Secretary at War a decade before he rose to the top post, and had been expelled by the House of Commons. Even while Chancellor of the Exchequer, he indulged in trading with contraband goods from the Continent. In 1717, he resigned from that post in protest at the dismissal of his brother-in-law, Lord Townshend. When King George I refused to accept it, Walpole repeated his resignation request 10 times before he got his way. He was also suspected of insider dealing in the infamous South Sea Bubble scandal. He sold his shares, having made a 1,000 per cent profit, just before the bubble burst in 1720. He became Prime Minister on the back of the affair, with the task of sorting out the national mess from which he had so handsomely profited.

LOSING A MIND – AND AMERICA

William Pitt, Earl of Chatham, the Younger Pitt's father, had not one, or two, but three mental breakdowns during his political career and still endured to reach the premiership. It was hardly a dynasty from which one would expect national leaders to emerge. Pitt's brother and four out of his five sisters were all mentally unstable. For much of his own premiership, Pitt was on the verge of insanity. Only three months after becoming Prime Minister in 1766, he retreated from the pressures of Westminster to the seclusion of his house at North End in the Hampstead suburbs, from where he ran the affairs of state, in a manner of speaking. A contemporary observer described the Prime Minister's demeanour: 'He sits most part of the day leaning his head down upon his hands, which are rested on the table.' He hardly talked to anyone, not even his wife, and rather than communicate by speech he would silently motion his wishes with hand signals. His main preoccupation appeared to be avoiding his fellow ministers and the problems they brought. Thus unsupervised, his Treasury team laid the seeds for the loss of the American colonies by imposing the taxes on the settlers that would lead to the move for independence.

Losing It All

Lord North, Prime Minister throughout the American War of Independence, had a reputation for falling asleep on the Government front bench in Parliament and snoring loudly. He had such poor eyesight that he could not make out who was speaking on the opposite side, and was renowned as being extremely careless in guarding the confidences of his office. His Cabinet colleagues were known to feel it was dangerous to trust him with any state papers as he 'perpetually' mislaid them. A letter 'of first political importance' written to him by the King, was found after a long search, lying wide open in his water closet where he had evidently been reading it while on the toilet.

The Quiet Man

During the two and a half years of his second premiership, from March 1807 to September 1809, the **Duke of Portland** never spoke in Parliament. He rarely even attended Cabinet meetings.

Politics from the Bottle – But Not the Baby's

Pitt the Younger is famed not only for the unprecedented age at which he arrived at the top as Prime Minister – 24 years and 205 days – but for the uncouthness of his drinking habits. Addicted to port as a result of bizarre medical advice to drink a bottle daily as a health tonic (it was up to three a day by the end of his life), he often appeared in the House of Commons drunk. Pitt was premier at the time of the Napoleonic Wars. Like Churchill a century and a quarter later, the leader responsible for the greatest national war effort of the age was a notorious and prodigious imbiber. By 1800, when Prime Minister, he had to live for a period with Henry Addington, Speaker of the Commons, and a close friend, because he could not look after himself. His habit rarely seemed to interfere with his official duties, however. He once left his seat on the Government bench to be sick behind the Speaker's chair, keeping a careful ear on the debate while he did so, and returned to respond as if he had missed none of the argument.

Summoning Up the Courage

Henry Addington, himself Prime Minister for three years immediately following Pitt, evidently picked up some of his mentor's habits too. A poor debater, he steeled his nerves by regularly drinking up to 20 glasses of wine at dinner before going into the Commons Chamber to speak.

War by Other Means

The **Duke of Wellington**, war hero and victor at Waterloo, never quite got the hang of civil administration. When he became Prime Minister in 1828, his first Cabinet meeting did not go as he expected He described it afterwards as 'an extraordinary affair. I gave them their orders and they wanted to stay and discuss them'. He is one of only two Prime Ministers to have fought a duel while in office (the other being the Younger Pitt). His sense of honour was so intense that when he felt he had been insulted by Lord Winchilsea over an about-turn on policy (when he brought in the Catholic Emancipation Bill), he challenged his opponent, and fought the duel in Battersea Park. They both deliberately missed and honour was restored.

53

Spending Time With the Family

Earl Grey, Prime Minister between 1830 and 1834, is likely to be better known to the general public for his tea than as a political leader. He rose to the highest office from complete obscurity. He had been in Parliament for 44 years, but only had 15 months of service as a minister behind him when he became Prime Minister. Historically, he is one of our most significant PMs, leading the Great Reform Act of 1832 that started the 19th century's journey towards electoral democracy by extending the vote. He passed the first Factory Act to limit child labour and abolished slavery throughout the Colonies. He also indulged in the old-fashioned trammels of office too. He enriched his own family egregiously. On appointment, he immediately gave official posts or pensions to 20 of his relations from which, after the four years of their patriarch's tenure, they had netted £202,892 from their Government's coffers (amounting in modern values to some £16 million).

A Most Unlikely Chaperon

Lord Melbourne, Prime Minister in 1834 and then more sub-stantially for six and a half years between 1835 and 1841, was at the helm at a pivotal point in British history. He cuts his best-known figure as the fatherly guide to the young Queen Victoria who ascended the throne in 1837 aged just 18. Melbourne, then nearing his sixties, became her mentor on public affairs, tutoring the young Queen.

It was a distinctly unlikely prospect. Melbourne's private life, not always secret, was far from a palatable one. He was a womaniser of serial proportions. He has the unique record among Prime Ministers for being cited twice in court actions brought by husbands alleging adultery with their wives. One of them, in 1836, he had to defend while still serving as premier. Being married for 23 years to Caroline

Lamb, who conducted a scandalous affair with Byron to Melbourne's public embarrassment, could not have helped instil stability into his approach to life.

Even darker aspects of his other side only emerged in the late 1990s. Research amongst Melbourne's unpublished letters showed he indulged in flagellation and had an unhealthy interest in whipping, especially children. Melbourne told the Queen that his tutor at Eton had not flogged him enough. 'It would have been better if he had flogged me more.'

He appears to have been equally indulgent to the children he fostered when he and Caroline could not produce a family of their own. According to one biographer, at least one of the children was still writing to Melbourne in old age recalling the 'chastisement room' where beatings would take place, and reminding him of his apparent revelling in the pain inflicted by enquiring hours afterwards whether the victim was still hurting. Oxford academic Leslie Mitchell, who uncovered the letters, concluded that 'he was, in modern terms, a sadist and a child abuser'.

He also had the unappetising practice of cutting illustrations of children being beaten out of a collection of French erotic literature called *Les Dames Galantes* and sending them to his mistress, Lady Elizabeth Branden. She sent him similar cuttings in return.

As far as public duty goes, he is regarded as the most indolent of all our Prime Ministers. He refused to move into 10 Downing Street because he did not want to be at the centre of political affairs or be troubled by his ministers. Instead, he allowed himself to be installed for most of his premiership at Windsor, where he would spend up to six hours every day with the young Queen.

Throughout his life he had the unfortunate knack of falling asleep in the middle of a discussion. He once did so three times during an audience with Victoria. Rather disconcertingly, he also talked loudly to himself.

Dubious Beginnings

Lord John Russell, who would become Prime Minister in 1846, was legally under age when first elected to Parliament (he was a younger son of the Duke of Bedford so was able to stand for the House of Commons). He won a by-election in May 1813 when he was only 20 years and nine months old, three months short of the legal minimum for sitting in the House. According to the Parliamentary bible, *Erskine May*, he took his seat in the Commons before his 21st birthday. It was all technically illegal, but in those days, such formalities counted for little, especially when the unusual (to us) circumstances are appreciated. He was being elected in the family borough of Tavistock in Devon, which was effectively owned by the Bedfords, he had no other candidate standing against him and he was not even in the country at the time when his election took place.

It was hardly going to be challenged. The Prime Minister at the time was **Lord Liverpool** who had been elected even younger, just 11 days after his 20th birthday. At least he waited until he had passed his coming of age before taking up his seat.

Age Shall Not Weary Them

Lord Palmerston, elected to Parliament at the age of 26, was 71 when he formed his first ministry in 1855, the oldest of all the Prime Ministers at their first appointment. He was a notorious womaniser, was cited for adultery at the age of 78 – which only seemed to enhance his popularity – and is rumoured to have fathered an illegitimate child when nearly 80. Queen Victoria never forgave him for trying to rape a lady-in-waiting while staying as a royal guest at Windsor in 1839 when he was Foreign Secretary. He took a fancy to Mrs Brand over dinner, and boldly marched into her room during the night. She resisted, Victoria got to hear of it and the Prime Minister Lord Melbourne had to use all his fatherly charm to get the next most senior politician in the country off the hook. One excuse was that he had entered the room by mistake. On delving deeper, the explanation was less than excusing – he claimed he had been aiming for the bedroom of another woman, not his wife, who *was* expecting him.

The Greasiest Struggle

Benjamin Disraeli competes with Melbourne and Palmerston for the title of the 19th century's most colourful premier. Prime Minister for a year in 1868, and then between 1874 and 1880, he secured some of the high points of Britain's imperial history. He bought half ownership in the Suez Canal for Britain in a dramatic diplomatic coup, and made Victoria Empress of India. Domestically, he passed some of the Victorian era's most forward-thinking social reforms. He was universally regarded as the Queen's favourite – and most sycophantic – premier.

This historical reputation that he carved out for himself successfully buried an earlier less salubrious phase of his life that led to perhaps the strangest launch of any political career, and one he would always be keen to draw a veil over. He won his first election triumph actually trying desperately to keep *out* of the public eye.

Dodgy Dossiers

The victory, in the Kent seat of Maidstone at the General Election of 1837, was his fifth attempt to win a place in the House of Commons. He was 32 and heavily – very heavily – in debt from unfortunate speculation in foreign mining shares.

He had been attracted to the opportunity to make apparently easy money in the stock market boom of 1823 to 1825. Some idea of the fevered atmosphere can be gained by the astonishing returns possible. Shares in one Anglo-Mexican enterprise that had been bought for £10 the previous year were selling at £150 in January 1825, near the peak of boom. Then a young solicitor's clerk, Disraeli got even more ensnared during that fateful year.

He had been deputed by his employers to draw up prospectuses for three mining opportunities in Central America. These misleadingly exaggerated the potential of the mines' outputs. They were in fact seriously fraudulent. Some biographers maintain that he did so unwittingly, not knowing the information with which he had been supplied by the promoters of the schemes to be suspect; others that he was all too fully aware of the likelihood that he was committing a gross deception, but that he had been sucked up by the enormous gains to be had. He was still only 20 years old.

He himself borrowed heavily to invest in such schemes. By his own estimate, he had sunk £6,000 into various companies (some £400,000 in current values). In December 1825, one of the worst financial crashes ever in British history occurred. The stock market imploded and 73 banks in Britain suspended business or failed entirely. It wiped out all the value of Disraeli's shares. The debt he now had would hang over him well into his middle age. More immediately, he had a mental breakdown, which lasted more than four years. He also had to leave the country for a while to escape his creditors.

On his return to England, he embarked on his five-year effort to get into Parliament. His luck turned when the opportunity arose to join his friend Wyndham Lewis, who was one of the two MPs for Maidstone, in the dual-seat constituency at the General Election occasioned by the death of King William IV and the accession of Queen Victoria, the monarch with whom he would, decades later, form such a personal bond.

Give Me Your Vote, Not Your Attention

When he and Wyndham travelled down from Westminster to Maidstone for the campaign, they kept a very low profile, all the time alarmed that Disraeli's creditors would make a grab for him en route. He had been keeping himself in virtual self-imposed isolation for months. It was hardly a promising tactic for seeking public office. He had to be quietly secreted into the Conservative Party office in Maidstone, where he was safely away from intruding eyes.

He spent most of the election campaign trying not to draw attention

58

to himself. In these pre-democratic days, success came by other means than appearing openly in public to press one's case. Wyndham's wealth – he was said to be worth £11,000 a year (about £800,000 in modern values) – was a godsend to Disraeli in a constituency which was reputed to be 'universally corrupt' and where votes could cost anywhere between £5 and £50. Wyndham generously advanced him the proceeds necessary for victory. At the poll, he came second to Lewis, well ahead of the only other candidate, and was elected. He was to sit in Parliament continuously for the next 44 years until a month before his death.

The connection with Wyndham turned out, in a way, to be life long. When his co-member suddenly died the next year, Disraeli took up with his bereaved wife, Mary Anne, even though she was 45 and he only 33. She did, however, have a legacy from Wyndham of £5,000 a year (£350,000 today) and a house at Grosvenor Gate in London's plush Mayfair. It turned out a ringing success. They were happily married for 33 years until her death in 1872.

Great Expectations

Disraeli's early Parliamentary career was also built around a ruthless and undisguised scramble for rapid advancement. Disloyalty and one significant lie were central in laying the ground for his future glittering success.

After just one term in the House, he expected the Party leader, Robert Peel, to give him a ministerial post in the Government following the election in 1841, and he wrote pleading for a job. He did not get it. Embittered, he turned against his leader and as Peel became ensnared in an economic crisis over the Irish famine and the laws keeping corn prices high, which would eventually bring him down and split the Party for a generation, Disraeli saw his chance to get rid of the obstacle to his own progression.

It was personal, very personal. Destroying his leader became, in his words, 'the ultimate object of my political life'. He became an enemy within to Peel, made outrageous attacks on his own Party leader in the House and led a cabal of dissidents to undermine the Government. The split he cultivated would leave the Conservatives divided for nearly three decades. When it came together again, surprise surprise it was Disraeli who had emerged at the top of the pile to forge the new Conservative Party.

The Nearly Man

It could have been so very different. Disraeli came within a whisker of blowing his ambition when he found himself neatly trapped in debate by Peel after one of his greatest assaults on the Prime Minister at the height of the Corn Law crisis in May 1846 and had to lie to the House of Commons, the most grievous of offences that any member can commit.

Peel had responded to the attack with mock puzzlement. He asked the House why, if Disraeli so detested the Government, he had asked so keenly to join it? Disraeli, taken off guard, lied in reply and denied he had ever written asking for a post. He took an enormous risk, not knowing whether Peel would produce the letter there and then. Had Peel done so, he would have had little option but to resign in disgrace. Accounts differ as to whether Peel had the letter with him. Some say he had it among his papers, but could not find it in time; others that he had had it in his pocket, but that his own honour restrained him from reading out a private communication. Not for the first, or last, time Disraeli scraped through a potentially fatal moment. Not for nothing did he later acquire the nickname 'Dizzy' as his fortunes went from strength to strength.

Dangerous Liaisons

In 1993, biographer Stanley Weintraub published evidence that strongly showed Disraeli to have fathered two illegitimate children, a boy and a girl, by different mistresses, in 1865, three years before he first became Prime Minister. (Disraeli was then just past 60 – his wife, Mary Anne who, as we have seen, was much the senior partner and had never given Disraeli children, was 72.) One mistress, Lady Dolly Walpole Nevill, a cigar-smoking, renowned social rebel of her day, virtually acknowledged Disraeli as the father of the boy, Ralph, towards the end of her life, confessing, 'I have known [Disraeli] in every possible way.' The other birth, to an unknown mother, was quietly hushed up and the baby, Kate, fostered under arrangements made by Disraeli's lawyer. She was said to have grown to bear a striking resemblance to Disraeli. Her existence only came to light when a note was found in the lawyer's papers regarding Disraeli's will which was drawn up a few years later. In cold Disraelian fashion, it referred to an infant beneficiary, to whom no provision was to be made.

Jekyll and Hyde

William Gladstone was the Victorian era's 'Grand Old Man'. His political career lasted 63 years – the third longest of any British Prime Minister. He was premier four times – the last stint started when he was 82 – and he was still in the top office when he retired from politics in 1894 at the age of 85. Attlee regarded him as the 'W.G. Grace of politics'. He defined the political era he inhabited, and is the epitome of 19th-century values of stentorian probity, ultra religiosity and stern devotion to public duty. Disraeli's sharp eye caught the light in which Gladstone was seen by his contemporaries: 'He has not a single redeeming defect.'

Yet behind the façade, Gladstone was a tortured soul. Having nearly taken holy orders when considering his career after leaving Oxford University, and been deeply involved in the ferment of the religious reform movements that swept early Victorian Britain of the 1830s and 40s, religion was the bedrock of his life and the backbone of his public service. But his diaries, which only became available in their entirety to scholars in 1994, tell an eloquent, if coded, story of the inner struggles of a personality that was riven with conflicting urges. They were deeply spiritual in tone, a veritable daily account to God of his failings, lapses and self-doubts. A frequently recurring symbol in the shape of a whip was deciphered as an indication that he had scourged himself as a punishment – or perhaps compensation – for what he had done – or not done – the previous night.

61

Nocturnal (E)missions

The 'other side' of him was his practice of 'night walks' through the seedier parts of London, which persisted for 30 years, including while he held the highest political office, ostensibly to rescue prostitutes from their fallen state. He was oblivious to the warning his inner circle gave him on many occasions. Rumours spread. He acquired the nickname 'Old Gladeye' as he seemed to prefer trying to save the younger and prettier type.

One peak in his activity was the early 1850s, when he was temporarily out of ministerial office. In the first half of 1852, he met with various prostitutes 50 times – an average of twice weekly for six months, and each carefully noted in his diary. Frequently, he would record his encounters cryptically as 'strange, questionable' occasions and then document the flogging he inflicted on himself when he returned home. As late as November he was consorting with a favourite, Elizabeth Collins, whom he saw dozens of times since first coming across her in 1851. Incredibly, none of this behaviour impinged on his political prospects. A month later, he reached his highest office so far when he was appointed Chancellor of the Exchequer.

Such conduct astonishes the modern mind. Was it the high-minded missionary zeal of a deeply religious spirit who felt immune to worldly comment, or a succumbing to the mortal urges of a deeply fractured psyche? At the time, and now, it's almost impossible to tell with Gladstone.

In a confession late in life, worthy of the tightly drawn circum-locutions of a Bill Clinton, Gladstone told his clergyman son that he had never been guilty of 'the act which is known as that of infidelity to the marriage bed'. Biographers interpret this to mean he denied ever having full sexual intercourse with the women. What he thereby did not deny doing is left to the imagination.

Most biographers have fought shy of sordid speculation and sweep this aspect of Gladstone's character under the carpet, so astounding they find it that he appeared to casually lay his reputation open so publicly to such risks on a nightly basis.

Relaxing With His Chopper

One of Gladstone's more bizarre ways of gaining release from the pressures of the day was to chop down trees at his Hawarden estate in Flintshire, North Wales. He found it the ideal remedy for pent-up energy. He once explained how it helped rest his brain: while chopping down a tree, one only had time to think of 'where your next stroke will fall'. He felled hundreds during his 30 or so years there. It was not uncommon for visitors to make a pilgrimage there to see the old man in action. Even at the time, his political adversaries looked disdainfully on the practice. Winston Churchill's father, Randolph, then high-flying in the opposition Conservatives, sharply observed that 'the forest laments in order that Mr Gladstone may perspire'.

BORN TO LEAD

Lord Salisbury, far less known to the modern mind than Disraeli, his predecessor as Conservative premier, actually served nearly 14 years as Prime Minister, more than twice as long as Disraeli did, and by the end of his career was seen as nothing short of the epitome of stolid late Victorianism. Bred from the ancient Cecil family that had served monarchs as far back as Elizabeth I, he was always going to have a gilded public life. But his personal characteristics were deeply inauspicious. He suffered a complete mental breakdown while at university and had to be sent away on a round-the-world voyage to recover. He would suffer from depression and 'nerve storms' throughout his life. When under stress, he would sleepwalk to his bedroom window apparently trying to prevent 'the mob' from storming in.

Temperamentally, he hated the public duty of socialising. He was easily bored by the forced necessities of public office. When Foreign Secretary he regularly had to see ambassadors from abroad, which disinterested him intensely. He kept awake by jabbing himself in the legs under the table with a paper knife.

63

He had such a lack of interest in other people that stories multiplied about his failure to recognise faces that should have been familiar. He failed to recognise his Chief Whip, had to ask who a dinner guest was to discover he was a Cabinet member who had been serving for more than a decade, mistook his gardeners for two envoys he was about to despatch overseas and even thought his eldest son was a visitor. He was overheard in 1901 castigating a photograph that he took to be of General Buller, who had been the disastrous Commander-in-Chief of British forces in the Boer War. The picture was of King Edward VII.

Bob's Your Uncle

Nepotism was Salisbury's political Achilles heel. So many relations were appointed in his final ministry in 1900 that the Government was ridiculed as the 'Hotel Cecil'. Three nephews were given key posts, First Lord of the Treasury and Leader of the House of Commons (effectively deputy Prime Minister), Board of Trade and the PM's Parliamentary Private Secretary. A nephew-in-law was put in charge of the main House of Commons committee for managing the flow of business, and a son-in-law was First Lord of the Admiralty. *His* son became a minister in the Foreign Office. The Liberal Opposition sarcastically congratulated Lord Salisbury on being 'the head of a family with the most remarkable genius for administration that has ever been known'. Salisbury's reaction suggests just how out of touch he was with modern expectations. He pointed out that the number of relations in the Government was the same as had been the case five years earlier. As he had won both general elections that had been held in between, he could only draw the conclusion that the electorate evidently did not mind.

WHO YOU ARE, NOT WHAT YOU BELIEVE

Showing that quixotic and unorthodox beliefs were no barrier to leading the country if you had the right connections, Salisbury's nephew **Arthur Balfour**, Prime Minister from 1902 to 1905, had earlier served (for a year in 1893) as the President of the newly formed Society for Psychical Research, which had startled the scientifically assured Victorian era by extolling the mysteries of the paranormal. It promoted the study of telepathy, hypnotism, mediums, ghosts and the afterlife, a wacky brew of ideas in which even a modern politician might resist professing belief. Balfour had got involved through his eldest sister, Nora, whose philosopher husband, Henry Sidgwick, had founded the Society.

Balfour had won his first ministerial appointment in 1885 at the age of 36 in his uncle's first Government, became Secretary for Scotland a year later, and served throughout Salisbury's administrations in one office or other, taking over the premiership on his uncle's retirement in 1902.

LOVE STRUCK LEADER

Herbert Asquith, Prime Minister for eight years until halfway through the First World War, became so besotted with his daughter's best friend, 25-year-old Venetia Stanley, that between 1912 and 1915 the premier, a man in his early 60s, spent many Cabinet meetings writing love letters to her. In the first three months of 1915, he wrote to her 151 times. The letters, which became known about in the mid-1960s but were only published in 1982, could be read as revealing Asquith as a distracted individual at a time when the country was hurtling towards, and then in 1914 beginning to fight, the First World War (although one biographer chivalrously points out that he would have spent less time writing to Venetia than he might have spent had he actually been consummating a physical affair). Quite how much his mind was on affairs of state can only be left to speculation.

As the reality of the war sank in – the troops would not be 'home by Christmas' as had been confidently predicted at the beginning – Asquith began to be seen as indecisive and procrastinating. By 1915, he was heading a coalition Government, and by the following year he had resigned when Lloyd George emerged as a more decisive leader.

Lost Leader

There had long been question marks over Asquith's drinking, although his Conservative adversary Bonar Law once said that 'Asquith, when drunk, could make a better speech than any of us sober'. He was an imbiber of potent amounts of brandy, which, unknown to him, his wife used to water down. He was christened 'Old Squiffy', a term that entered the language as a tag for being worse for wear. During the committee stage of the landmark Parliament Bill in 1911, he was slumped in his Prime Ministerial position on the front bench in the House of Commons too drunk to speak. The following year, 'very flushed and unsteady in gait', he sunk into his place and fell asleep during a debate on the Welsh Church Bill, which two of his ministers, Herbert Samuel and Rufus Isaacs, were handling. The opposition leader, Balfour, pointed out to concerned Welsh folk that their religious interests were 'in the hands of two Jews who are sober and a Christian who is very patently drunk'.

TEFLON MAN

Compared to **David Lloyd George**, Asquith was a saint. Lloyd George was nevertheless one of Britain's greatest Prime Ministers, in war and in peace, and probably to last to have been able to 'get a way with it'. He acquired his nickname, 'The Goat', because of his serial womanising. Skeletons? They were not just in a cupboard but all over the house. A story, told of his daughter and possibly apocryphal, captures the man to his core. She was standing in a queue at the post office in her father's north Wales constituency becoming more and more frustrated at the wait. She eventually called out angrily, 'Don't you know that I am Lloyd George's daughter?' The postmaster replied, 'There's plenty of girls round 'ere could say that.'

His secretary had become his mistress four years before he became Prime Minister in 1916, and remained so for nearly 30 years until his wife died in 1941. He then married her two years later.

Lloyd George's premiership was also troubled in 1922 by a huge scandal surrounding his dispensing of honours for financial contributions to the Party. Allegedly, anyone could get a peerage for £50,000. Knighthoods went for £15,000. It led to changes in the law that set up the modern system of vetting honours by a civil service committee. Ten years earlier, while Chancellor of the Exchequer, he had also been involved in controversy in a share scandal. He had bought £2,000 of shares in the American division of the Marconi electronics company just before the English arm of the company won a valuable contract from the Government to build radio stations across the Empire, and which sent the share values of all the company's branches rocketing. Although it was never proved that Lloyd George used inside knowledge of the Government's plan to award the contract, there was deep suspicion over his behaviour and judgment.

Rocking the Boat

Perhaps the most biting criticism over his judgement came long after Lloyd George had left the mainstream political scene. As Nazism emerged on the Continent, he appeared to become an admirer of Hitler as a saviour of peace. In September 1936, he spent two weeks in Nazi Germany, visiting the Führer in his Bavarian retreat at Berchtesgaden. Hitler is recorded as having been bewitched by the Welsh Wizard, then 73 years old but lacking little of his characteristic energy. They talked for three hours. Lloyd George likewise was elated at the experience, and spellbound by Hitler's personality, declaring, 'He is indeed a great man ... he is a born leader – a statesman.' They met a second time the next day.

When he returned to England, he wrote an effusive article in the *Daily Express* lauding Hitler's achievements (he was the 'George Washington of Germany'), and intoning with evident confidence that those who feared a rising Germany had nothing to worry about. 'Those who imagine that Germany has swung back to its old

Imperialist temper cannot have any understanding of the character of the change. The idea of a Germany intimidating Europe with a threat that its irresistible Army might march across frontiers forms no part of the vision . . . They have no longer the desire themselves to invade any other land . . . The Germans have definitely made up their minds never to quarrel with us again.'

Such strong views raised eyebrows among the political elite in Britain and did his own reputation considerable harm. His later attempts at spirited criticism of the subsequent war effort on which, as an experienced war leader himself, he might have been thought to have something to offer, were, as a consequence, insignificant.

THE NATION'S GREATEST?

The variety and length of **Winston Churchill**'s career has created both an enduring historical image and much opportunity for darker sides of his character to lapse back into the shadows.

In the Lurch

Churchill's daring escape from a Boer War prisoner-of-war camp in December 1899 established his public reputation for bravado and for having a larger-than-life character. It turned the unknown 25-year-old adventurer, stuck for a career and trying his hand at war reporting, into a national hero and a symbol of British success at a time in the war when the Boers firmly had the upper hand. It eased his journey into national political life. Within three months of his return from South Africa in the middle of the following year, he won election as an MP and embarked on his historic career.

The escape, however, sparked a bitter round of recriminations between Churchill and his two camp colleagues who ended up remaining behind. They accused Churchill of abandoning an agreed plan to escape together and, in his own selfish bid for freedom, deserting his comrades.

Aylmer Haldane, who eventually rose to be a general, died before he could write a public account of his side of the story, but a letter he wrote in 1931 which only came to light in 1997 set out the bones of his complaint that Churchill's account of individual enterprise was 'fiction'.

Haldane had been irked by Churchill's flamboyant autobiography *My Early Life*, which came out in 1930 and retold the story of the Boer War escape. Haldane claimed that he and another man, one Sergeant Major Brockie, had already devised a joint plan to escape when Churchill came into the picture. Churchill 'perfectly understood', Haldane wrote, that the three were to go together. They tried once but discovered a sentry posted outside the latrine where they had spotted an unlit part of the perimeter. The next night they tried again. According to Churchill, Haldane and Brockie were so hesitant he feared they would spend another night in indecision. He jumped the wall to show it could be done without detection. He maintained that he waited for his colleagues for more than an hour and half on the other side, always in grave danger of being discovered, before deciding to go it alone. He even claimed he tried to pass messages back across the wall to Haldane trying to persuade him it was safe to come across.

According to Haldane, it was much simpler than that: 'He slipped off without myself or the third man, whose abuse of Churchill I shall not forget.' Haldane eventually escaped three months later. He had wanted to tell his story soon after his own return to England but, as Churchill's star rose, he claimed he kept quiet about the affair because of pressure from Churchill's friends. *My Early Life*, however, infuriated him for presenting a travesty of an episode that in truth revealed Churchill more as cad than hero.

Haldane's letter, written to a senior Conservative politician, explained he was not intending to publish the allegation as it was one man's word against another. But it was a cry from a betrayed friend. 'I do not wish to harm him, though I do not have much faith in him.'

Churchill biographers are inclined to believe Haldane's account, saying it has an authentic ring about it. It points to Churchill breaking the code of honour between gentlemen officers. Breaking the rules was a common facet of Churchill's life and career. As historian Andrew Roberts noted, 'It was the secret behind his success.'

Gas, Boys, Quick!

While Secretary of State for War at the end of the First World War, Churchill vigorously pushed for the use of poisonous gas in future conflicts. Despite the appalling casualties that chemical warfare caused on the Western Front, where Churchill himself had seen active service for six months between 1915 and 1916, records released only in 1997 showed that when his military advisers were tasked with considering future war strategies, he intervened to stress the military value of the weapon, despite the horrific injuries it caused.

He wrote in an official memorandum in May 1919 that had the war continued into 1919, 'gas would have been almost our most formidable weapon'. He could not understand the 'squeamishness' of those who objected.

Churchill's passion for gas had been seen during his management of the last year of war as Minister of Munitions. In just five months between April and August 1918, British production of gas shells more than doubled. By as early as May 1918, every third shell fired on the Western Front by the British Army was a gas shell.

When he took over at the War Office in early 1919, his task was to prepare the country for future threats, and the current menace facing the Western democracies of the Bolshevik Revolution in Russia. In April 1919, a month before his memorandum to the generals, he authorised the use of gas against the Red Army in the campaign that Allied troops had been fighting since 1918 in their intervention in northern Russia. His only concern was that it might give away the secret of the weapon, which was one of the new poison gases developed in the final months of war. As for the military effect, he wrote that 'of course, I should very much like the Bolsheviks to have it'. Gas experts and cylinders of the top-secret gas were sent to North Russia in May and attempts to deploy were made almost immediately. The absence of any wind, however, stalled plans for a month until engineers came up with their own improvised solution. History's first gas bombs were made and dropped on the Russians from the air. More than 2,700 were thrown from Allied planes into the forests around Archangel, causing 'great panic' among the enemy, before the British withdrawal in October.

Churchill had even fewer qualms about using gas on 'uncivilised tribes'. When Britain took responsibility after the First World War for administrating former Turkish provinces in the Middle East, it faced frequent rebellions against their occupation. Faced with a revolt by Kurds in Mesopotamia (modern Iraq) in 1922, British planes bombed villages with gas in one of the world's earliest examples of targeted deployment of weapons of mass destruction. Mesopotamia came under the political responsibility of the Colonial Office. The Colonial Secretary at the start of the revolt? Winston Churchill.

It was just in time. Poison gas as a weapon of war was prohibited under international law in 1925 by the Geneva Protocol, which at the same time formally banned biological warfare.

Fighting for a Reputation

Churchill's heroic leadership in the war against Hitler not surprisingly cast him in the mould of 'saviour of the nation' for following generations. He is remembered by post-war generations as the embodiment of resistance and determination against the odds. For much of the period since the war he has been the sheer epitome of the British bulldog spirit. It was undoubtedly the genuine sentiment of a thankful nation. Yet Churchill's lasting heroic image was very different to the one he had earned in the longest portion of his political career. Had Churchill died before ever becoming Prime Minister (he was well into his 66th year when he became premier), history would have painted a very different portrait – of spectacular potential thwarted by a series of colossal misjudgments.

Churchill fancied himself to be in same mould as his famous antecedent John Churchill, Duke of Marlborough, the 18th-century warrior supremo who never lost a battle and won victories that still resonate today – Blenheim, Ramillies, Malplaquet, Oudenarde. For

71

these he won his dukedom and enough financial reward to build Blenheim Palace, where Winston would be born. Winston would later write a two-volume biography of his forebear, reliving each military challenge and achievement as if his own.

But as war leader himself, his skeletons were legion, and his own credentials not at all inspiring. Although he turned in a famously successful youthful career as a cavalry officer in the Hussars, he failed his entrance exams to the Royal Military College at Sandhurst twice and only got in on the third attempt, and then with marks too low to qualify for the socially superior infantry, to the huge disgust of his father Randolph.

A(n)twerp

Churchill's irresistible urge to get involved left him with a legacy of question marks over his true military prowess. As First Lord of the Admiralty at the outbreak of the First World War, he was unable to contain himself when hostilities neared home. As German forces moved on the Belgian port of Antwerp, a vital entry point behind German lines for the Allies to hold, Churchill enthusiastically charged off himself to lead the defences of the city. When he got there, and after a few days found he was needed back in London for Admiralty business, he even telegraphed Asquith, the Prime Minister, offering to resign from the Cabinet to coordinate the action on the ground 'provided I am given necessary military rank and authority, with full powers of a commander'. Asquith later wrote in a private letter that the proposal had been received by the Cabinet 'with a Homeric laugh'. Asquith went on to point out the absurdity of Churchill's thinking, 'W is an ex-Lieutenant of Hussars, and would if his proposal had been accepted, have been in command of 2 distinguished Major Generals, not to mention Brigadiers, Colonels & c.' A few days later, Asquith is complaining in another letter that 'Winston persists in remaining there, which leaves the Admiralty without a head, and I have had to tell them to submit all decisions to me.' Despite all Churchill's efforts to stiffen defences, four days after he returned to London, Antwerp fell.

A turkey Effort

Churchill's 'noisy mind' (a description given him by Margot Asquith in a pen picture on his 40th birthday in November 1914) was immediately focused on the next big idea. He was convinced the Allies needed a vigorous offensive policy in the face of the German onslaught. He initially wanted to launch an aggressive assault across the North Sea on Germany directly, but when the prospects of an even more dramatic option emerged, he seized it. Always on the lookout for the unorthodox, the vision of the surprise attack from an unexpected quarter materialised. He almost single-handedly forced on the Cabinet the ill-fated operation that would scar his reputation for 20 years – Gallipoli, the sea-borne invasion in April 1915 of a tiny peninsular of land in Turkey, with the aim that it should lead to the capture of Constantinople and – even more fantastically – be the start of a march into the 'soft underbelly' of the enemy.

Gallipoli ended up as a bloodbath from the unexpectedly stiff Turkish defences that prevented the invasion from ever leaving the beaches. Of the half million Allied troops committed, more than half became casualties, 42,000 of whom died in the nine-month disaster. Badly planned and ignorant of the terrain – generals were supplied with tourist guidebooks bought in Egypt that were at least 10 years out of date – the Allied forces all had to be evacuated in January 1916. As one historical authority has put it, 'With the possible exception of the Crimean War, the Gallipoli expedition was the most poorly mounted and ineptly controlled operation in modern British military history.' It would hang around Churchill's neck for the next two decades, casting doubt over his judgment. Such a pedigree was hardly a recommendation for a war leader to bring with him.

A General's View

During the Second World War, his dealings with generals were usually fraught, although to the outside world a solid image was preserved of unity in adversity. In diaries that were only fully released in 2001, Field Marshal Sir Alan Brooke, Churchill's Chief of the Imperial General Staff, the highest military adviser to the Government, a post he held from 1941 to the end of the war, confided that he thought Churchill 'a public menace'. After a dispute in 1944, he wrote of the Prime Minister: 'He knows no details, has got only half the picture in his mind, talks absurdities, and makes my blood boil to listen to his nonsense. The wonderful thing is that three quarters of the population imagine Churchill is one of the great strategists of history, a second Marlborough, and the other quarter have no conception of what a public menace he is.' According to historian A.J.P. Taylor, Churchill at various points during the war proposed to dismiss every one of his leading admirals, although he did not succeed in every case. Churchill was unrepentant. When told that Hitler bullied his generals, Churchill acknowledged that 'I do the same'.

One of the Few Who Dissented

He famously sacked Sir Hugh Dowding, his Air Chief Marshal responsible for victory in the Battle of Britain, just weeks after the battle was over because he had deigned to contradict Churchill on a decision earlier in the war. Churchill rarely forgave such open dissent. The treatment rankled with the Battle of Britain pilots for years afterwards. When Dowding died in 1970, one of those who served with him said in tribute, 'There was unanimous agreement that he was treated rather shabbily. Never in the military history of this country has a successful commander been treated like him.' Legendary pilot Douglas Bader added his own powerful testimonial. 'Lord Dowding is probably unknown to most of the younger generation, yet it was because of him as much as any other man that they have been brought up to the English way of life, speaking the English language. They might have been speaking German.'

Dowding was unquestionably the man for the job in the dark days of 1940. He was single-minded, lonely and aloof, was nicknamed 'Stuffy' by his colleagues and was, in the words of his *Dictionary of National Biography* entry, 'not a man to compromise, thereby provoking anger, exasperation, respect and devotion, sometimes all of these in a single day.' He got public recognition of a sort in September 1969 when he received a standing ovation to a trumpet fanfare at the premiere of the film *Battle of Britain*. He took his place in the stalls surrounded by 350 of the pilots he once commanded. On his death four months later, the bitterness returned. His former personal secretary remarked sadly, 'Seldom in our history has a man deserved so much of his fellow countrymen and wanted and received so little.'

Strategic Ideas

Churchill clashed on many occasion over strategic decisions, as perhaps any political supremo would. But some of his pet obsessions bordered on the quixotic. Perhaps still living his First World War strategy, he laid great store on a second front through southern Europe – what he would continue to refer to as the 'soft underbelly of the Axis'. Historians pointed to the inaptness of such a view, as any understanding of geography showed the Mediterranean hinterland to be anything but soft, it being almost all mountainous terrain and difficult to penetrate. Reality also showed that in the end no Allied Army had managed to reach Germany from the south before the war ended. 'Doing something' was often more important to Churchill than doing what was right. He overruled Admiral Pound, his First Sea Lord and chief of the naval staff, about the wisdom of sending two of his largest and newest warships, the *Prince of Wales* and the *Repulse*, to the Far East in 1941 to act 'as a vague menace' against the Japanese. They had no air cover, and were both sunk a week after they had arrived in the region in their first engagement with the enemy. Eight hundred and forty men were lost, at the cost to the Japanese of four aircraft. As one historian said of the episode, 'It was Churchill all over; if he could not do something effective, he would do something ineffective.'

'Mobilising the English Language'

One aspect of Churchill's wartime leadership would be imagined to be untouchable – his unparalleled command of the English language. He left to posterity some of the most memorable lines ever uttered. He seemed imbued with the knack of conjuring up the perfect phrase for the moment – 'Blood, toil, tears and sweat', 'Never . . . so much owed by so many to so few', 'Not the end; not even the beginning of the end, but the end of the beginning', 'the Iron Curtain'. American broadcaster Ed Murrow put it into words when he said of Churchill in an 80th birthday tribute in 1954, 'He mobilised the English language and sent it into battle.'

Churchill's magic with words was, indeed, unprecedented for a politician. Few other leaders have left such a rich legacy. But if it is thought that these phrases were pristinely new inventions, one would be wrong. Most had a pedigree. Churchill's breadth of reading, his joy at using language to telling effect and his literary endeavour – he was an accomplished historical writer and the Nobel Prize he won in 1953 was for literature, not for political service – gave him an edge over the average politico. The hint of a skeleton in his cupboard lay in his adoption of the phrase as a seamless part of his own speech. Others might have felt a twinge of an obligation to acknowledge the sentiment as deriving from someone else.

'Blood, toil, tears and sweat': Churchill's first speech to the House of Commons on 13 May 1940, three days after becoming Prime Minister, introduced his new Government and made clear to the nation the challenge that lay ahead. Belgium, Holland and Luxembourg had been invaded by Hitler's Blitzkrieg on the day Churchill became Britain's leader, and German forces had just crossed the border with France for the first time. His message was famously defiant, 'You ask, What is our aim? I can answer in one word – Victory – victory at all costs, victory in spite of all terror, victory, however long and hard the road may be', but full of foreboding too: 'I would say to the House, as I said to those who have joined this Government: "I have nothing to offer but blood, toil, tears and sweat."'

No inkling that this last phrase might be a borrowed one. But to the literate, the lineage was long. The poet John Donne had first used a similar tag in 1611: 'Tis in vain to do so or mollify it with thy tears or sweat or blood.' Byron, in *The Age of Bronze* (1823) had also used it, 'Year after year they voted cent per cent / Blood, sweat and tear-wrung millions / why – for rent!' And Lord Alfred Douglas used it in the introduction to his *Collected Poems* (1919): 'It [poetry] is forged slowly and patiently, link by link, with sweat and blood and tears.'

In America, Theodore Roosevelt, future US President, used another close formulation in a speech to the national Naval War College in 1897 when Assistant Secretary of the Navy: 'Every man among us is more fit to meet the duties and responsibilities of citizenship because of the perils over which, in the past, the nation has triumphed; because of the blood and sweat and tears, the labour and the anguish, through which, in the days that have gone, our forefathers moved on to triumph.'

Some researchers believe Churchill also drew inspiration from Garibaldi, the Italian revolutionary, who used a comparable construction to the one Churchill offered the House of Commons when facing an equally dire situation defending a besieged Rome in 1849. Garibaldi's appeal to his small band of supporters for their sacrifice is uncannily similar: 'Let those who wish to continue the war against the stranger come with me. . . . I offer hunger, thirst, forced marches, battles and death.'

So by the time Churchill came to prepare his remarks, the context and the phrase had well-developed roots. But it is Churchill's rendition that history remembers, and remembers entirely as his own.

'Never in the field of human conflict was so much owed by so many to so few': Churchill's tribute to the RAF during the Battle of Britain in August 1940 became the legendary instance of the use of this striking formula, but it was one that he himself had worked up in his early writing several times. In his *History of the English-speaking Peoples*, which although not published until after the war, was largely written in the 1930s, he cites the phrase as being borrowed from 'a contemporary' to describe an English rout at the hands of a Scottish Army during the English Civil War: 'Never so many ran from so few with less ado.' It crops up in Churchill's early speeches. One, referring to a Nile dam in 1908, had the construction: 'Nowhere else in the world could so enormous a mass of water be held up by so little

77

masonry.' Sources have pointed to the 18th-century memoirs of military commander Sir John Moore who described the 1794 siege of Calvi during the Napoleonic Wars: 'Never was so much work done by so few.' And Churchill would have been very familiar with Shakespeare's creation in *Henry V*: 'We few, we happy few, we band of brothers.' So, again, a rather more time-worn phrase than perhaps was realised then, or now.

'Now this is not the end. It is not even the beginning of the end. But it is, perhaps, the end of the beginning': Churchill's celebrated appraisal came after the first major Allied victory against the Axis, at El Alamein in November 1942. Many at the time were tempted to see it as the turning point in the likely fortunes of the two sides. (As it turned out, they were broadly correct: Churchill would later famously reflect in his memoirs that 'Before Alamein we never had a victory. After Alamein, we never had a defeat.'). But in 1942, Churchill needed to temper the optimism since he was well aware of the prolonged struggle that still lay ahead.

There is evidence that Churchill borrowed the formulation from a colleague. A generation earlier, at the start of the First World War, Churchill, then First Lord of the Admiralty, shared a platform at a political meeting in September 1914 with his great friend and fellow member of Parliament, F.E. Smith. As *The Times* reported, Smith spoke of a pessimist whom he had heard the previous week 'when the news appeared for the moment to be gloomy', announce that it was the beginning of the end. 'He was wrong. It was only the end of the beginning,' Smith quipped, to cheers from the audience.

Smith's biographer noted that it would seem Churchill quietly pocketed the clever riposte, dusted it off three decades later, and is now the one remembered for it by us all.

'An iron curtain has descended across the Continent': Churchill's phrase, used in his speech at Fulton, Missouri in 1946, to describe the post-war division of Europe as Stalin overran the Eastern states, became the enduring label for the 40-year Cold War that followed. The phrase encapsulated the multitude of perceptions the West had about the Communists – the air of menace and threat, the

sense of decisiveness in action and intent, the aura of division, harshness and secrecy. It was a marvellously all-embracing expression. It was also far from Churchill's creation.

An early use of the phrase, in a similar context, is found in H.G. Wells' *The Food of the Gods* (1904): 'An iron curtain had dropped between him and the outer world.' Queen Elizabeth of the Belgians used the phrase to describe her poignant position (she was herself German) as the First World War started: 'Between them [the Germans] and me there is now a bloody iron curtain which has descended forever.'

Author George Washington Crile, writing in 1915 in *A Mechanistic View of War and Peace* carried on the image: 'France . . . a nation of forty millions with a deep-rooted grievance and an iron curtain at its frontier.' And specifically in the Russian context, as the Communist revolution unfolded, commentator Vasily Rozanov wrote in *Apocalypse of our Time* (1918), 'With a rumble and a roar, an iron curtain is descending on Russian history.' Traveller and political writer Ethel Snowden, who reported on the early revolutionary days in *Through Bolshevik Russia* (1920), wrote on arriving in Petrograd that, 'We were behind the "iron curtain" at last.'

Perhaps the least commending, and the closest, of the antecedents was the use of the phrase by Nazi propaganda chief Josef Goebbels as the Second World War drew to a close. In February 1945, he wrote in the weekly newspaper *Das Reich* a chillingly similar forecast to the one Churchill would deliver just over a year later. The remarks were widely printed in British newspapers: 'Should the German people lay down their arms, the agreements between Roosevelt, Churchill and Stalin would allow the Soviets to occupy all Eastern and South-Eastern Europe together with the major part of the Reich. An iron curtain would at once descend on this territory.' Germany's Foreign Minister, Count Schwerin von Krosigk, also used it in a broadcast to the nation on 2 May 1945. As the Soviet armies overran the country, 'In the east, the iron curtain behind which, unseen by the eyes of the world, the work of destruction goes on, is steadily moving forward.' The broadcast was also widely reported in the British press.

Churchill appears to have picked this up because just 10 days later he used the very phrase in a telegram to US President Truman to describe his own anxieties about not knowing what the Russians were up to in Eastern Europe.

So at Fulton, 10 months later, he expressed the sentiment to a wider audience – and it would be his embracing of the phrase that the world would remember.

Order Out of Chaos

Churchill's working practices were characteristically unorthodox. He preferred to work in bed and did much of his speech writing there, as well as working on Government papers. It was by no means a private affair. He would still collect around him his secretarial staff for dictation – and his pets. Cats were almost ever-present. Nelson and then Smokey would sprawl at the end of the bed. At one time, Churchill also had a budgerigar called Toby. He would be free to fly around the room, but spent much time perched on the Prime Minister's bald head. To protect the pate from bird droppings, Churchill put a sponge on his head. One observer of these bizarre arrangements recorded in his diary, how the secretary taking notes 'had somehow to retain her composure while taking dictation on matters of state from the Prime Minister of the United Kingdom in bed with a sponge balanced on the top of his head and a budgerigar balanced on the sponge'.

His tireless and energetic style meant that when he was deep in a piece of work, he was truly absorbed. He took inordinate amounts of time over his speeches – he was one of the last premiers to write most of them himself. For major occasions in the House of Commons, he would be writing and revising right up to the last minute. His secretaries often recounted having to try to type in the car, type-writer balanced on knees, as Churchill was driven through winding country lanes up to London from Chartwell, his Kent retreat. Kathleen Hill, his personal secretary throughout the war, recalled an occasion when Churchill had already started his speech in the Commons while she was outside typing up later pages. Sheets were passed in to him as he spoke.

Churchill's insistence that those around him worked just as

manically is well known (he invented 'Action This Day' tags to attach to instructions which filled recipients with dread). One secret kept from the public in the early part of the war was the still relaxed working practices of the Foreign Office. Churchill's Private Secretary Jock Colville records in his diary, one senses with no small hint of achievement, in November 1940 – more than a year into the war – 'The FO now begin work at 9.00am – two hours earlier than normal.'

Hidden Pleasures

His personal habits were likewise unorthodox. His alcohol intake was prodigious for any human being, let alone a Prime Minister and war leader. Daily, he had whisky and soda after breakfast, followed by a bottle of champagne for lunch, washed down with brandy and whisky, cognac for dinner and more whisky into the night when he preferred to do much of his work. Measured against modern recommendations for healthy drinking, Churchill's daily consumption amounted to what a normal person should imbibe in a week. And it was *every* day. Although Roosevelt is recorded as once saying Churchill was 'drunk half the time', remarkably his Prime Ministerial aides almost never saw him worse for wear. His Private Secretary described Churchill's room in the Admiralty Building where he worked at night during the war: 'At the side of his desk stands a table laden with bottles of whisky etc.'

He also smoked huge cigars, up to seven a day according to one biographer. They became a fixture in his iconic image during the war. In later life, it was revealed in 1997, it was more show for the cameras. He confessed to an associate in 1950, when he was 75, that he had virtually stopped smoking, but no one was allowed to know in case it harmed his image of undiminished vitality (he would return as Prime Minister the following year for another three-and-a-half years at the top). He told the confidant, 'I have a trick for the photographers. I always keep a half-smoked cigar on me and produce it at just the right moment.'

81

A Life in a Phrase

His wartime close friend, Lord Beaverbrook, observed that 'Churchill on top of the wave has in him the stuff of which tyrants are made'. Another, Robert Boothby, put it rather more starkly: 'Winston was a shit, but we needed a shit to defeat Hitler.'

NOT SO MODEST

Clement Attlee, who succeeded Churchill as post-war leader, was probably the most unassuming Prime Minister ever to occupy the office. Said by historian Eric Hobsbawm to have had the charisma of an average building society branch manager, he was intensely private, taciturn, seemingly enlivened only by the cricket scores and *The Times* crossword, and harbouring a secret wish to be a poet rather than a politician, he was the most unlikely inspirer of men. He was so shy at university that he attended the debates at the Oxford Union but could not summon up the courage ever to speak in one.

It emerged in 1998 that Attlee's First World War service record was doctored when he became Prime Minister in 1945 to beef up its content. As an officer in the Tank Corps, Attlee had served in Gallipoli and the Middle East for the first two years of war, but had seen no action at all until his first battle in 1916, in which he was wounded and had to be returned to England. According to his own memoirs, he made only a few visits back to the Western Front after that.

The Public Record Office revealed more than 50 years later that his official file had been surreptitiously amended in 1945 to claim that Attlee had returned to the Corps after his injury and had served continuously in France to the end of the war in 1918. The issue had arisen when his old regiment had asked the Prime Minister's office for confirmation of Attlee's record. A letter had been sent to the regiment containing the altered information. The PRO said that there was no clue as to who had instigated the changes. It was clear, however, that Attlee was aware of what was being sent and had not queried its accuracy. Even in 1945, it seems, concern for image and spin had begun to be a fixation in No 10's way of working.

MURKY WATERS

Anthony Eden was first identified by Churchill in 1942 as his intended successor. The heir apparent had to wait 13 years, as the grand old man dithered for most of the early 1950s about when to retire (a precursor of the more recent Blair–Brown imbroglio). Eden then had his reputation shattered by the Suez crisis almost as soon as he arrived at No 10. His tenure was to be dominated by the affair, and lasted just 21 months. Eden resigned in January 1957 shortly after the collapse of the Anglo-French invasion of Egypt. He appeared doomed to be remembered by history for simple political mismanagement. But the real skeleton in his cupboard was more devastating. Documentary proof finally emerged 40 years after the event that confirmed a nagging allegation that Eden had always denied – that the whole Suez affair was a put-up job and that Eden had systematically lied to his colleagues and to Parliament at the time.

Eden had fallen for a bizarre scheme proposed by France to secretly use Israel as a Western stooge in the Anglo–French confrontation with the Egyptian firebrand Nasser who had taken over the Suez Canal and was effectively holding the great powers to ransom. If Israel could be persuaded to mount their own invasion of their mortal enemy, Britain and France could intervene, appearing to the world to be the honest peace brokers and secure the canal again for international use. That is exactly what happened in October and November 1956, although the unexpected American opposition that followed ended hopes of restoring Allied control over the waterway.

A 40-Year Deception

Eden had won his Cabinet colleagues' support for British action by telling them of the Israeli plans as if it was merely the diplomats' and intelligence services' assessment of what appeared to be brewing, not that a deliberate plan had been hatched with the Israelis to engineer it. Virtually no senior official outside Eden's narrow inner circle was let into the secret. The military could not be told either, so did not start their own preparations until hostilities actually broke out, leaving them a fortnight behind in mobilisation.

When challenged in the House of Commons on 20 December about rumours of collusion with Israel, Eden told a blatant lie – the most heinous of Parliamentary sins – by denying 'quite bluntly' that he had been aware of Israel's intentions. He said he wanted to 'emphatically deny' that the Government had been involved in 'some dishonourable conspiracy'. It was all untrue, and Eden well knew it at the time.

Proof was not forthcoming – until 1996. Then, a BBC research team in Israel, preparing a documentary for the 40th anniversary of the affair, discovered in an archive in the remote Negev Desert the Israeli copy of the agreement, signed by all three parties at a secret conference at a villa in Sevres, near Paris, in October 1956 just two weeks before the Israelis acted.

More details emerged when Ted Heath, the Government's Chief Whip during the crisis, published his memoirs in 1998. He recounted personally witnessing the Cabinet Secretary leaving the Cabinet room with the British copy of the Sevres Agreement, having just had instructions from Eden to destroy it. Eden had been furious to discover that the secret pact had been written down. He instructed diplomats to demand that all three copies be destroyed, but the French and Israelis refused.

Eden resigned three weeks after his lie to the House, broken physically by the months of strain and, in political terms, humiliated by policy failure. Only four decades later, and long after his death in 1977, did it emerge that to that roll call of defeat should be added deception and dishonour too.

Succession Planning

When history records that, following Eden's demise, **Harold Macmillan** succeeded, both meanings of the term 'succeed' are applicable. He was factually the one who followed Eden. But he succeeded in the other way too – succeeded in outwitting potential rivals to the top job by bravura Machiavellian tactics. A biography of Eden published only in 2003 provided what a reviewer called 'chilling' evidence that during Eden's troubles over Suez Macmillan, then Chancellor of the Exchequer, was already manoeuvring to be his successor. He appears to have made several visits to the American Ambassador in London, at a time when the Americans were deeply upset by Britain and France's actions and refusing to support their campaign against Egypt. The purpose of the calls appeared to be to establish his own credentials as a more reliable and pro-American premier than Eden was showing himself to be.

His positioning did not go unnoticed. One colleague noted how 'until about a week ago Macmillan, whose bellicosity was beyond description, was wanting to tear Nasser's scalp off with his own fingernails. Today he might be described as the leader of the bolters.' More acerbically, but perhaps still as accurate, opposition spokesman Harold Wilson described Macmillan's approach to Suez as 'first in, first out'.

Macmillan eventually did prevail, over Rab Butler, in the miasma of a process the Conservatives had at the time to select a new leader, by which the preferred candidate 'emerged' from furtive 'soundings' by the great and the good of the Party.

Behind – the Scenes

The other skeleton in Macmillan's cupboard was the sham of his apparently perfect marriage to Dorothy, a daughter of the Duke of Devonshire. They married in April 1920 when he was 26 and on the verge of beginning his political career. She was just 20. Although the marriage formally lasted nearly 50 years until her death in 1966, and they had three children in quick succession (the first in January 1921, barely nine months after their wedding, the others in 1923 and 1926), by 1929 she had been driven by Macmillan's apparent lack of attention for her into an affair with Robert Boothby, a flamboyant political colleague of Macmillan, which led to a fourth child in 1930. The Macmillans came to an understanding that allowed the affair to last on and off until Dorothy died. No public knowledge of it emerged throughout Harold Macmillan's glittering career. It only emerged after Dorothy's death in 1966, long after Macmillan himself had retired.

THE IMAGE MASTER

Harold Wilson was one of the first premiers to exploit the dark arts of television to win the public's attention. The 1964 election was the first television campaign, and Wilson's first election as Labour leader. The practice then was for the evening news broadcast to cut live to campaign rallies for an excerpt from a Party leader's speech. For everyone else, they got the excerpt that the speaker happened to have reached when they chose to cut across. With Wilson, it was brazenly different. According to veteran No 10 watcher, Michael Cockerell, Wilson well knew how the BBC would go live to his speech for a minute or so during their bulletin. 'As soon as he saw the red light on top of the camera glow – which meant he was on air – he would stop in mid-sentence and pick up a piece of paper which contained a crisp, sharp paragraph for the benefit of the viewers.' As soon as the light went off, he returned to the standard speech. He reached millions through the trick that looked natural to those at home and left the impression that the small part they had seen was the mere tip of an oratorical iceberg. In masterful fashion, it left them eager for more.

Pipe-Trick

Wilson's other trick, pandering to the new needs of the media, was his trademark pipe, which Cockerell discovered originated entirely as a television prop. He had the habit of forcefully raising his fist to emphasise his points. This looked threatening on the small screen, so advisers gave him a pipe to hold in his hand instead. The appendage came to almost define Wilson down the years. It was a closely guarded secret that he actually preferred cigars.

The Bag That Held a Secret

Wilson's 'kitchen cabinet' at 10 Downing Street in the late 1960s acquired a reputation for intrigue and backstairs goings-on that would have rivalled a television soap opera of the modern era. His personal secretary, strong-willed Marcia Williams, exerted a mysteriously magnetic influence over Wilson which few even today have been able to explain. It led to plentiful rumours of some undisclosed secret. (She became notorious for her habit of ostentatiously tapping her handbag in front of Wilson and colleagues at times of tension, as if hinting . . . something). This appeared to get official confirmation in 2005, 10 years after Wilson's death, when official papers were released covering a squalid legal case dating from 1974 involving another of Wilson's No 10 advisers who had died from stress and overwork four years earlier, caused mainly, it was alleged by the bereaved wife who was claiming compensation, by the demanding Williams. The legal suit contained a reference to the existence of a secret that, had it been revealed, would have brought Wilson down. Only the adviser, Williams and Wilson knew what it was. Wilson successfully dragged the case out until the wife gave up. Wilson is now long dead. Only one person alive, now in her late seventies, knows what it is, and she is unlikely to be telling.

KEEPING THE IRON LADY GOING

Margaret Thatcher would seem an unlikely candidate to be harbouring dark personal secrets. But her personal assistant divulged in 2003 Thatcher's fondness for all-night drinking while premier. Cynthia Crawford, who served Thatcher throughout her 11 years as

Prime Minister between 1979 and 1990, revealed that at times of stress Thatcher would stay up all night with a continual supply of Bell's whisky. (Husband Denis was renowned for his fondness for a tipple.) Crawford had to do the same. The Falklands War in 1982 was a particularly stressful period. 'By the end, I'd become hooked on whisky and soda,' Crawford said.

She also disclosed that part of the secret of Thatcher's legendary tireless energy was down to vitamin injections. She had B12 regularly injected into her bottom. Another stress-managing technique Thatcher indulged in was from the Indian Ayurveda system of medicine. Her treatment bizarrely involved being given mild electric shocks while lying in a bath of water. Given her strident and rarely popular style of governing Britain, she must have been awfully trusting of her therapists.

THE SECRET LIFE OF THE FÜHRER

The rise of **Adolf Hitler** to power is by now a well-honed narrative: the deranged individual with messianic powers of persuasion over others, coinciding with a moment in history when Germany, burning with grievance from defeat in the First World War, is pitched into the economic destitution of the 1930s, and Hitler the saviour sees the opportunity for national revival by force of arms against the supposedly weak and dissolute democracies. Historians have long argued over how far Hitler planned and engineered his actions on his terms and how far he took opportunistic advantage of the fecklessness of his adversaries. But, essentially, the story is of a ruthless political and military calculator, different from everyone else in the game, as the historian A.J.P. Taylor observed, because he knew what he wanted to achieve, while everyone else knew only what they wanted to avoid.

That depiction is unlikely to alter in its fundamentals. But modern revelations have added intriguing new perspectives on other forces that impelled Hitler along. In 2002, new research revived a long-buried story that Hitler recruited the services of a clairvoyant in the crucial year before he ascended to power. And not just any anonymous seer, but Germany's most famous psychic, Erik Jan Hanussen. Although unknown today, Hanussen was a public sensation in the Berlin nightclubs throughout the 1920s. He easily adjusted his act to the debauched levels Berlin became famous for. His pièce de resistance, it seems, was to hypnotise women into a sexual frenzy and induce them to orgasm – on stage.

New Directions

His entry into politics came in March 1932 when he published an unlikely prediction that within a year Hitler would be leader. At the time, Hitler was still regarded by most players as too much of an outsider from the political mainstream to be considered a viable candidate. Most of the public regarded the rabble-rouser from Munich as a megalomaniac buffoon, not a chancellor-in-waiting. As the year progressed, his fortunes appeared to have peaked and to be declining. In elections that November, the Nazis had fallen back losing 15 per cent of their vote and a similar proportion of seats in the Reichstag, the national Parliament.

In the turmoil, Hitler frequently turned to Hanussen. It was in the strictest secrecy. It would have been the death knell to his credibility if he had been exposed consulting a fortune-teller. He had about a dozen consultations with him. One, in early January 1933, took place in Hitler's Berlin headquarters. Hanussen once again prophesied Hitler's success. Inside the month, Hitler had indeed risen through the fiendishly complex deal-broking negotiations and emerged as Germany's new leader, albeit with only two of his Party with him in Government and everyone else in the new administration feeling they had cleverly boxed the maverick into their plans for controlling him like a puppet.

Shooting Star

The surprisingly welcome outcome of these events boosted Hanussen's status with Hitler – and Hitler's confidence that destiny was on his side. But Hanussen's star was to fall suddenly. Barely a month later, on the eve of the Reichstag fire, which it is now believed was ordered by Karl Ernst, the head of Hitler's Stormtroopers, the SA, Hanussen forecast at a séance attended by Nazi officials that 'a great house' would go up in flames. Whether it was a genuine psychic call, or whether Hanussen, who was now brushing shoulders in exalted circles, had picked up inside information, his position was now highly tenuous. As the accusations flew in the aftermath and the Nazi regime vigorously denied responsibility and produced an imbecile Dutch communist as the culprit, Hanussen may have been seen as a potential threat to the cover-up. It may not be without significance that it was the SA that arrested Hanussen in March and summarily executed him.

Hitler's dabbling in the occult is far from lacking in credibility. The roots of Nazism went deep into Germanic and Aryan mythology. But one aspect of the whole affair that would have given the Nazis at least one other reason for burying his relationship with Hitler was that, far from being the Danish nobleman Hanussen purported to be, he was in fact a Czech Jew.

Relative Concerns

Other secrets from Hitler's background provide fascinating insights into the Führer's personal world, providing startling new facets to an already complex personality. In 2005, historians found a family secret that, if it had been disclosed during Hitler's lifetime, might have caused no small grief to his political and personal standing. They discovered that one of his cousins was an inmate of a mental institution, who was gassed in 1940 during the first year of a programme which Hitler had launched to systematically purge Germany of citizens who were judged less than pure – racially, mentally or physically. It may explain Hitler's legendary reluctance to talk about his family. To acknowledge a familial link to any such 'impairment' would have seriously tainted his position given the importance that Nazi medical and biological philosophy attached to genetic linkages.

The programme to eliminate 'defectives' had begun in 1939. It first dealt with disabled children. By January 1940, a national programme for the euthanasia of adults deemed to be 'useless existences' was under way. During the war years, some 200,000 mentally and physically impaired patients were gassed in a network of institutions across the Reich. One of them, in Vienna, housed Aloisia, a cousin related to Hitler through his father's side, a line of the family steeped in mental instability. She was two years younger than Hitler. She was killed in December 1940 because, according to the medical notes uncovered, she suffered from 'schizophrenic mental instability, helplessness and depression, distraction, hallucinations and delusions'. It is not known whether Hitler ever found out about her death. He certainly would not have wanted his family relationship to have become common knowledge.

Was Hitler Jewish?

It was not the only family skeleton Hitler despaired over. If he worried he might be revealed as hailing from a line of 'defectives', his other fear was even deeper – it was that he might himself be part Jewish.

Hitler's complicated family genealogy opened up this possibility. His father, Alois, had been illegitimate. Alois' mother – Hitler's grandmother – had not married until her son was five. When she did, Alois kept his mother's maiden name – Schicklgruber – strongly suggesting that the man, Johann Heidler was not his biological father.

Fast forward to late 1930, with grandson Adolf now on the brink of his political breakthrough. Hans Frank, Hitler's personal lawyer, received an instruction from Hitler to examine his family background in intricate detail. The Party leader was being blackmailed with the allegation that Alois's true father, his grandfather, was Jewish. His anxiety that this might be made public was evident from the urgency with which Frank was told to conduct the investigation. It suggests he felt there may have been some substance to the claim.

Frank duly discovered that a Jewish family, the Frankenbergers, in whose house in Graz Alois's mother had served as a maid, had paid her child support money until her son was 14 years old. Frank, recounting the episode in his memoirs, recalled that the family's 19-year-old son was the suspected father. He did not say where the evidence came from,

91

vaguely referring to it being in long correspondence between Alois's mother and the family. The letters demonstrated the 'common understanding of the participants that the ... child had been conceived in circumstances which rendered the Frankenbergers liable for the paternity allowance'. Frank wrote that the discovery was 'to the highest degree painful' for Hitler. The letters, though, have never surfaced.

Some historians have cast doubt on the story. Research suggests that there were no Jews in Graz until 1856, having been driven out of the city in the 15th century. That is 20 years after Alois was born. However, that may not be the most important aspect. In the view of historian Robert Waite in his seminal 1977 biography, the first psychological study of Hitler, the fact that Hitler *thought* he could have Jewish blood 'constituted a psychic reality for Hitler. It helped to shape his personality and to determine public policy'.

Another piece of evidence that revealed Hitler's inner anxiety was his decision in March 1938, given in orders directly by him, to demolish the Austrian village of Döllersheim ostensibly to make way for a firing range. The inhabitants were ejected, all the buildings razed, the parish registers removed and the cemetery left unrecognisable. Hitler had personally ordered it to be that village, and no other, despite there being thousands of empty acres that could have been used without all this effort. The likely reason? Döllersheim was the birthplace of his father Alois and the site of the grave of Alois's mother, the grandmother he suspected of tainting his blood.

RED ENIGMAS

The health of political leaders has been a constant source of cover-up and deception. Many have gone to extreme lengths to avoid the politically fatal image of a sick or dependent leader, reflecting a perverse but persistent supposition about electors' views of their politicians: that they need to be assumed to be above the normal human frailties.

Ruled by a Dead Man

It was disclosed in 1988 that for the last six-and-a-half years of his life, Soviet leader **Leonid Brezhnev** was virtually a dead man standing (or more usually, slouching, in a brainless stupor). In the spring of 1976, he had disappeared from view for seven weeks. It later emerged that he had had a massive incapacitating attack – details are still not known but observers surmised either a stroke or heart attack. Doctors had declared him clinically dead, but he had 'recovered' sufficiently to carry on leading the country. He eventually died in 1982. He did, however, 'stop taking in what was going on around him' according to the account by respected historian Roy Medvedev, and could not carry out even the simplest of duties. He 'worked' for no more than one or two hours a day. Meetings of the ruling Politburo were especially shortened for him – to only 15 or 20 minutes a time. He rarely even went to his Kremlin office.

The true extent of his illness was known to four senior Politburo members and a clutch of doctors. Elaborate deceptions were prepared for his public appearances in order to keep the unsuspecting populus ignorant. Hidden escalators allowed him to climb to the top of the Lenin mausoleum for the usual display of the leadership on national occasions. For speeches, his writing team were under strict instructions not to use long words. It was always a matter of doubt whether he would successfully complete a public address and safely get back to his seat.

Momentous decisions of the period now appear to have been made by a shadowy power structure and an unknown leadership, including the invasion of Afghanistan in 1979 and the crackdown on dissidents which became a PR disaster for the late Soviet period as figures like Alexander Solzhenitsyn and Andrei Sakharov (who was awarded the 1975 Nobel Peace Prize for his efforts) established themselves as favourites of the West in the propaganda war.

The Child as Father of the Man

Thanks to the collapse of the Soviet Union in the 1990s, and the opening of the state archives, more is also known of the background of

Lenin that throws fresh light on the forceful urges that impelled him to the top. It seems that Lenin's drive to challenge authority was less a rational and thought-out one developed in maturity and more a deeply ingrained personality trait going back to his earliest childhood days. Rather than the traditional image of an unemotional, coldly calculating political operator, we have a picture of a character formed by the consequences of a disruptive childhood and parents unable to cope.

In 2000, authors combing the Kremlin archives uncovered a secret handwritten account by Lenin's elder sister Anna describing their early lives. The memoirs had been confiscated by the authorities shortly after Lenin's death in 1924 and consigned to a sealed vault ever since. They revealed a deeply disturbed young Lenin who, because of his unusually big head and weak legs, was literally an unbalanced little toddler who had a tendency to topple over frequently. When he did so, he would furiously bang his head against the floor in frustration. One excerpt told how 'the wooden structure of the house made it into an echo chamber and the floors and walls resounded as the little fellow went on crashing his head on the carpet – or even the floorboards.'

It apparently became such obsessive behaviour that his cultured parents worried that he would become mentally retarded. They had no idea how to control him. The disruptive trends carried on through childhood. When three years old, he deliberately stamped over his brother's precious collection of theatre posters, and a toy horse given to him as a birthday present had each of its legs systematically twisted off.

The revelations added a fresh perspective to one of the mysteries of the founding of the first Communist state and one of the 20th century's most oppressive dictatorships. They shed more intimate light on how the hatreds and animosities grew inside Lenin's personality. The less flattering conclusion emerging is that in his formative years Lenin was essentially a spoilt and uncontrolled little brat, whom his parents did not handle very well. Russia, and the world, paid a terrible price for their failings.

The Greatest Turncoat?

Evidence emerged in 2001 that even **Stalin**, whose reputation one would imagine has been fairly well set in stone now, had an astonishing dark secret that had remained hidden for nearly 90 years. It outlasted him, and the Soviet Union.

In a new biography of the dictator who, on conservative estimates, ordered the murder of up to 20 million of his citizens because of their supposed opposition to Communist rule, American historian Roman Brackman suggested that in the turbulent period immediately before the 1917 Revolution, Stalin was in fact an agent of the Okhrana, the Tsar's feared secret police, and had been planted inside Lenin's movement to spy on its insurrectionary activities. Brackman postulated that the purges of the 1930s may have been driven by Stalin's paranoia that his secret would be exposed.

Allegedly, Stalin's Okhrana file, identifying the agent only as 'Vasily' but clearly containing some other identifying information, had been discovered in 1926, nine years after the revolution. It was just at the point when Stalin, his allegiances now clearly shifted to the winning side, was manoeuvring in the power struggle which engrossed the new regime after Lenin's death two years earlier.

The file found its way to Felix Dzerzhinsky, founder of the Communist state's own secret police, the OGPU, forerunner of the KGB. According to the theory, Stalin found out that the file had been discovered and shortly afterwards Dzerzhinsky suddenly died of a supposed heart attack at the surprisingly early age of 49. The new allegations suggest he may have been poisoned by Stalin.

The file languished in Dzerzhinsky's papers until found by a junior officer in 1929. An attempt to get the material to Stalin's sworn enemy, Leon Trotsky, then in exile, failed when the plotters were caught and executed. No one dared to reveal to Stalin that the file had been rediscovered, so the new head of the OGPU hid it again until 1936 when, at a time of high discontent with Stalin's rule, a group of military officers planned to publish the evidence. Before they could do so, they too were arrested for unrelated reasons, paraded in a show trial, convicted and executed. It was at this point, according to

Brackman, that Stalin finally got his hands on the file and destroyed it for good.

Although some historians remain sceptical, if true, the revelation casts a different light on the motivation of many of Stalin's actions. At heart, it would show that Stalin, far from being an ideological zealot, was simply driven by the thirst for power and willing to jump from one vehicle to another to obtain it.

We are unlikely to know the truth. But one small facet of Stalin's past may now make sense and offer a clue to the strength of the claim. It has long mystified historians why Stalin spent such great effort as he rose in the ranks after the revolution to falsify his birth records. Although by the time he had risen to power, his date of birth had been officially documented as 9 December 1879, it is now known that he was actually born on 6 December 1878. Why would Stalin, in the middle of his life, worry about making such an apparently irrelevant change to his records? The new revelations offer a plausible reason. Could it be that he feared that the secret file for agent Vasily would emerge containing details of his real date and place of birth that would expose him? Is that why he went to so much trouble to make the otherwise inexplicable alteration?

Chinese Whispers

More is now known of Chinese communist strongman **Mao Tse-tung** than ever emerged during his lifetime. The hero worship fanaticism cultivated in post-war China and the legendary maxims on Party orthodoxy spread through the *Thoughts of Chairman Mao* (the 'Little Red Book') created his iconic image as the fount of doctrinal purity, the personification of unwavering service to the cause and, moreover, espouser of the simple life. He was meant to be, and was believed by nearly a billion people to be, the clean broom sweeping in after centuries of corrupt and self-serving Chinese emperors.

The truth was rather disappointing. To his close associates, whose inside stories began to emerge in the 1990s nearly 20 years after the Great Leader's death, Mao was an echo of the imperial past.

He operated on the Taoist belief that sexual activity prolonged life. He was fixated with pornography and sexual excess. His doctor recorded in his memoirs how Mao was an obsessive womaniser, and a supply of peasant virgins was maintained for his use, something that remained a closely guarded secret during his lifetime. When in 1961 he became a carrier of an infection, he refused simple treatment that would have cured it and stopped him from passing the infection on, simply on the grounds that it was not affecting his own health. He remained a carrier for the rest of his life and infected at least 1,000 girls.

Mao had an extreme lack of personal hygiene. According to his doctor, he never bathed. He never brushed his teeth, but, in the tradition of Chinese peasants, rinsed them daily with green tea. As a result his dentures turned green.

For the leader of a proletarian revolution, Mao liked his perks, which were little different to the emperors he had supplanted. His favourite, an indoor swimming pool, was an unheard of luxury in 1950s China. While he luxuriated, tens of millions of his countrymen died through famine and economic dislocation caused by his policies. A 2005 estimate put the number killed at 77 million, surpassing the totals of Stalin and Hitler.

The personality cult that grew up around Mao, which he avidly cultivated, may itself have held back China's economic and military advance. In the more relaxed era of 1994, a Chinese newspaper brazenly calculated that the 4.8 billion metal lapel badges that China produced during the Cultural Revolution, which became mandatory adornments for loyal citizens to wear, used up aluminium that could have made 39,600 MiG jet fighters.

3

America – (Uh) Oh America!

Politics across the pond has always possessed an exuberance that the mother country could never truly compete with. If anything, though, down the years the respective political cultures seem to have been diverging. If British politicking appears to be less coarse than it used to be, America looks to have gone in the other direction. The more modern the politician in the land of the free, the more extreme the secrets that have had to be covered up.

FROM HIGH IDEALS
TO REAL LIFE

The family indulgences of **Thomas Jefferson** were covered in the opening chapter. While in office as America's third President between 1801 and 1809, he extended the territory of the republic massively by his purchase from France of 800,000 square miles of Middle America, and managed to keep the country out of the Napoleonic Wars. However, his Embargo Act, which prohibited any trade with European powers, caused immense hardship to American commerce and shippers, and has been described by historians as the most repressive and unconstitutional legislation ever enacted by Congress in time of peace. Jefferson himself spared little in the way of personal comfort. During his eight years at the White House, he racked up a personal wine bill of $10,835. That's equivalent to nearly

$200,000 in modern values, $25,000 a year or just over $2,000 every single month of his presidency.

A No-Nonsense President

Andrew Jackson, war hero President between 1829 and 1837, suffered more wounds through love of duelling than in his formal war encounters as a major general in the war of 1812. The principal source of so many duels was a personal scandal he had got himself into early in life when he married his wife Rachel wrongly believing she had divorced her first husband. She had not, and the husband widely accused Jackson of living immorally with a bigamist. As soon as the official divorce was through, Jackson married Rachel a second time, properly, and vigorously defended his reputation by fighting duels against anyone who resurrected the affair. In this way he fought dozens of duels as he climbed the political ladder. He killed at least one of his opponents.

He had a bullet lodged in his chest from an 1806 duel. It led to abscesses and lung pain, causing him trouble for the rest of his years. He incurred a shoulder wound in another duel seven years later. That bullet, too, could never be removed. It left a wound that was always vulnerable to bursting open, which it did occasionally. While President, he used to bleed himself regularly to try to ward off the danger of accidental internal haemorrhaging. He would use a penknife to open up a vein and have a servant hold a bowl 'and bleed himself freely'.

His blood-thirsty reputation was lifelong. As a militia commander sent in 1813 to quell the Creek Indians in the southern Gulf region (in modern-day Louisiana), his troop massacred the Indians at Horseshoe Bend and kept a body count by cutting off the tip of each dead Indian's nose as a record.

99

A Sensitive Soul

Despite the heroism of his war exploits by which history tends to remember him, Jackson has been described as one of the most emotionally unstable men ever to reach the top office. He was paranoid about attacks on him and his wife. Apparently no looker – Rachel was described as 'plump, quiet and unassuming' – she had died suddenly in December 1828, after his election but before he was sworn in, in deep distress because of overheard comments made by two society ladies who opined that she would never fit in to the Washington scene as First Lady. She had a nervous breakdown, took to her bed and within two weeks died of a heart attack. They had been married nearly 40 years. Jackson harboured the grief about her treatment. When a similar affair arose two years into his Administration with the wife of his Secretary of War being socially snubbed by Cabinet members, he sacked all but one of them.

IMAGE ISSUES

Abraham Lincoln is America's most cherished President of the 19th century, famed by history for his openness and candour (his nickname was 'Honest Abe'). He was, in fact, one of the earliest learners of the art of media spin. In an era when photography was just becoming a tool of the politician's art, Lincoln was at a signal disadvantage. His looks were severely unimpressive. The Washington correspondent of *The Times* during the American Civil War described him as 'a tall, lank, lean man, considerably over six feet in height, with stooping shoulders, long pendulous arms terminating in hands of extraordinary dimensions, which, however, were far exceeded in proportion by his feet'. American newspapers were less refined. One called him the 'Illinois baboon'. Another described him as 'a horrid looking wretch . . . sooty and scoundrelly in aspect, a cross between the nutmeg dealer, the horse-swapper and the night-man. He is a lank-sided Yankee of the uncomeliest visage and of the dirtiest complexion.' (Medical historians now think he suffered from Marfan's syndrome, a genetic disorder that is recognisable from unusually large extremities and a gaunt appearance. It was not identified until 30 years after Lincoln's death.)

So when he stood for election to Congress, he asked his photographer to touch up details of his portrait so that he looked less scraggy. It is one of the first examples of manipulative photography. When he ran for President in 1860, it got even worse from the modern eye. There were so few full-length portraits of him that publishers put Lincoln's head on other people's bodies. It has been found on the torso of Andrew Jackson and Martin van Buren, two earlier Presidents, as well as other notable senators. It seems it was a common practice in early America, with no untoward inference being drawn from the deception.

KEEPING UP APPEARANCES

One of the most notorious deception campaigns in American politics was the concealment that **Franklin Roosevelt** was wheelchair-bound. Having suffered from a crippling attack of polio in 1921 at the age of 39 when his political career was just taking off – he had just been the Democratic vice-presidential candidate in the 1920 election, which the Party lost – he never regained the use of his legs. In public, he adopted the use of leg braces underneath his trousers, which enabled him to apparently 'walk' with the subtle help of a cane and a steadying arm from an aide. Although his closest political associates knew, and senior members of the press corps often saw the President being lifted from his wheelchair to his desk before press conferences, an unspoken but rigidly held pact ensured that no one revealed to the outside world the secret of the extent of his disability. He was never seen in public in a wheelchair for fear it would imply weakness in the presidency, and by extension the Government. Some idea of the extent of the deception can be gained from the fact that of the 35,000 photographs that are kept in his presidential library, only two show him in his wheelchair.

Pretence to the End

Roosevelt's tenure of office, from 1933 to 1945, was one long crisis – the world was going through the Great Depression at the start of his first term, and finishing the Second World War at the end of his last. He referred to his braces publicly for the first time just five weeks before his death in 1945. He had just returned from the major post-war conference at Yalta, was already very ill and dying, and had had to ask for the indulgence of Congress for making his report to them sitting down. Even his last Vice-President, Harry Truman, was kept in the dark about the seriousness of his failing health in 1944 as Roosevelt did not want to affect his public image while seeking an unprecedented fourth term, which he duly won. It meant that on his sudden death in April 1945, three weeks before the war in Europe ended, Truman was totally ill-prepared for the rigours of the top office at a pivotal moment in world history.

SHADOW ADMINISTRATION

Woodrow Wilson, President during and just after the First World War suffered such a serious stroke in October 1919 that his final year and a half in office was, unknown to the outside world, effectively run by Edith, his (second) wife of fewer than four years. It was a crucially delicate time after the ending of the war with the debate raging in America whether the Senate should approve joining Wilson's personal project, the League of Nations, the first attempt to create a world organisation for peace and forerunner of today's United Nations. It was universally felt in the White House that if the Vice-President Thomas Marshall took over, as was the proper course of action, it would be a disaster. Marshall had almost physically collapsed with nerves at the prospect. So Edith stood in, unofficially. She sat in on every one of Wilson's meetings, became gatekeeper to Cabinet members and congressman wanting to see him, filtered all the papers sent to the President and pre-digested the business to advise him what to do. Wilson was too weak even to sign his own name. Edith would guide his hand as he approved official documents. Sometimes, to the concern of Congress, the shaky signature gave every suggestion that she was, in fact, forging the President's moniker. Her dominant role became a source of friction and suspicion amongst senior politicians, especially Wilson's enemies, but the true extent of Edith's overall control of public affairs never fully emerged until after his term of office was over.

Doctored Image

Perhaps the strangest deception over a President's health involved **Grover Cleveland** who had half his jaw removed because of a cancerous growth just after he had begun his second term in 1893. The operation was hushed up as it was feared that concerns over the Chief Executive's health would further affect the economy, which was in the throes of the worst downturn of the 19th century. Two hundred banks had failed, 8,000 business corporations had gone bankrupt in just six months, and unemployment was running at 20 per cent. Amid huge subterfuge, and in order to reduce the chances of discovery, the surgery was performed on a yacht cruising in New York's East River. He was given a false rubber jaw that fitted inside his cheek to give his face a normal appearance which, it seems, was highly successful. Remarkably, he was able to conceal the fact from the public for the rest of his term of office, and beyond: the story did not emerge until 1917, nine years after he had died.

Camelot Was a Fairy Tale After All

To modern readers, **John F. Kennedy** is now rather better known for his darker side than for his political achievements while in office. His serial, bordering on obsessive, womanising has become the theme of

103

his presidency – he is alleged to have had a threesome at one of the balls held on his inauguration evening while his wife danced downstairs. Even less known, though, but of perhaps more importance for the quality of his decision-making while occupying the most powerful office on the planet, is the fact that Kennedy was to all intents and purposes a highly dependent drug addict throughout his term of office, developing a strong dependency on amphetamines and being boosted by his personal doctor up to four times a week.

Kennedy suffered from constant back pain from an old football injury, worsened by active service as a patrol boat commander in the Pacific during the Second World War. He sought relief by permanently wearing a tight and uncomfortable back brace. But in 1960, during the election campaign which he was to win, he encountered a New York doctor, Max Jacobson, who specialised in injecting amphetamine-laced concoctions of multi-vitamins, hormones, steroids and ground-up animal organ cells to celebrities in the early days of the emerging drug culture of 1960s America. Not for nothing did he acquire from his clients the nickname 'Dr Feelgood'.

Kennedy, wearied by a gruelling schedule, needed relief to prepare for the first televised debate with rival Richard Nixon. It turned out to be the crucial encounter of the campaign, one which election folklore says sealed Kennedy's success by showing his youthful and powerful image and mastery over an (also, incidentally, ill but more visibly suffering) opponent.

According to Jacobson's own account, that first injection instantly took away all Kennedy's bodily pain, instilled a warmth throughout his system and made him feel both calm and alert at the same time. Four months into his presidency, Kennedy turned to Jacobson again for his back pain and the injections became more regular. In the beginning, the doctor's visits were once a week. They were soon as many as three or four weekly. Kennedy never asked what was in the injections; Jacobson never told him.

By the summer of 1961, Kennedy was clinically dependent on amphetamines. The 'treatment' continued right up to his assassination, the last one being just seven days before his fateful visit to Dallas.

A Pill-Popping, Mind-Blowing Cripple

Contrary to the youthful and vigorous image he cultivated, Kennedy was a physical wreck from a range of complaints that plagued him in addition to his back and for which his official doctors also prescribed multiple pills and injections (up to eight different medications a day). He was doped with hydrocortisone and testosterone to control Addison's disease, a potentially fatal condition affecting the adrenal glands; codeine and methadone as orthodox painkillers; thyroid hormone and Ritalin as liveners, barbiturates to calm him down and help him sleep; and gamma globulin to combat infections. The amphetamines would also have provided a short-term stimulant and mind boost. He therefore appears for much of the time to have been on uppers and downers simultaneously. They kept him alternately alert and groggy depending on the moment.

There's no doubt that he needed drastic treatments. So intense was the physical pain that he had to continually shield his infirmities from the press. He could not put a sock or shoe on his left foot unaided. In 1961, he had to be hoisted onto *Air Force One*. Out of sight of the media, he went up and down the steps of his helicopter one step at a time. One biographer estimates that with the afternoon naps and early bedtimes, Kennedy spent half his days as President in bed due to ill health.

The effects of amphetamines were not well known at the time, although studies in the late 1950s were already suggesting the possibility of damaging consequences. They are now recognised as being responsible for substantial mood-altering effects, hence their popularity among recreational drug users. These include delusions of paranoia and persecution, along with hallucinations, both visual and auditory (in other words, 'seeing things and hearing voices'). According to one medical reference, amphetamine induces a psychosis that comes closer to mimicking schizophrenia than any of the other drugs of abuse.

The World in His Hands

And that was the condition of the leader of the Free World at the height of the Cold War. On his watch, the West was faced with the two pivotal crises of the post-war face-off with Communism: the Berlin Wall and the Cuban Missile Crisis. That we escaped a nuclear holocaust may now look rather more of a lucky break than perhaps we had realised.

A LIT FUSE

Not only was **Kennedy** a womaniser and a misuser of drugs. Evidence which only came to light nearly 35 years after his death added a fresh, third dimension never hinted at before which sank the Kennedy reputation into new depths of mire. It suggested that he took bribes from defence companies seeking multi-billion dollar Government contracts. He may also have been trapped into being blackmailed by an arms manufacturer. It looks increasingly evident that assassination saved Kennedy from an ignominious array of threats that would almost certainly have eventually toppled his presidency.

Veteran investigative journalist and Washington insider, Seymour Hersh stunned the political world in November 1997 with his exposé of the real Camelot. Laying out details of Kennedy's sexual pecca-dilloes added little to the mountain of misdemeanours already largely known. But detailed revelations of improper financial behaviour were a new angle. Kennedy may have been known for being unable to control his urges, but he had never been suspected of being bought.

The connection was a former girlfriend of Kennedy's pal Frank Sinatra, Judith Exner, with whom Kennedy conducted a two-year affair that started during his 1960 election campaign and continued until the middle of 1962. Its existence was a close secret. But shortly after it ended, her flat was mysteriously broken into by the sons of the head of security at General Dynamics, the arms manufacturer. At the time, the company was in a fierce competition with Boeing to build the next generation of combat fighter planes, code-named the Tactical Fighter Experimental (TFX). (It was to become the F-111, one of the worst-performing jets the US military ever had.)

The Multi-Million Dollar Silence

Why the Pentagon chose it was a hotly disputed question at the time. The new suggestions point to a darker answer. General Dynamics were desperate for the contract. It had lost $400 million the previous year. The $6.5 *billion* TFX contract was a lifeline. The strong favourite to win the contract was General Dynamics' rival, Boeing. They were recognised at every stage of the competition to be the front-runner. So when the announcement was made in November 1962 that General Dynamics had won in the last stretch, few in the industry or Congress could understand the decision. Hersh suggests that General Dynamics had become aware of the Exner affair, purloined incriminating evidence from her flat and used it to sway the decision.

Exner confessed to Hersh that during her affair she had been used as a bribes mule to take payoffs from California businessmen involved in seeking Pentagon contracts directly to Kennedy in the White House.

So aberrant was the TFX decision that the Senate started hearings on the matter. They were suspended by Kennedy's death and never resumed. General Dynamics built the TFX, costs for which had tripled by 1966, producing a Navy version which turned out to be too heavy actually to land on an aircraft carrier. The Navy cancelled their part of the contract in 1968. An admiral testified before Congress that 'all the thrust in Christendom couldn't make a fighter out of that airplane'. The air force took fewer than a quarter of the planes they had originally planned. By 1970, the cost of each had risen nearly tenfold, from the starting estimate of $2.8 million to $22 million.

In all, the US military estimated $400 million ($2 billion in current values) was wasted. And all to protect a little secret from coming out.

LIES ON THE WAY TO STARDOM

Kennedy managed to engineer himself into a war hero from his exploits in the Pacific as a 26-year-old Navy Lieutenant in charge of a torpedo patrol boat. Through connections, he got himself appointed to command one, and in the summer of 1943, his boat was rammed by a Japanese destroyer. Two of his crew of 13 were killed, but Kennedy's leadership saved the remainder as he corralled them and swum to a nearby island. Kennedy helped one of his men who was too injured to swim by grabbing the man's life vest in his teeth and dragging him for hours through the water to safety.

His reward was the Navy Medal and the Purple Heart, and instant fame as a heroic member of a famous American clan. Only afterwards did it emerge that the incident should probably never have happened at all. Kennedy had stationed as lookout a man whose eyesight was so bad he was almost clinically blind. He never saw the huge destroyer coming.

Other questions surfaced almost to the point that Kennedy could and should have been court-martialled instead of decorated. It emerged that he had secretly replaced the boat's life raft with a heavy gun, endangering his crew, and had allowed some of his crew to sleep on the patrol, contrary to procedures. However, the officer conducting the inquiry that followed was an old friend of the Kennedy family. He got him off any charges, and better still got medals thrown in.

As the plaudits were all raining down on the golden boy from America's most famous family, those who were in the know played down this awkward fact which cast a different gloss on the quality of Kennedy's leadership. Within four years, he had entered Congress and the 29-year-old never looked back.

Fame, Courtesy Of . . .

While a senator, Kennedy won lasting fame for his considered historical appreciation of the political convictions of eight of his Senate forebears in his book *Profiles in Courage*, which won the prestigious Pulitzer Prize for Biography in 1957. It is still today viewed as a classic tome analysing how celebrated American legislators faced the key political challenges of their age, and Kennedy soaked up reflected glory, and increased the public's sense of his own political acumen, by his deftly crafted and highly literate portrayals. Except that it now looks very likely that he hardly wrote a word of it.

Soon after publication, rumours abounded that Kennedy's counsel and speechwriter, Ted Sorensen, had actually ghosted it (Kennedy paid tribute to Sorensen in the preface to the book saying it was to him that he owed his 'greatest debt'.) Sorensen and Kennedy both denied the allegation at the time. Kennedy was left to bask in the plaudits.

In 2008, on the publication of his memoirs to mark his 80th birthday, Sorensen told the *Wall Street Journal* that the rumours were, in fact, largely true. He had been responsible for preparing a first draft of most chapters, and 'helped choose the words of many of its sentences'. Kennedy had surprised him shortly after publication by offering him half the royalties for the first five years. Sorensen said that this generosity made him disinclined to press for further recognition.

First Time Around

It was not the first time Kennedy played loose with authorship. His first book, *Why England Slept*, an account of Britain's slowness to re-arm in the 1930s, was published in 1940 when Kennedy was leaving Harvard. Supposedly his undergraduate thesis, it was in fact partly based on research provided by a political columnist and friend of Kennedy's father, Arthur Krock. It then won the notice of the wider public by a glowing review in *The New York Times* – written by the same Arthur Krock.

TRICKY DICKY COPYCAT

It seems that **Richard Nixon** followed suit in 1962. As defeated presidential candidate in the 1960 election, Nixon was under-occupied immediately afterwards and turned his hand to a Kennedy-esque volume. It was, likewise, to become a book that would cast the author as an insightful political analyst. *Six Crises* told Nixon's personal political odyssey from Congressman to Senator to Vice-President, taking its title from six crises that Nixon had faced during his career. He claimed that writing the memoir was a 'maturing' experience. It turned out that, apart from the last chapter covering the recent presidential election, it was all written for him by an Associated Press journalist, one Alvin Moscow, a famed 'ghoster'. In hindsight, it perhaps tells more about Nixon's approach to character than even he intended to reveal.

THE BEAST

Kennedy's successor, **Lyndon Johnson**, introduced some of the most progressive social change in America in his 'Great Society' programme. He was also one of the crudest Presidents to occupy the Oval Office in modern times. Beneath the surface dignities of the most powerful office on Earth lay the unrefined simplicities of a true Texan red-neck. You can take the man out of the backwoods, but . . .

A consummate Washington operator – his is the second longest congressional pedigree of any President, 12 years in the House of Representatives, followed immediately by 12 in the Senate – Johnson was a driven politician determined, since a teenager, to reach the presidency. (When he faced risking his Senate seat by becoming Kennedy's vice-presidential running mate in the 1960 election, he had Texas law changed so he could run for both offices at the same time so if he failed in his bid with Kennedy he would keep a political foothold in Washington for another try.) His moment came unexpectedly, in the midst of the trauma of Dallas in November 1963. His first words to Kennedy's mother as he was about to be sworn in just two hours after the assassination, were unfortunate, ambiguous but perhaps deeply revealing: 'Mrs Kennedy, we feel lucky.'

Strange Behaviour in Dallas

Some said of him that he would have killed to be President. Some have claimed he did just that. Before she died in 2002, Johnson's mistress at the time, Madeleine Brown, recalled Johnson's mysterious behaviour the night before the assassination – he had arrived in Dallas ahead of the President – as the culmination of three years of bitterness at Johnson's not getting the presidential nomination at the 1960 election. By late 1963, the theory goes, Johnson was getting worried that he was about to be dropped as Vice-President for the next election, which was soon to kick off. He was being implicated in bribery allegations that were about to come before a congressional investigation. He was, according to Brown, becoming too hot for Kennedy. Brown told interviewers, 'Had the assassination not happened the day that it did, Lyndon would have probably gone to prison; they would have gotten rid of him – he was so involved with some of this.'

According to Brown, almost as soon as he arrived in Dallas, Johnson attended a late-night Party of senior anti-Kennedy figures. Brown was surprised that he would devote time to come to a social event given his busy schedule. Immediately he arrived, he disappeared with some of the politicos into another room and closed the doors. A short time later Johnson, anxious and red-faced, reappeared. He came over to Brown, squeezed her hand 'so hard it felt crushed from the pressure, and spoke with a grating whisper – a quiet growl into my ear, not a love message but one I'll always remember: "After tomorrow those goddamn Kennedys will never embarrass me again – that's no threat – that's a promise."'

No wonder Johnson 'felt lucky' so soon after his President had been blown away. According to *Rolling Stone* magazine in April 2007, Howard Hunt, long time shadowy CIA operative, who ended up as a conspirator in the Watergate scandal, corroborated the story to his son shortly before his own death in January 2007.

Management Extraordinaire

As President, he exercised a strong but strange political influence, which became known to insiders as the 'Johnson treatment' – a concoction of abuse and affection in overwhelming quantities. A commentator described it picturesquely as a mixture of 'grabbing, touching, goosing, cajoling, flattering, threatening, promising, horse-trading, swearing, kissing, doing anything required to have his way, and uncannily sensing what it would take.'

His manners were rural. William Doyle's 1999 exposé of presidential idiosyncrasies *Inside the Oval Office* records a congressman describing Johnson as 'damn crude – always scratching his crotch and picking his nose in mixed company.' His sexism was legendary. Another biographer recounts how he berated any secretary who put on weight. He made it clear that he expected 'the view' would be good as they walked away from his desk. 'I don't want to look at an Aunt Minnie. I want to look at a good, trim back end.' He bullied even minor assistants, once leaving a note on a junior secretary's untidy desk instructing her to 'clean it up right now or I'll come back tonight and do it myself'. It was so unimportant that the irresistible conclusion was that Johnson simply liked being a threat to everyone around him, however insignificant they were. (A psychological profile of him suggested that it was the effect of his overprotective mother. She was desperate for him to succeed, overwhelmed him with affection and forced him to take ballet and violin lessons. Johnson, the theory goes, spent a lifetime trying to prove his manliness. He even invented an ancestor whom he claimed had died at the Alamo.)

He would often invite aides to continue a policy conversation in his private toilet as he sat on the lavatory. Aide Arthur Goldschmidt has recorded that Johnson conducted a discussion on United Nations affairs in this way. 'I stood at the bathroom door while he took a crap, then shaved and showered, all the while continuing his conversation as though what he was doing was the most normal thing in the world.'

Nothing private seemed to get in the way. It had been a long-standing habit of Johnson's. A story is told of him doing the same when he was a senator, except it was a female secretary to whom he continued dictating while he ostentatiously urinated (into a washbasin) in his Capitol Hill office.

Nothing to Hide

When a senator, he had suffered a serious heart attack in 1955 and had been bedridden under doctor's orders. A visitor described calling on him to find Johnson conducting business lying on his side in bed, with aides and a secretary by the bedside and a nurse also in attendance. Three televisions were blasting away in the room as Johnson was simultaneously shouting dictation to his secretary. And then it dawned on the new arrival why the nurse was there – she was administering an enema.

On occasions his private demeanour spilled over into public action. In his magisterial account, biographer Robert Dallek tells of when Johnson drove at 90mph down a highway, a glass of beer in one hand, with his Secret Service entourage (and the press corps!) desperately trying to keep up. He once took a bevy of female reporters out in his car on his Texas ranch and sped in similar fashion scattering his frightened cattle. In those early 1960s days of a deferential press, the episode did not receive much publicity – but it showed the man in his true irreverential colours.

In summing up the 'warts and all' Johnson revelations that have emerged over the last two decades, the conclusion is almost inescapable: Johnson was mostly wart.

BOMBING UNDER THE INFLUENCE

Richard Nixon's foibles were all too exposed in the long drawn-out nightmare that was Watergate. Less well known, until years after his death in 1994, was the extent of Nixon's mental state throughout the 'good times', before scandal and cover-up overwhelmed the White House. According to Anthony Summers' biography in 2000, Nixon took mood-altering drugs that caused his advisers so much concern that they instructed military chiefs not to take orders from him without seeking confirmation from the Defence Secretary or the Secretary of State.

As early as 1970, two years after winning the presidency, and without the knowledge of his official White House doctor, Nixon secretly began taking Dilantin, a drug whose side-effects include changing the patient's mental state, confusion, memory loss and impaired cognitive function. He was then charting the build-up of

113

the war in south-east Asia and beginning secret bombing of Cambodia. Defence Secretary at the time, James Schlesinger, confirmed the account, describing himself as proud to have performed the backstopping role in the apparently dysfunctional Oval Office. 'You could say it was synonymous with protecting the Constitution.'

Nixon was also a heavy drinker, often mixing sleeping pills with the alcohol. For more than one emergency, he was incapacitated. In 1969 when an air force spy plane was shot down by North Korea, a drunken Nixon contemplated unleashing a nuclear bomb in retaliation. The military simply ignored their Commander-in-Chief.

Acting the Part

According to Henry Kissinger's memoirs, published in 1999, another side of Nixon emerged which could have been equally as dangerous. He was, Kissinger had observed, intensely insecure. He liked to use the trappings of office to impress friends and visitors. When Palestinian hijackers seized an American airliner in 1969 and were involved in a standoff at Damascus airport, Nixon received the call informing him of the emergency while surrounded by several friends. Apparently to impress them, he simply said into the phone 'Bomb the airport'. The next day, when Nixon asked Kissinger whether anything had been done, and received the answer 'no', Nixon simply replied, 'good'.

Kissinger believed Nixon acquired his reputation for being 'Tricky Dicky' simply because of his aversion to face-to-face conflicts. If he disagreed with a proposal, he would tend simply to decide differently but fail to tell those concerned, who then felt tricked and misled. He nurtured a tough-guy image in compensation, often dreaming up 'extravagant' policies to impress aides but which he did not really want implemented. The trouble is, when surrounded by willing acolytes hanging on every word and keen to do a master's bidding . . .

Kissinger certainly concluded this. 'Some of the more bloodcurdling orders on the White House tapes . . . have their origin in this proclivity – as I believe to have been the origin of Watergate itself.'

The Hollywood President
With Inspiration from the Stars

Ronald Reagan's eventual emergence as one of the most successful Presidents in recent history (at least in American eyes) for winning the Cold War tends to mask the skeletons that started to rattle very early in his tenure. His age was always a problem – he was the oldest to win election at 69 in 1980 and was just shy of 78 when he left office. Within months he was being labelled as a 'dilettante' President for working only two or three hours a day. An aide was quoted in August 1981 – just seven months in – how there were times they 'really need him to do some work and all he wants to do is tell stories about his movie days'. Aides joked about a report saying the President worked six hours a day: 'That wasn't a day in the life [of the President]. That was a week in the life.'

The real shocker came in 1988 as the Reagan years were winding down. Memoirs by former White House Chief of Staff, Donald Regan, revealed that almost every major scheduling decision for Reagan had to be cleared in advance with an astrologer by his wife, Nancy. Joan Quigley's name quickly emerged from the brouhaha, but Regan had never known her identity. Her role in setting the President's timetable was so extensive, Regan wrote, that at one point he kept a coloured calendar on his desk to remind himself which days the astrologer had marked out as being good (green), bad (red) or 'iffy' (yellow). According to veteran Washington insider Bob Woodward, writing of the period 10 years later, Regan believed it was the most closely guarded domestic secret in the Reagan White House.

A Secret Closely Held

Quigley, from San Francisco, had been advising the Reagans since the 1970s. Major events such as signing key arms control treaties with the Soviet Union, the timing of the invasion of Grenada in 1983, and when to bomb Libya in 1986 were all finessed by a call to Quigley. The Reagans' dabbling with astrology went back to their California days (Reagan was Governor there between 1967 and 1975). He had taken the oath of office in 1967 in the middle of the night on the advice of an astrologer – there were claims it was the celebrated seer Jeanne Dixon – who had decreed this to be the most propitious time. Nancy Reagan had warmed to Quigley when she had warned her of the dangers of Reagan's assassination, pointing to March 1981 as the danger period. Reagan was indeed shot that month.

Reagan used the secret service to chart all their movements in coordination with Quigley's decisions. She would send a computerised spreadsheet to Nancy Reagan every three months, which would be passed to the aide responsible for drawing up the President's forward schedule. Determined to trust no one, Mrs Reagan had a private telephone line installed which by-passed the White House switchboard. She would coordinate details of travel, often with the aide on one line and Quigley on the other, passing times between the two to fine tune arrivals and departures.

On 'red' days, Reagan was banned from leaving the White House, but no one outside the inner circle of the aide, Regan and Nancy, would know the reason. Even the President was often kept ignorant of the good and bad days.

He occasionally let the cat out of the bag. In 1985 when he greeted the incoming President of Brazil, he regaled his astonished visitor with his first words that 'your zodiacal sign and mine are compatible and therefore we cannot have anything but the best relations between our two countries.' The Brazilian leader was described as being 'left speechless'.

Americans seemed less flustered than the rest of the world at the news that their leader had been guiding them through some of the rockiest moments of the Cold War on the word of a soothsayer, when he was actually paying attention to being President. The Speaker of the House of Representatives was reported as saying, 'I'm glad the President was consulting somebody. I was getting worried there for a moment.'

By-Passing the Information
Superhighway

Bill Clinton's skeletons barely had a chance of staying in the cupboard in the modern era of intrusive and 24-hour news coverage. His financial dealings and sexual dalliances were dissected in the press and on television almost continuously through the eight years of his presidency. He was a very modern President. It was on his watch that the modern telecommunications revolution unfolded, in the shape of the Internet, email and mobile telephony. Clinton claimed to be at the vanguard of the new technology. In speech after speech he marvelled at the 'limitless possibilities' of the Information Age. In a 1998 speech to the Massachusetts Institute of Technology, he lauded how, over the previous four years, information technology had been responsible for more than a third of America's economic expansion and how 'all students should feel as comfortable with a keyboard as a chalkboard, as comfortable with a laptop as a textbook'. Listeners could not have guessed how far Clinton had personally embraced the challenge.

Three years after his departure from the White House, staff at his presidential Library revealed that their archiving of the 40 million or so emails that his staff produced had shown that Clinton himself had made rather parlous use of the system. He had sent just . . . two. One of these did not officially qualify as it was a test message to check that he knew where the 'send' button was. In actuality, it appeared that he only sent one real message – to an orbiting astronaut in a publicity stunt.

Skip Rutherford, the Library's President, commented, seemingly unnecessarily, that Clinton was 'not a techno-klutz'.

On the Record

Although **Richard Nixon** was brought down in the Watergate scandal through his secret Oval Office tape-recording system, he was by no means the only President to record his conversations surreptitiously. Almost all the incumbents from Franklin Roosevelt (who hid a microphone in a desk lamp) did so. None it seems ever disclosed to their visitors that they were recording them, which invites new question marks over their moral attitudes.

More intriguingly, the recordings, which only became available for scholars in the late 1990s, reveal telling aspects of Presidents' characters that often jar with the more polished historical personas we usually have in mind. They capture the rawness of personality since, bizarrely, most of them appear to have quickly forgotten they were recording themselves. The tapes present unvarnished portraits that can be stunningly unflattering at times.

Hitting the Wrong Note

Roosevelt, who used to hold press conferences at his Oval Office desk, used taping to ensure he was not misreported. Some of his remarks, however, suggest a forgetfulness of the all-hearing machine. To civil rights leaders in September 1940 who had come to complain about discrimination against Negroes in the armed services, Roosevelt suggested that the way to improve blacks' treatment in the navy was to draw on their musical ability and create ships' bands 'because they're darn good at it' and it would 'increase the opportunity' for advancement in the ranks.

War in Peace

Eisenhower, War General and D-Day supremo-turned-President, gave out a public demeanour of quiet simplicity and peaceful serenity during his eight years at the helm between 1953 and 1961. On the few tapes that exist, however, a starkly regimental streak emerges. He is heard castigating staff for over-burdening him with paper. When presented with a 25-page brief on Philadelphia in advance of a visit, he exploded that 'it only took a six-page directive to get me into Normandy.' He railed on another occasion that 'if a proposition can't be stated in one page, it isn't worth saying'. Dogged throughout his presidency by heart problems, he complained that his 1955 heart attack was caused by being constantly interrupted on the golf course by unnecessary phone calls from the State Department. Aides spoke of his 'flashes of anger of great intensity'. Even the White House animal life got to him. A passionate golfer, he would practise his shots on a putting green that had been laid right outside the Oval Office. His predecessor, Truman, had fondly fed the resident squirrels which now plagued the area. On one tetchy morning, Eisenhower ordered staff, 'The next time you see one of those squirrels go near my putting green, take a gun and shoot it.' They were all quietly rounded up and despatched to a park on the far side of Washington.

Gadgets Galore

In the last 18 months of his presidency, **Kennedy** developed the rudimentary taping system into what has been described as the White House's first fully fledged secret recording network. It was an entirely private set-up installed by the Secret Service. It seems that no one else knew of its existence. The level of deception was extreme. It was consistent with what we now know was a life full of secrets, but at the time few would have imagined it from this young, modern President who arrived at the White House as a breath of fresh air personifying a new era of politics. Not content with a solitary microphone, he had installed a patchwork of devices in the Oval Office, the Cabinet Room and even the private residence, the Mansion. On his desk in the Oval Office, the ornate pen and pencil set hid the secret on/off switch. There were microphones in the light fittings along the walls, under the foot well in the desk, under the coffee table near the fireplace and in all the table lamps.

Ironically for history, much of the 260 hours recorded covered prosaic political affairs. It did cover the Cuban Missile Crisis, perhaps Kennedy's pinnacle moment. It failed – mysteriously! – to capture any of the misdemeanours Kennedy is now more famous for. Within hours of his assassination, the system was removed by the same Secret Service agent who put it in.

Telephone Mania

Lyndon Johnson thrived on communicating orally rather than on paper. As we have already seen, his forceful character leant itself to the personal touch. His obsession with the telephone became legendary to insiders. He made up to 100 calls a day. He loved direct-dial facilities, then a modern cutting-edge touch. At one point, his phone on his Oval Office desk had 42 different buttons, one each for a regular contact. At his Texas ranch he had installed special floating phones for his pool, and he had three phones just in his official car – one witness observed that he would often speak on all three at once while also holding a discussion in the limousine and shouting instructions to the driver.

He was known for interrupting his secretaries who might be on the phone by grabbing the handset, terminating their call and making his own – without a word of apology. When he once failed to reach an aide who had gone to the bathroom, he ordered phones to be installed in all the men's rooms in the White House. Soon, he had them throughout the place – on every coffee table, under dinner tables so he did not have to rise from the table, on window sills, and, of course, in all bathrooms.

The predilection for crudities that we have already seen could not be resisted even when he knew he was recording a conversation. Of some of the more printable comments the tapes picked up, he is recorded as saying of a new staff member, 'I want loyalty. I want him to kiss my ass in Macy's window at high noon and tell me it smells like roses.' About a group of congressmen who were not cooperating, he told his aides to set up a Christmas reception for them. 'Let's be over there and smile and shake hands and thank everybody, and then just cut their dicks off and put [them] in your pocket when they do us this way.'

Expletive Deleted

Nixon's travails with his tapes are well documented, and eventually led to his downfall. When he lost his legal attempts to prevent their publication as part of the Watergate investigations, the transcripts became famous for the multitude of excisions that had to be made ('expletive deleted') because of the foul language Nixon regularly used. It was the American public's first introduction to the coarseness of their Commander-in-Chief.

4

War – Nasty Realities

By its nature, war challenges historical truth. No one ever confesses to wanting war, so the regular outbreaks of violence that litter (some would say make up) history tend to be recorded in one's own annals as the opponent's fault, one's own resort to combat merely the unavoidable action pressed upon an unwilling victim. During war, morale requires the burying of bad news, the inflating of the good, the twisting of information for the common perceived good. And after war, when the histories get written, the orchestration of facts can be free and unrestrained. Churchill famously said to an opponent that history would vindicate his view, 'because I will write it'. He did, and it still largely does. The sacrifices of war – human and material – force the telling of the tale in heroic terms, in part as justification to those surviving and the generations that follow. Not surprising, then, that the history gets moulded in the telling.

INNOVATION IN EVIL

One of the British military's darkest skeletons in the cupboard is the legacy of being the force that turned the concept of the **concentration camp** into a strategy of war and developed it on an industrial scale.

It was originally conceived, in the Boer War, supposedly as much for humanitarian reasons as military, but the unintended results were disastrous. Even at the time, the camps contributed to appalling suffering, but worse came when the concept, refined by Nazi Germany in the Second World War, created the juggernaut of mass death and the means for an altogether more monstrous purpose.

Although there had been earlier small-scale precedents for the practice – the Spanish rounded up civilians into camps when dealing with an insurrection in their Cuban colony in the late 1890s – the British endeavour took the idea to an altogether different level of organisation.

Kitchener's Bright Idea

The military mind responsible was Lord Kitchener, later to be immortalised as the figure on recruiting posters imploring the nation's men that 'Your country needs YOU'. His reputation has always been controversial. Cited in 1998 as a war criminal by Sudan for the alleged massacre of 10,000 dervishes at the Battle of Omdurman in 1898, Kitchener became the Chief-of-Staff to Lord Roberts, the British military commander on the ground, in early 1900 after initial setbacks in the Boer War. By the end of the year, Roberts was gone and Kitchener was in charge of the campaign.

By then the style of war had shifted from the orthodox set-piece battle the British had been familiar with to the Boer's inventive hit-and-run, guerrilla tactics. This presented Kitchener with a dilemma. How to solve the problem of Boer farms being used as bases for attacks and supply depots. The solution was to remove the population, and destroy the farms. There was also a humanitarian angle too. Boer commanders had publicly threatened to drive out of their homes the families of Boer soldiers who had surrendered to the British.

In early 1901 a plan was cobbled together – Kitchener left all the details to subordinates, but insisted on rapid action – to deal with the civilian problem. One historian of the campaign cites the scheme's four factors that appealed to Kitchener: it was big, ambitious, simple and cheap. These made it almost certain to result in a catastrophe.

Systemic Chaos

Twenty-four camps were planned, each staffed with a small administration stretching to not much more than a superintendent, a solitary doctor and a few nurses. Civilians would be fed on a reduced military ration, which at first banned meat for the families whose men folk were still fighting as an inducement to their surrender. Generally, the diet lacked nutrition – no vegetables or fresh milk – and hygiene was poor with inadequate supplies of soap and fresh water, and horrendously poor sanitation (there were reports of latrine buckets not being emptied and left standing in the blazing sun for hours, making living downwind unbearable and deadly). They were conditions guaranteed to produce disease and, almost immediately, typhoid broke out.

By May over 60,000 men, women and children had been rounded up and interned in the increasingly overcrowded camps. Concerns began to filter back to London, but, although he never visited one, Kitchener replied to a worried Government back home that the inhabitants of the camps were 'happy'. In fact there were epidemics breaking out all round and spreading like wildfire.

Britain in Denial

In the face of mounting criticism, the Government maintained that the camps were well run and designed to induce the enemy to surrender. But Parliamentary campaigners produced startling figures. Death rates by July were running at an annual rate of 12 per cent. The allegation, broadly true, that the Government was waging war on women and children was an incendiary one. The Government replied in what to modern ears sounds a familiar lament. The policy had been forced on them by the actions of the guerrillas. They were ultimately responsible for their hardship. Some of the families had been helping the enemy; but others had been abandoned by their men folk. Either way, the argument ran, women and children could not be left out on the veld to starve.

In a House of Commons debate, the Government Minister responsible denied 'altogether' that not enough had been done 'to make these camps sanitary and to preserve human life'. He also denied that conditions were deteriorating. In fact, it was the opposite, 'so far from going from bad to worse, [conditions] have been steadily ameliorating'.

By August 1901, there were nearly 95,000 housed in camps, and deaths were increasing exponentially – 550 in May, 782 in June, 1,675 in July. By October, the Boer camp population was over 111,000, with deaths running at over 3,000 a month – described as being of 'plague' proportions. Expressed as annual rates, this amounted to a 35 per cent death rate for all inmates. But for children, rates were even higher, nearing (and surpassing in Transvaal province) 60 per cent. In the worst camp of all, Mafeking, the October rates represented an annual death rate of 173 per cent. If judged by modern standards, it would be difficult to avoid labels of ethnic cleansing and genocide.

Action at Last

The Government had to act. In November, instructions were issued from London for the High Commissioner to satisfy himself everything was being done to control the unfolding disaster. As a result of a women-only review of the camps – a modern Florence Nightingale exercise – some reforms were introduced, such as boilers to cleanse water and introducing rice and vegetables to the diet.

Death rates began to fall, and by the start of 1902 the worst was over – 16 per cent in January, 7 per cent in February and 4 per cent in March. The war itself would come to an end in May. But the toll was appalling. In the end, some 27,500 Boers had died (22,000 of whom were aged under 16) along with at least 14,000 black Africans (who were kept in separate camps) out of a total incarcerated of barely 150,000. And almost all had died from epidemics of disease, particularly measles and typhoid, which were entirely preventable.

The Dove Is a Hawk

Franklin Roosevelt's approach to American involvement in the Second World War has always been controversial. Throughout the 1930s, as Europe teetered from one Nazi-instigated crisis to another, and the likelihood of war grew, Roosevelt publicly adopted a firmly isolationist stance in keeping with the national mood. Until Pearl Harbor, two years after the outbreak of war in Europe, his public line was crystal clear: 'We are keeping out of the wars that are going on in Europe and Asia,' he said in April 1940 as Britain and France were reeling from Hitler's invasion of the West. In July, he was clearer: 'We will not send our men to take part in European wars.' By October, clearer still: 'I give you one more assurance. I have said this before, but I shall say it again and again and again: your boys are not going to be sent into any foreign wars.'

Leaving aside the controversial claims — which are unlikely to be proven one way or the other — that Roosevelt deliberately man-oeuvred Japan into attacking Pearl Harbor to provide the excuse he needed to go to war, Roosevelt's attitude to war preparation was in fact considerably more bellicose than this public image suggested.

FDR Presses for Action

As early as the Munich Crisis of 1938, his instinct was, in fact, to prepare vigorously for early entry into war. He wanted to order a massive fleet of several thousand bombers for an air war that would devastate the civilian population of Germany. 'This kind of war,' he claimed, 'would cost less in money and casualties and would be more likely to succeed than a war by land and sea.' It was his military advisers who baulked at the prospect, and it would be 1943 before American bombers first raided German territory, and then with disastrous losses.

Japan Gets the Blame

America's entry into the war, immediately after the surprise attack on Pearl Harbor, has cemented itself into history as the natural action of a victim responding to outrageous provocation. It emerged only in 1991, however, that six months before the Japanese attack, America had itself agreed on plans to bomb Japan in September 1941, three months before Pearl Harbor. Had it done so, at a time when the two countries were still officially friendly states, it could well have prompted from Japan the same reaction as Pearl Harbor prompted from the US. History would then have recorded for posterity a rather different legacy about which country was the catalyst for war in the Pacific.

A 97-page document was found in the US National Archives, dating from between 10 May and 18 July 1941, detailing the plan to bomb industrial areas on the Japanese mainland in support of China with whom Japan had been engaged in a bloody conflict for four years. The plan was signed off by Roosevelt on 23 July. The bombing was intended to take place in under two months. However, it turned out that the American Air Force were unable to carry out the raids as by then Britain had asked for more US bombers for the European theatre. They went there instead, the attacks were put off and history now paints Japan as the villain 'who started it' in the Pacific.

DITCH THE POLES TOO

Britain's apparent loyalty in supporting **Poland**, after the acknowledged shame of betraying Czechoslovakia at the Munich Conference in 1938, became the trigger for the outbreak of hostilities in September 1939, when Britain declared war on Germany two days after the Nazi invasion of the country. What was not known at the time, and only emerged 60 years later, was that a secret last-minute attempt had been made by Britain to persuade Germany to accept another Munich-style agreement to settle the Polish dispute. In short, notwithstanding the Czech humiliation a year before, Britain was at it again in the summer of 1939 trying to avert war by selling out an ally. In the end, the scheme failed and history portrays plucky Britain as valiantly standing alongside its wounded friend and selflessly committing itself to war on another's behalf.

Britain had made its public commitment on 31 March that it would come to the aid of Poland if attacked by Germany, just a fortnight after Hitler had broken the undertakings he had given at Munich and occupied the remnants of Czechoslovakia. As the crisis over Poland deepened during the summer and war looked ever more likely, Britain's 'guarantee' of Poland began to look like an awkward millstone. So, as it now appears, Britain tried to wriggle out of it.

Mission to Betray

The attempt to once again buy off Hitler only emerged in August 1999 from the private papers of the sole living survivor of the effort, Lord Aberconway. He and six other businessmen had been asked by the Foreign Office to travel to Germany to meet Hermann Goering, the head of Hitler's Air Force and one of the most senior Nazis, in early August 1939 to see if a deal could be cut to avoid war over the Poland crisis.

The British team travelled to the remote German island of Sylt, off the Danish coast, for the meeting. Each of the seven businessmen travelled by a different route as far as Hamburg to avoid drawing attention to the plot. They were then driven to a farmhouse on the island on Monday 7 August for the encounter with Goering and his delegation.

Over two days, the British team tried to persuade Goering that Germany could achieve its 'living space' goals in Poland peacefully. This would be done through another four-power conference that would redraw Poland's borders. It was, Goering told the British, 'definitely the last territorial claim Germany had in Europe'. (Hitler had used the same phrase over the Sudeten Czechs the year before.)

The British returned from the visit impressed by Goering's apparently genuine wish for a peaceful settlement. It was soon clear, however, that the attempt had failed. Two weeks later, Hitler announced his pact with Stalin, which would enable Germany and the Soviet Union to carve up Poland without difficulty. The die was cast, war followed, and Britain found itself hitched to the Polish falling star.

A Reputation Undeservedly Saved

We now know that Hitler had fully worked up his invasion plans for Poland by July 1939, and as the Nazi–Soviet Pact was being finalised he was instructing his armies to be ready to invade on 26 August.

In the event, delays pushed it back a week to 1 September. The last-minute British attempt was almost certainly doomed from the beginning. What it does appear to have confirmed, for Hitler, was Britain's unwillingness to fight, which gave him an extra spur to get a move on. He was surprised when Britain did declare war in the end, but by then action on the ground was past recovery for both the Poles and its reluctant ally. The only solace for Britain was that its moral position was boosted by its apparent selfless act. At least the record of history would be on Britain's side – until now.

HORSES FOR COURSES

Planning for war had been typically British. As late as 1937, Britain's priorities for the new era of military conflict were still out of kilter. The budget for the Army's riding school was £20,000 (about £1 million in today's values) for its 38 students. The Tank Corps School was granted slightly more than double (£46,000) to cater for its 550 trainees. The Army still produced a detailed manual for riders. *Cavalry Training 1937* contained 23 pages devoted solely to sword and lance exercises. It just about acknowledged the newer world, having a supplementary chapter which began with the reassuring message for novices: 'The principles and system of Cavalry Training (Mechanised) will be as laid down in *Cavalry Training (Horsed)*, with certain modifications laid down in this chapter.' It went on to inform the reader that 'the principles of training in field operations given in *Cavalry Training (Horsed)* are, in general, applicable to armoured car regiments.'

BLUE PROPAGANDA

Archive papers discovered only in 2004 cast a new – and grubby – light on the lengths British propagandists went to in order to hit at

German morale. Researchers found evidence that a systemic campaign amounting to pornography over the airwaves was organised by Whitehall's political intelligence department to undermine the Nazis both at home and on the front line. Organised by a tabloid journalist, Sefton Delmer, it prompted intense anxiety within Government circles appalled at the extreme content. Sir Stafford Cripps, a senior member of the War Cabinet, went so far as to complain in June 1942: 'If this is the sort of thing that is needed to win the war, why, I'd rather lose it.' He said he had refused to have his letter to Foreign Secretary Anthony Eden typed because he did not want his 'young lady' secretary exposed to the scandalous contents. He objected to 'such filth being allowed to go out of this country'.

Sounds Disgusting

Delmer broadcast obscene radio plays directed at German troops on active service. They purported to be underground German broadcasters revealing the extent of sexual debauchery at the heart of the Nazi regime. Some of the material was highly obscene, describing in intimate detail orgies by senior officers, alleging that soldiers' sons were being raped by male Hitler youths and that wives were having lesbian sex because they were lonely.

This kind of material was far beyond the coy and suggestive propaganda that had gone before. Leaflets were disseminated at the front depicting black forced labourers in Germany having sex with stereotype peasant German women, and running sweepstakes as to how many German wives they could sleep with. Fake photographs of Fascist leaders were shown in the embrace of naked women – a pioneering step for the times.

Cripps decried the effort, claiming Delmer was running 'a beastly pornographic organisation'. Before his death in 1979, Delmer is said to have acknowledged to his daughter that the campaign might have gone too far and had been 'wrong but necessary'.

Black Propaganda

Sanctioning the distasteful is not normally seen as a British trait – the Government famously turned down a proposal from its military attaché in Berlin to assassinate Hitler nearly a year before the Second World War began because it regarded such actions as 'unsportsmanlike' – so revelations of skulduggery jar. The most notorious propaganda episode of the First World War is similarly little known, involving the explosive assertion that the German authorities were using their war dead to produce much-needed domestic supplies. The then Foreign Secretary permitted the story to have wide coverage in the national press, despite suspicions that they were unfounded, because of the short-term gains to be made. Few ever wondered about what the long-term effects would be on the public's attitude to Germans, and how far such tales seeded deeper anti-German sentiment that outweighed any immediate advantage obtained.

The story was a concoction of probably unconnected elements that became woven into a nauseating tale that was seen to suit the needs of the time. A German press report in April 1917 detailed the operation of a factory being used to convert 'cadavers' into domestic fats and oils. Days later a Berlin newspaper ran a story of the discovery of a trainload of dead German soldiers in Holland, supposedly en route for the homeland. A Belgian paper then ran a story claiming the dead soldiers were being returned to be boiled down into soap. British intelligence investigated the story, but could find no further evidence of what was going on. They did obtain testimony from British officers confirming that the Germans had been seen removing their war dead from Vimy Ridge, and pointing to the noticeable absence of war graves.

Spreading the Word

On the basis of these fragments, the story was fostered that human bodies were being turned into household goods. Despite suspicions that the 'cadavers' referred to in the original story were horses, the British authorities encouraged the atrocity account to run. Foreign

Secretary Arthur Balfour took the pragmatic – if unelevated – view that given the 'many atrocious actions of which the Germans have been guilty' there did not appear to him 'to be any reason why it should not be true'.

Ministers themselves promoted the allegations to give them greater credence. Lord Curzon, the Lord President of the Council and one of the five members of the inner War Cabinet – someone, the public would reasonably think, 'should know' – pushed the message on an audience in Derby a few days after the story appeared. *The Times*, also authoritative enough a source to give an aura of truth to the tale by merely reporting Curzon remarks, recorded him saying: 'No horror that human ingenuity can devise is too bad for the Germans. They have not even, as we have read in the papers, spared the corpses of those who have fallen for them in battle.'

The value of the boost to Allied morale about their cause may have overcome any doubts about truth. The story appeared just days after America had at last entered the war and, perhaps with a sense that the tide was turning, the unsavoury affair was judged to be worth it.

DID CHURCHILL TRY TO
BUY OFF MUSSOLINI?

Diplomacy and war are always complex siblings. **Churchill's** unequivocal conviction on the Allies' political and moral righteousness in the conflict against Nazism was second to none. But it did not prevent him sanctioning some secret shady dealings to buttress the case. Only emerging long after the war, it now seems that in persuading potential enemies to think again as to their loyalties, Churchill not only relied on their own political calculations but he also nudged them in our direction with rather more earthly inducements.

A long-standing historical mystery was revived in 2000 when an 86-year-old former Italian partisan was reported by a Milan history journal to have confirmed the accuracy of a claim that shortly before

Mussolini joined the war in June 1940 on Hitler's side, Churchill had written privately to the Italian dictator offering him large territorial concessions, including parts of Britain's ally France, if he stayed neutral. Although originals of the letters no longer existed – it is claimed that Churchill travelled to Italy under the guise of a holiday in September 1945 to buy them back in order to destroy the evidence – unknown to Churchill, photocopies had been made and were said to be buried somewhere in the Italian Government archives.

Secret Missives

Luigi Carissimi-Priori told the journal that he had retrieved copies of the letters in 1946 when he and a fellow partisan had ransacked an ex-Fascist Party member's office in Como in northern Italy and uncovered a file of papers which consisted of 62 letters exchanged between Mussolini and Churchill between 1936 and 1940. The sheaf was later passed to the post-war authorities, leading Carissimi-Priori to his belief that they were lying somewhere in the state archives.

The incriminating letter from Churchill was one of the last to be sent, in the early summer of 1940 as France was being overrun by Hitler and with Mussolini still on the sidelines. Carissimi-Priori says that the letter contained a promise from Churchill of several territorial gains Mussolini could have. These included Nice, in southern France, the French island of Corsica, most of the Dalmatia coast lying opposite the Eastern coast of the Italian peninsula, a large swathe of Tunisia which lies just across the Mediterranean Sea from Sicily, and even Malta which at the time was Britain's military bastion in the region.

The ploy failed to persuade Mussolini, who concluded that hitching himself to Hitler offered even more gains and in June he declared war on the Western allies and invaded southern France. Churchill was clearly so embarrassed by the prospect of his promises being revealed after Mussolini's death that he took extreme measures and subterfuge to get them back. But he was unaware of the existence of the copies.

A Mystery Still

Historians still dispute whether the claims are true. Circumstantial evidence beyond the assertions of Carissimi-Priori lends some weight to the possibility. It was near Como that Mussolini was captured in April 1945 while trying to escape to Switzerland. He was carrying a briefcase of papers said to be his 'insurance policy' in case he was caught and tried.

In the end, he was summarily shot. Another angle that only emerged in 1996 claimed that a British Secret Service agent was involved in his capture and ordered the execution to prevent Mussolini from exposing the embarrassing contacts. The fate of the briefcase in unknown, but copies of its contents are alleged to have been what was found a year later by the partisans.

French Manoeuvres

These were potentially awkward times for Churchill. His willingness to give away parts of France had a strange reverse counterpart at the end of the war that was brushed under the carpet by the Allies, and is little known even today. In May 1945, the victorious Charles de Gaulle tried to snatch a large portion of the Italian border area for France, which led to a tense stand-off in the spring and summer of that year, and eventually involved the American President Harry Truman instructing de Gaulle to back off. Interestingly, Churchill is not mentioned at all in the episode, and appears not to have been involved. If his own proposed land dealings had become known to de Gaulle and the other Allies, he would have been in a deeply embarrassing position, and the Allied position against de Gaulle severely weakened.

De Gaulle had invaded the Val d'Aosta in the Italian Alps as soon as the occupying German forces had surrendered on 2 May 1945, two days after Hitler's suicide. They penetrated 40 miles up the valley to within 12 miles of Turin and 60 miles along the Mediterranean coast as far as Savona, three-quarters of the way to Genoa. They did everything they could to foster an anti-Italian mood, setting up local committees of collaborators to persuade the populace to demonstrate in favour of French annexation. The French commander promised enticingly attractive offers – distribution of food, which was in short supply, promises of no taxes for several years and a promise to build a long-desired tunnel through Mont Blanc.

By the end of the month, France had 19 battalions of soldiers on Italian soil, and resistance was increasing. Italian partisans blew up the French police HQ. By the middle of June, matters were serious enough that Truman had to be asked to intervene. He threatened the withdrawal of all supplies to de Gaulle if he did not retreat. De Gaulle had no option, and the last troops left Italy on 10 July.

Churchill adopted a low-key role in the diplomatic tussle, and let the Americans do the Allied arm-twisting of de Gaulle. It may have seemed curious at the time – after all, Churchill had known de Gaulle very closely throughout the war; by contrast, Truman was just weeks into his presidency after Roosevelt's sudden death – but in the light of the new knowledge of Churchill's own compromised position, it now makes sense that he decided to keep his head down.

Success in Spain

We may never know the truth about Churchill's manoeuvrings. However, extra credence is added to the story of the Mussolini bribe by revelations that show that Churchill had form in this regard. In late 2008, new evidence came to light from papers in the US and British archives that showed that Churchill bribed another potential adversary, Spain's **General Franco**, to keep out of the war, this time successfully.

Churchill was desperate to avert Spain's entry into the war on Hitler's side. Franco's fascist regime had been strongly helped to victory in the Spanish Civil War by Nazi military assistance. Had Spain returned the favour and become active in the Axis cause, the Straits of Gibraltar – the crucial shipping route into the Mediterranean – and Gibraltar itself would have been lost to the Allies. The campaign in Egypt and North Africa would have to have been supplied from around the southern tip of Africa, and in that case may have been impossible to sustain at all. The whole course of the war may have been very different.

At the time when Franco's allegiance was uncertain (again it was the summer of 1940), Churchill authorised millions of dollars in bribes to be channelled to Franco's generals to persuade them to dissuade Franco from joining in. A respected banker, Juan March, who had acquired a fortune in the First World War through dealings in contraband tobacco, appeared the ideal conduit. The British authorities put $10 million (in the region of $150 million in modern values) in a New York bank account, and March used it to pay off as many as 30 generals in the Spanish Army.

Hitler Thwarted

The crude move worked and Franco stayed out, despite Hitler's entreaties. These peaked in October 1940, just months after the bribery scheme had begun, when Hitler met Franco for the only time. He travelled all the way down to the French–Spanish border, Franco was late and, when he arrived, he presented an outlandish shopping list of demands. Hitler gave up. It seems the insidious influences from inside then helped to keep Franco from ever wanting to do anything else. Spain remained a 'non-belligerent' (they still duplicitously provided naval bases for Nazi submarines) and after the war Franco remained in power for another 30 years until his death in 1975. If Mussolini had played his cards differently . . .

MYTHS THAT BIND A NATION

It is a fact of history that some of war's most famous and heroic endeavours turn out in reality to be rather less than that etched on our collective memory. Through a blend of mythologising and a reverence for the bravery of those making the effort, some events have been burned into the public consciousness as having a defining impact. The truth turns out very differently.

The Little Boats

At the heart of the common folk memory of the evacuation of Allied troops from **Dunkirk** in the spring of 1940, as British and French forces reeled from the onslaught of the German invasion, is the supposed decisive contribution of the flotilla of 'little boats' that heroically made the difference between success and disaster. Research in the 1980s began to reveal a different story. By 4 June, at the end of the nine-day logistical miracle, 338,000 had been rescued from the beaches and returned to England to fight again. However, of that number, 200,000 were taken off by British and French warships and 115,000 by large passenger ferries, manned mainly by naval or merchant marine crews. In fact, only some 18,500 – around one in 20 – were actually brought back by one of the privately organised, civilian-crewed vessels.

The image of an Army of volunteers flooding forwards in the hour of need was a myth. The operation itself was cast in so much secrecy that the evacuation did not become public knowledge until 31 May, when it was more than half over. So few boat owners could volunteer for a mission they knew nothing about. It certainly served morale in those desperate days to cultivate the 'all hands to the pump' mood. Indeed, the 'Dunkirk spirit' has entered our language as the embodiment of communal effort in adversity. It served a political purpose when needed, but historical reality is only now starting to catch up.

Vive la France!

The **French Resistance** emerges as another 'necessary myth'. Far from being a decisive thorn in the side of the Nazi occupation, modern research has shown how ineffective and insignificant it actually was.

In 1996, the first authoritative critique of the French wartime secret services, by American intelligence academic Douglas Porch, concluded that the Resistance had had negligible impact. Its inflated reputation was the result of a political imperative. The post-war leader, Charles de Gaulle, needed his country to convince itself it had resisted the Nazis, otherwise the populace would be demoralised and incapable of assuming the great role in the world that de Gaulle's vision had for the future France.

Although 95,000 French men and women (undoubtedly bravely) sacrificed their lives, the Nazi leadership is recorded as regarding the Resistance to be 'non-existent'. Uncomfortable facts tend to support this view. Half of all Resistance radio operators were captured; as late as 1943, 40 per cent of Resistance broadcasts were on frequencies that only the Germans were capable of picking up. A good deal of the information gleaned and passed on to Allied sources turned out to be wildly inaccurate. Porch cited the view from a British Secret Service report that the best intelligence came not from patriotic French resisters but from 'outright purchase from venal people'.

They were even chastised by their own countrymen. Most of the population simply wanted to forget that they were occupied. Resistance leaders acknowledged that support from within their own communities ranged from apathy to actual hostility. Shortly after the war, de Gaulle offered a more realistic assessment. He is reputed to have said, 'The Resistance was just a bluff that came off.'

The Myth of the Few

The **Battle of Britain**, when 'The Few' defended the island homeland from the Nazi air onslaught, was certainly the most decisive battle in the early phase of the war. Had the invasion of Britain been successful, the last Allied toehold in Europe would have fallen and along with it the likelihood of America ever taking up arms. The bravery of the RAF is not in doubt, and the significance of the victory is clear. Later research has, however, demonstrated that the balance of forces, epitomised by Churchill as the grossly uneven battle between the German hordes and 'The Few', was a well-honed myth.

British intelligence at the time genuinely believed that Fighter Command was outnumbered, but the evidence is that it actually always held a slim advantage. Reputed British historian Richard Overy, who brought the true picture to light in a 60th anniversary retrospective in 2000, documented how, at the start of the campaign, the RAF had 1,032 fighters against the Luftwaffe's 1,011 (and had the added advantage, of course, of fighting over home ground with shorter supply lines). The RAF was better placed with airmen too, having 1,400 pilots, several hundred more than the Luftwaffe.

Britain also continued to produce more aircraft than Germany throughout. In the critical three months of the battle between June and September 1940, nearly three times as many new fighters came off the assembly lines in Britain (1,900) compared to Germany (775). Germany ran out of new aircraft and spares; the RAF had plenty of both. By the end of the battle, German aircraft losses would be double the RAF's (1,733 to 915). Overy neatly summed up the real position: 'If Fighter Command were the "Few", German fighter pilots were fewer.'

Some historians actually see in Britain's misplaced over-estimation of German strength part of the reason for eventual success. Thinking the enemy larger than it was made commanders more cautious in their operations and determined to get maximum return for any action. Fighter Command used small formations to tackle the larger Luftwaffe bomber fleets, again creating an impression of being out-numbered.

The practical reality of the engagements was very different to the image that we have settled on today. While the story we believe is of the effectiveness of radar in pinpointing enemy raiders and efficiently targeting our scarce fighters so as not to waste effort, analysis of sorties after the battle showed that in fact on 69 per cent of occasions when fighters were directed to a specific location where controllers thought the enemy were, pilots found nothing.

Tactically, Goering, the Luftwaffe chief, committed a fatal error in mid-September by turning the focus of attacks from the RAF airfields to Britain's cities. Relieving pressure on Fighter Command, it tipped the balance. By then, as Hitler was reassessing the chances of his sea invasion plans that the Luftwaffe was supposed to have paved the way for, Germany was losing aircraft at twice the rate of the RAF, with reserves running out. Days after Goering's switch, Hitler concluded that his chance had gone and he cancelled the invasion for good.

But at that point in 1940, with Britain standing alone, the myth of 'The Few' was too powerful a weapon for boosting morale to allow uncomfortable facts to get in the way. And after the war, it continued to penetrate deep into the national psyche as a totem of defiance against all odds.

An Overblown Affair

The celebrated **'Dambusters Raid'** of May 1943 in which Guy Gibson's 617 Squadron destroyed the Eder, Möhne and Sorpe dams in the heartland of the industrial Ruhr is remembered as one of the most outlandish operations of the war, primarily from Barnes Wallis's inventive bouncing bomb developed especially for the mission. Success came at a high price. Eight of the 19 Lancaster bombers taking part were shot down and 56 of the 133 airmen taking part – over 40 per cent – did not return. But the real tragedy of the affair was that the intended disruption to Nazi war output never materialised. Ten days after the attack, other reservoirs in the region had recovered local water capacity to 96 per cent of that before the raid. And production in the steel and weapons factories was not interrupted even for a day. Some 1,200 civilians were killed in the deluges caused by the collapse of the dams. With the negligible military outcomes that ensued, it remains a good example of how our memories and reality often fall out of synch.

The Other Blitz

Since its inception, the aerial **bombing offensive** against German cities was always the most controversial aspect of the Allies' war strategy. Our received wisdom is that it played a vital, if unpleasant, role in defeating Nazism. It was undoubtedly conducted partly in retaliation for the Blitz on British cities, but primarily to meet a calculated military objective of destroying transport and industrial infrastructure while, undoubtedly too, also with the aim of fracturing civilian morale.

After the war the German Federal Statistical Office estimated that 593,000 people, mostly civilians, died. Almost every major German city had more than 50 per cent of its built-up area destroyed. Some were particularly severely hit. Cologne suffered 61 per cent destruction, Hamburg 75 per cent, Bremerhaven 79 per cent and the Bavarian industrial town of Wurzburg 89 per cent. Wuppertal, in the Ruhr area, suffered only one raid – but it destroyed 94 per cent of the city.

Fifty-five thousand RAF airmen also perished. The rate of attrition in Bomber Command was higher than for officers on the Western Front in World War One. Even though moral qualms surfaced almost as soon as the raids started, their justification stood firm in the RAF's – and Churchill's – mind on the grounds of military effectiveness.

Since the end of the war, however, detached expert assessments have increasingly cast doubt on the military value of the strategy. As early as 1946, an official review of the effectiveness of the bombing campaign compiled by the British Bombing Survey Unit, concluded that the bombing of German cities 'had little effect upon either the trend of production or upon the morale of the German worker'. At the height of the campaign in 1944, when between March and December Bomber Command conducted 102,811 sorties (an average of nearly 2,400 every week) the bombing only accounted for an overall loss in war production of 7 per cent.

Churchill's vindictive streak showed itself in a particularly harsh light in his attitude to bombing. When in 1942 German reprisals for the assassination in Prague of Reinhard Heydrich, one of Hitler's top SS leaders, led to the notorious killing of all the males in the Czech village of Lidice and its razing to the ground, Churchill pressed his Cabinet to allow the RAF to wipe out three German villages in revenge, and then to announce the reason for doing so afterwards. His fellow ministers blocked the plan. Churchill is recorded as saying he would 'submit (unwillingly) to the view of the Cabinet against'.

We Will (Not) Remember Them

The cheery images of the **Home Front** that we still get in our minds from the available media, especially the uplifting newsreels, have tended to mask the uncomfortable realities of the wartime experience in Britain. We tend not to know of some of the awkward things that emerged:

- Within two weeks of the outbreak of war, the RSPCA estimated that some 200,000 dogs had been taken to vets for destruction. A secret burial ground had to be constructed in London's East End and

80,000 carcasses were buried in a single night. One historian of the period has written that 'never, perhaps, was there such a holocaust of pets as in the month of September 1939'. London Zoo elected to kill its entire collection of poisonous and constrictor snakes.

- Dogs (or any other animal) were not allowed inside public shelters. They had to be locked or tied up nearby. In London's Hyde Park, the authorities thoughtfully provided dozens of white posts, replete with chains and leads, so owners could safely tie up their dog before entering the shelter to see out the air raid.

The mass of bureaucracy and regulation that descended on the country was mind-boggling in its detail. The Emergency Powers Act had been passed a week before the outbreak of war, which allowed the Government to make regulations almost on a whim. Even before war started, the first hundred-odd regulations had been published; more followed almost every day. Some seemed extreme:

- Every car, however expensive, had to have a white edging painted on its running boards, bumpers and mudguards for the blackout. Only one headlight, duly masked according to the regulations, was allowed, the bulb having to be removed from the other. The use of illuminated arrow-type direction indicators was permissible only if they were reduced in width to one-eighth of an inch. Dashboard lights were entirely prohibited. (As a result, the number of people killed on the roads in the autumn and winter of 1939 was 1,000 a month, double the 1938 level.)
- It was an offence to leave a car unattended if it had not been immobilised against theft – usually by having to remove part of the engine – the rotor arm of the distributor became the most common method. If the police found a car not obviously immobilised, they had the power to prevent it from being moved. This was usually done by deflating all four tyres.
- Babies' prams needed lights to be on a highway at night (four women in Walsall were summonsed for not doing so).
- It was an offence to display a lit cigarette during an air raid.
- Travellers out of the country had to leave their newspapers behind when leaving British territory. Women could leave

wearing wedding and other rings and watches only up to a value of £12. Anything more was liable to be forfeited.

- Edinburgh and Dundee city councils closed their reservoirs to anglers because of the risk that saboteurs could masquerade as fishermen to poison the water supply.
- Press photographers were forbidden to use flash bulbs in the open.
- Illuminated shop signs were illegal, even in daytime.
- Car radios were banned (seemingly for fear they might be turned into transmitters). The ban initially extended to caravan dwellers too. After complaints, the Home Office relented on the latter, provided the caravan had no engine or wheels attached at the time of use. (Curiously, there were no proscriptions against individuals carrying radios, or riding a bicycle with one.)
- It was an offence for anyone to own a map on a scale more accurate than one mile to an inch. An alien could not own a map more accurate than 12 miles to an inch.
- Signs revealing railways station names were only allowed if they were under the station roof and indecipherable from the air or the roadway. Elsewhere on the station, the name had to be given in lettering no larger than three inches high.
- It was an offence for a confectioner to put sugar on the exterior of any cake, biscuit, bun, pastry, scone or bread roll after baking.
- It was an offence to keep pigeons without a permit.
- Kite flying was banned, as a precaution against illicit signalling.
- All household attics, unless reachable by a fixed staircase, had to be emptied of all movable and combustible material.

The first few months of the evacuation programme for children was largely ineffective. The Board of Education acknowledged by the end of 1939 that 43 per cent of evacuees had drifted back into the cities. In Glasgow, the figure was 75 per cent, double that of London (30 per cent of evacuees from Clydeside had returned even before the end of September). Ninety per cent of the mothers with children under five went back to city life. When the Blitz began the following year, a second evacuation was hardly more successful. The number of children of school age remaining in London in the winter of 1940 (520,000) was still more than the total that had been billeted throughout England and Wales.

A survey of air-raid shelters in 1940 found that many surface brick-built ones had been wrongly constructed due to an ambiguity in the Ministry of Home Security's circular that led to a misunderstanding as to the correct cement content. Five thousand in the London region alone had been built with lime and sand mortar containing no cement at all and were, in the words of a reviewer, 'barely strong enough to withstand a direct hit from a free-wheeling bicycle'.

At the height of the Blitz, only a small minority of people in central London actually used shelters. A census in November 1940 estimated that nine per cent of the population slept in public shelters, only four per cent used the Underground and 27 per cent used their domestic shelters. Numbers in the outer suburbs were even lower. The rest – a staggering 60 per cent – simply stayed in their homes.

According to the 1957 official history of the Home Defence preparations, inexperienced civilian contractors building pillboxes constructed many of them facing the wrong direction.

The habit of carrying gas masks never really took on. In the first weeks of war, fewer than 75 per cent obeyed the instructions from the Government to have them when out in public. By November, only a minority did so; by the following spring, almost nobody bothered.

The Government's apparently urgent campaign in July 1940 at the start of the Battle of Britain for housewives to donate their aluminium pots and pans for 'turning into Spitfires and Hurricanes, Blenheims and Wellingtons' was largely a fake exercise, even though the appeal was compellingly desperate: 'The need is instant. The call is urgent. Our expectations are high.' The public responded, reportedly stripping their kitchens. Months later, though, aluminium goods were still on sale in hardware shops. The Government was well aware that few of the domestic items would yield the high grade metal required for the aircraft industry.

Beer was never rationed, but was radically diluted. While the volume of beer consumption increased by 25 per cent during the war, the amount of alcohol taken in actually went down. And the price rocketed. Excise duty on a barrel increased from one pound and four shillings in 1939 to £7 by the second half of the war.

Striking had been made illegal in 1940 under the emergency powers. However, militancy still reared its head, despite the war. Three of the five war years saw a higher number of days lost through strikes than in the last peace-time year (1940 and 1941 were the exceptions). In 1944, there were 2,194 separate strikes, the highest number for 25 years, costing 3.7 million days, nearly three times the level of 1939. Despite the austerity required by the war, six out of ten strikes were disputes about wages.

A Different Take on Victory

One reputable British historian, Norman Stone, questioning the Allied attitude to fighting the war, produced a challenging critique in 1998 showing how British and American commanders tended to 'over-insure' themselves before combating the opposition. He argued that had they not cosseted themselves by always seeking massive superiority before venturing to engage the enemy, Germany might have been defeated by 1944, or even 1943 – two years earlier than actually occurred.

Stone pointed to the contrast with the Russian Army where there was one fighting man for one in the rear, looking after supplies and repairs. In the British Army the ratio was one to three; for the Americans, one to nine 'as the GIs were thought to be uniquely dependent on refrigerators and the like, and their supply lines became clogged with extra baggage'. The US Army often brought complete Coca-Cola bottling plants with them to keep the troops supplied. Three were shipped into North Africa after the landings there in late 1942. (In the Pacific war, the US Navy deployed an entire ship for the sole purpose of making ice cream for the ratings.)

On D-Day, the Allied superiority was in the order of 30 to one. The successful defeat of the Axis in North Africa – the hinge on which ultimate victory swung – takes on a different perspective when it is realised that British superiority over Rommel was nearly six-fold in tanks – 1,440 to just 260 German (alongside 280 'obsolete' Italian). And even then, Rommel managed two spectacular counter-offensives, the first dramatically seizing Tobruk to the Allies' deep embarrassment, and the second nearly breaking through to the Egyptian border and Cairo.

While America and Britain each lost some 400,000 soldiers killed in the war, Germany lost over three million and, from latest research, Russia is now thought to have lost up to 29 million fighters. In just two months during 1943, the Red Army lost as many men as the Americans and British lost in the entire war. It seems, Stone concluded, that Allied commanders simply did not dare to ask as much of their troops as their German (and especially Russian) counterparts. 'With dash and daring, Italy could easily have been . . . occupied in July [1943]. Instead, there was a very ponderous invasion of a barely defended Sicily and the Germans were able to regroup in southern Italy, making a step-by-step retreat over the next 22 months.' The 'most protected soldiers in history' lost sight of the dire state of the enemy's forces, failed to chance their arm without always having overwhelming material superiority and as a result, allowed the war to run on far longer than necessary.

Mechanics of War

Another perspective, however, perhaps suggests the Allies were wise to take precautions. Far from the slick, efficient fighting force we like to think took on the enemy, figures show that in the battle for France in 1940 under 25 per cent of all British tanks were lost through enemy action. The bulk had to be abandoned because of mechanical breakdown. Even this was better than the French effort. Of theirs, which were numerically superior to the invading Germans, more than half were lost simply because they ran out of fuel. French policy had been to limit each crew to just five hours' supply.

Picturing the Past

A number of the most familiar visual images of the Second World War, which frame our historical perception of events, are now thought not to be genuine but to have been faked in studio lots. In 1995, as the world commemorated the 50th anniversary of the end of war, the Imperial War Museum identified several examples where they believed existing documentary film did not portray actual events.

Celebrated footage of the D-Day landings is believed to have been enhanced on General Eisenhower's orders because foggy conditions on the day itself made the quality of film taken of the actual landings very poor. It is believed that film recorded during the rehearsal at Slapton Sands in Devon was interspersed with genuine takes.

Russian archive film used by Western documentaries portraying the battle of Stalingrad is now thought to have been stage-managed after the Russian victory had been secured.

One of the most celebrated Ministry of Information films, *Desert Victory: The Battle of El Alamein*, which won the 1943 Oscar for Best Feature Documentary, and was hailed by the British press at the time as 'the finest factual film ever made', is now known to have contained scenes filmed at Pinewood Studios as well as action shots filmed with the help of the British commander, Montgomery, well behind the front line and before the actual battle had begun. The director quixotically conceded 50 years on that they had 're-enacted without in any way distorting'.

The iconic photograph of St Paul's Cathedral, captured on the night of 29 December 1940 at the height of one of the worst raids on London of the entire war, and ever since used as a symbol of the indomitable spirit of survival amidst the raging of war, was revealed in December 2000 as having been doctored before its publication in the British press two days later. The image, of the dome apparently lit by the reflected glow of flames and rising ethereally amidst an enveloping sea of smoke, was snapped by Herbert Mason, a *Daily Mail* photographer who camped out all night on a Fleet Street office roof to get the shot. The raid that night produced an inferno twice as destructive as the Great Fire of London. When it published the photograph, the *Mail* caption read that it 'symbolises the steadiness of London's stand against the enemy; the firmness of Right against Wrong'. It also symbolised the artistic skills of the image staff who worked to enhance all the main aspects of the picture. Experts in 2000 said that two-thirds of the picture appeared to have been treated, to define more clearly the outlines of wrecked houses in the foreground, and to clarify the structure of the dome and the clock towers in order to accentuate its 'other worldliness' difference from the murkiness of the rest of the panorama. The picture attained its iconic status almost immediately, a symbol at the end of the dark year of 1940 of holding on by the fingertips against improbable odds.

The next most famous shot of the war – a cheery white-coated milkman on his morning round walking over the rubble-strewn ruin of a bombed London street, full crate in hand, an extra bottle tucked in his pocket, bearing a stoic look on his face – was a complete fake. Published on the morning of 10 October 1940, at the height of the Blitz, and after the 32nd consecutive night of German bombing, then and since it came to symbolise the determination of normal Londoners to get on with life despite extreme adversity. Except it was not a milkman. It was press photographer Fred Morley's young assistant, whom Morley had persuaded to dress up and pose for the camera. Morley did not intend it to be a propaganda shot at all. He wanted to portray the reality of the devastation caused by the raids. But a raw street scene would have been banned by the censors on the grounds of spreading despondency. The only way round was to mount the subterfuge. It worked better than he could ever have dreamed, turning into one of the most famous photographs in history.

SOME COULD HAVE BEEN SAVED

Ever since the end of the war brought the widespread realisation of the horrors of the **Holocaust**, in which up to six million Jews perished in the death camps, Britain has had to defend its sclerotic wartime response. Despite reports being received by Bletchley Park, the famous code-breaking centre, as early as 1941 about mass executions of Jews by special police units, the British Government effectively denied knowing of the unfolding catastrophe until late in the war. The Allies have been criticised for failing to bomb the railways lines that allowed the camps to function, or mount raids to disrupt the civilian deportations throughout Europe. The controversy whether more could have been done earlier is likely to continue without resolution.

What has emerged in recent years to Britain's further shame is evidence of how the British Government blocked an American plan in the middle of 1944 – a month after solid documentary evidence had arrived in London telling of mass gassings in Auschwitz – that would have enabled several thousand Jews in concentration camps to leave Germany by exchanging them for expatriate Germans being interned in Latin America.

British Objections

The Foreign Secretary at the time, and future Prime Minister, Anthony Eden, rejected the scheme. Despite the now known fate that the Jews faced inside Germany, he refused to agree to the plan because of concerns that the freed Jews would likely head for Palestine and cause trouble for the British authorities there, and that the returning able-bodied Germans would give Hitler a much-needed boost at a time when, just after D-Day, it looked as if the Allies had finally got the Nazis on the back foot.

The secret files were only made public by the Government in 1999 (they had originally been sealed for closure until 2021). Eden's qualms were given support by the British Ambassador in Uruguay who complained that returning the expatriates to their homeland would give rise to the idea that Britain had 'gone all soft and sentimental over the Germans'. The American initiative, proposed in July 1944, was pressed for months until, by early 1945, practical realities overtook it as the camps began to be liberated with what remained of their inmates.

Switzerland's Secret Shame

The role of any neutral in wartime is bound to draw ambivalent views from observers. Ireland's determined neutrality was pointedly a policy stemming from the ingrained sentiments of centuries of friction with the British rather than sympathy for Nazi Germany. Sweden's was seen as partially justified by her off-the-beaten track geography, but her economic links with Germany was a constant source of irritation for the Allies. Switzerland's position was more clear cut. Her neutrality was predictable and strictly in line with centuries of tradition. Her geopolitical position – mountaintops stuck in the middle of the Continent with few economic resources – offered little benefit to any neighbour. And for most of the post-war period, the country's reputation was as clean and crisp as the Alpine air. History taught that Switzerland was upright, honest and detached from the less salubrious motivations of surrounding powers. Until the 1990s.

The Spotlight Turns
The first, now well-known, dent in the gleam was the revelation in 1996 that Swiss banks had held on to the financial assets of Jews who disappeared in the Holocaust. Outraged at the slight cast on their banking industry, the Swiss Government quickly reached a $1.25 billion settlement in 1998 to pay claims of Jewish survivors and their descendants.

A second, lesser-known, dent emerged more recently, partially as a result of the Holocaust episode as historians became inclined for the first time to probe further the country's aseptic image. A panel of academics concluded in March 2002 that Switzerland's image of neutrality in the war was deeply compromised. The report was more damning than the Holocaust affair as it revealed a systematic policy by the Swiss Government to breach its official neutral stance to combatant nations.

Bankrolling the Axis
The Independent Commission of Experts and World War II revealed in its 12,000 pages of analysis that Switzerland actively engaged in

economic relations with Nazi Germany throughout the war, holding by the end over $1 billion of German assets. Instead of confiscating them and transferring them to the victorious Allies, as required under a 1946 war compensation agreement that aimed to use Nazi assets to compensate victims of Hitler's aggression, the Swiss quietly returned millions of dollars to their German owners after the war. Evidence also surfaced that Swiss banks willingly traded in securities from their German clients when there was good reason to believe these had been stolen from their legitimate owners.

The Swiss provided rail transit routes for economic resources and materials. The Commission found that during the war the volume of transit traffic expanded to three times the pre-war level. They also provided over one billion Swiss francs of loans (one estimate put this at around £500 million at modern values) to Nazi Germany and Fascist Italy to enable them to buy Swiss arms and other vital products such as energy (Switzerland was an important provider of electricity to the Reich), aluminium and machine tools. The Commission concluded that Switzerland's export trade during the war was 'active' and, in regard to treatment of all combatant nations, 'biased towards Germany'. It effectively helped to bankroll the German war effort.

One of the findings which drew particular ire was the discovery that the Swiss chemical giant Geigy was the supplier of the 'polar red' dye used in the Nazi swastika flag. It also concluded that deportation trains carrying Jews to their deaths in Nazi camps were allowed to pass through Swiss territory. In addition, up to 30,000 Jewish refugees who managed to reach the border with Switzerland were refused entry and returned to Germany, to almost certain extermination. The Swiss head of the Commission conceded that, 'Large numbers of persons whose lives were in danger were turned away needlessly. . . . The refugee policy of our authorities contributed to the most atrocious of Nazi objectives – the Holocaust.'

A Reputation Trashed
After the investigation, the commonly held image of Switzerland as a plucky, disinterested nation trying to ignore the war and insulate

itself from the mayhem of global conflict, lay in tatters. Within the space of six years, and on two fronts, the PR image of innocence upheld over 50 years had evaporated forever.

Clean Hands

General **Dwight D. Eisenhower** had had a 27-year military career by the time he was appointed Commander of US Forces in Europe in 1942 (subsequently elevated to Supreme Allied commander at the end of 1943 to lead the D-Day invasion) but, according to historian A.D. Harvey, had never seen a dead body before leading the invasion of North Africa in November 1942 – the RAF helpfully flew him over the battlefield to show him the carnage and the only time he had been near a weapon fired in anger was when he himself fired his .45 revolver to try to kill a rat that had invaded his private toilet at Caserta during the invasion of Italy the following year.

Patton's Strange Demise

General George Patton, American Second World War hero and famed for his no-nonsense approach to command – his men used to remark, 'You have never lived until you have been bawled out by General Patton' – had a secret that contrasted with his public demeanour. He held a lifelong conviction that he had been a soldier in up to six past incarnations. He told of recurring 'subconscious memories' of being a prehistoric warrior battling a mammoth; a Greek hoplite who fought against the Persian King, Cyrus; a soldier under Alexander the Great at the siege of Tyre; a legionnaire under Julius Caesar in northern Gaul; an English knight at the battle of Crécy; and a Napoleonic marshal. A good thing his modern-day commanders never found out.

Too Hot to Handle

Patton's well-established reputation for thirsting after military glory may have been too much for his political masters. Rumours abounded after his death in a car accident in December 1944 as he led the Allied assault into Germany, that he had been eliminated by his own side because of concerns that he would end up embroiling the United States in a new war with the Soviet Union.

There certainly were curious elements to his demise. He died after a troop truck hit his staff car outside Mannheim in southern Germany during a pheasant-hunting trip. The accident occurred just after both vehicles were starting up after stopping at a railway level crossing, so were going at less than 20mph each. Neither vehicle appeared to be badly damaged. Patton was the only person hurt, seeming to have struck himself on a metal seat partition. He was paralysed, with his neck broken.

Military historian Robert Wilcox claimed in a 2008 book to have identified a hit-man, Douglas Bazata, who confessed before he died in 1999 to engineering the accident and finishing off Patton by shooting him with a low velocity projectile that had broken his spine. Bazata said he was acting under orders from the forerunner of the CIA, the wartime Office of Strategic Services whose leader, 'Wild Bill' Donovan had described Patton as being 'out of control'.

Other intriguing aspects which Wilcox claimed pointed to a cover-up were the disappearance of the truck driver, who was whisked off to London before he could be questioned, and the absence of any post-mortem on the general. At least five documents on the accident appear to have been removed from the US Archives. According to Wilcox, 'the Administration thought Patton was "nuts"', and that 'he wanted to go to war with the Russians'. The world needed to be saved from him.

(RE)DEFINING SUCCESS

To conclude this chapter on war on a slightly lighter note, one of the most notorious of modern military PR offensives was unleashed in the 1991 Gulf War – one in which a wide panoply of 'smart' weapons took their operational bow. The US military proudly unveiled its surface-to-air **Patriot missile system** and quickly the world learned of its staggeringly effective defensive performance. Its supposed capacity to intercept incoming enemy missiles rendered it a potentially powerful media tool to show that Iraqi attempts to launch missiles into Western allies, Saudi Arabia and Israel, were doomed to fail. President Bush claimed that 41 of 42 Patriot launches success-fully intercepted Iraqi Scud missiles. The US military claimed even higher hit rates. A year after the war, reviews by the prestigious Massachusetts Institute of Technology revealed that most Patriots actually missed their target. No evidence in fact existed of the destruction of a single incoming missile. When challenged on the truth of the claims made during the war, military spokesman Brigadier General Robert Drolet stuck to his guns. He told reporters that the President's figures were still accurate: the Army's definition of 'intercept' was not 'destroyed', but that 'a Patriot and a Scud passed in the sky'.

5

Royalty – Regal Façades

The power of royalty lies in image and belief. After all, a mortal human being raised from among the populus, apparently endowed with mystical authority to govern, needs a good supporting story. The history that gets taught to successive generations of loyal subjects needs to buttress the institution of the monarchy itself, just as much as it dutifully preserves and respects the reputation of the current individual on the throne. The strength of the monarchy at any point in time relies on a solid, well-honed historical foundation. And that can mean leaving out some of the awkward bits that don't quite fit the picture.

LYING HEARTED?

Richard I, the Lionheart (1157–1199), although one of the best remembered of our monarchs, actually spent very little time in the Kingdom. Being also Duke of Normandy, Gascony and Aquitaine, Count of Anjou and Nantes and Overlord of Brittany, he lived mainly on the Continent or was on crusade in the Holy Land. He spent only 160 days of his 10-year reign in England, in just two visits. Modern research suggests his epithet to be more a shield than a true reflection of his manliness. He failed to produce an heir and he only consummated his marriage after five years, and that, according to one account, only as a penance imposed by a priest to whom Richard had confessed his homosexuality. A curious record, which only surfaced in

1948, has added weight to the theory he was gay. It recorded a chronicler writing that in 1187 Richard and the French King Philip II were so close 'that at night the bed did not separate them'. One academic opinion, however, maintained, perhaps a little optimistically, that it was an entirely political act, 'just two politicians literally getting into bed together, a bit like a modern day photo opportunity'.

ELIZABETH'S SECRET HISTORY

One of the most intriguing mysteries of British royalty – the failure of **Elizabeth I** to find a husband – may have been down to an abused childhood, according to a theory advanced in 1996 by child psychiatrist Dr Elinor Kapp. Publishing her analysis in the academic journal *Psychiatric Bulletin*, Kapp dissected the earliest portrait that exists of Elizabeth, as a 13-year-old during the last year of her father Henry VIII's reign.

Kapp identified signs in the face of Elizabeth that were symptomatic of the many abused youngsters she had witnessed as a practising child psychiatrist. Her expression in the portrait was one of 'frozen watchfulness' said Kapp, along with a 'haunting loneliness' that suggested 'obsessive secrecy'. Her tightly folded lips, and awkwardly set posture were all indicators of a child who had suffered significant personal trauma, possibly sexual abuse. All this made it unsurprising that in adulthood, like many similarly abused children, Elizabeth should find insurmountable difficulty in establishing relationships with men.

Elizabeth maintained a teasing elusiveness both before and after she became Queen, kept a 30-year on-and-off affair with courtier Lord Robert Dudley, whom she made the 1st Earl of Leicester. It is said she did not marry him because of her suspicions about the way in which Dudley's young wife had conveniently died falling down the stairs shortly after her own succession to the throne. When he died in 1588, she kept his last letter to her by her bedside for the rest of her life.

155

There were rumours she was not a 'proper' woman but Lord Burghley, her chief adviser, after consulting the royal doctors pronounced her 'very apt' for procreation. It may have been the politics that became too complicated, it may have been the public expectations that she resented . . . or could it have been memories of ill treatment early in life that were in fact responsible for giving Britain her Virgin Queen?

Behind the Façade

Elizabeth's regal bearing was artificially enhanced by stuffing her mouth with cloth when appearing in public to conceal her sunken face which had been caused by losing all her teeth. She endured a dental nightmare throughout her later life. Suffering from atrociously bad breath, she consumed huge quantities of sweets every day to mask the odour. The sugar eventually rotted her teeth, which made her breath even fouler, which she covered up with more and more sweets.

A BREAK IN THE ROYAL CHAIN? (1)

A mystery that dates from the mid-16th century, that remains unsolved, could cast doubt on the present royal line of succession. At issue is whether **James VI of Scotland**, who became James I of England in 1603 on the death of Elizabeth, was who his mother, Mary Queen of Scots, said he was. The reason for doubt lies in the macabre discovery in Edinburgh Castle in 1830 of a small coffin containing the remains of a baby. It was discovered in an antechamber long believed to have been the one in which Mary's son and future King was born in 1566. She was known for certain to have had no other children.

The discovery of the coffin raised the question whether the remains were indeed Mary's child, and whether the boy who grew up to be James I was an impostor, substituted in place of the dead child to maintain a line of succession. James himself was always said to be unsure of his legitimacy as he looked nothing like any of the other members of the Stuart family.

Historians generally agree that the room in which the coffin was discovered was most likely the birthplace of Mary's child. Reports of the find speak of the casket being of 'fine oak' with the baby wrapped in thick wool accompanied by a piece of cloth said to be silk, intriguingly embroidered with a letter 'J'. The cask and its contents were said to have disintegrated upon contact with air and whatever was left was re-interred.

As far as is known, and perhaps unsurprisingly given the potential ramifications, no efforts have since been made to attempt to relocate the remains.

A CATHOLIC STOOGE?

William of Orange, the Dutch monarch who became King of England after the 'Glorious Revolution' of 1688 which settled the British monarchy on a Protestant line, carried a secret with him that emerged only in 2001. Documents discovered in an archive showed that this ultra-Protestant, whose reputation for anti-Catholicism in Ireland still burns to this day, was quietly being funded by, of all sources, the Pope.

William's toppling of the Catholic James II, and his subsequent war of subjugation in Ireland, reinforced his reputation as a staunch leader of anti-Catholicism in Europe. The Battle of the Boyne in 1690 at which William defeated James is still marked to this day by the Unionist Orange Order as the pivotal moment in Anglo-Irish relations. The British monarchy has been Protestant ever since. The Bill of Rights, passed immediately as a consequence of the Glorious Revolution, and the later Act of Settlement of 1701, still in force, bars Catholics from the royal succession.

Religion and Politics Collide

The revelations in 2001 add an astonishing gloss on history. Far from the Vatican looking out for the interests of Catholics in England, the Pope at the time – the perhaps now inaptly named Innocent XI – appears to have been engaged in a complex Machiavellian game motivated by distinctly secular concerns: the growing menace of the French Catholic King, Louis XIV. As one of the strongest powers on the Continent, the attitude of the French was crucial, and they had been causing problems for the Vatican for years.

The haughty Louis contrived to humiliate and show disrespect for his supposed ecclesiastical betters. He picked fights – literally – with Innocent's predecessor but one, Alexander VII, in the 1660s by sending an ambassador renowned for his arrogance who on arrival prompted a brawl between his retinue and the papal guard that led to a breaking off of diplomatic relations and a near invasion of the papal territories by the French. It was the Pope who found himself having to back down and cravenly apologise.

By the time Innocent became Pope in 1676, Louis was at the height of his powers. Like Henry VIII in England a century and a half before, Louis objected to papal authority intruding into the governance of France. But, unlike Henry, he had no intention of relinquishing his Catholicism. He simply exerted his stronger force of arms against the Pope.

A strict theologian, Innocent was especially intolerant to laxity in doctrine. A dispute over who had rights over Church finances escalated to a point where the basic principles of authority between national monarchs and the Pope was at question. There was a repeat performance of the truculent French ambassador being sent, a papal expulsion and a threat from Louis to invade.

Seen in these terms, Innocent's concerns with France, which went to the heart of papal authority within the Catholic community, loomed larger than what the 'other side', the Protestants, were getting up to. So much so, according to the new evidence, that for years the Vatican found it politically expedient to undermine the threats from within by secretly supporting Louis's enemies, even though they followed a heretical faith.

The Enemy of My Enemy . . .

Before becoming Pope, Innocent had been head of the Vatican finance department, and herein lies the secret. Records show that Innocent's family connections had been used as intermediaries to channel Vatican funds to the Dutch King. It was not small beer either. An estimated 150,000 scudi was sent, equivalent to the Vatican's annual budget deficit at the time, and worth some £4 million in modern values. Scholars who uncovered the records presume that they were only part of the story – they happened to have been kept in the family's archives not the Vatican's – and that other records showing further transfers have been destroyed. The assumption is that it was impossible for the Roman Catholic Church to risk discovery that a Pope had played an important role in the overthrow of a Catholic King.

More evidence of the cover-up, and the impact the funds had in William's eventual triumph, comes from the disclosure that, after the Glorious Revolution, William offered to pay back the money by yielding to the papacy his lands in southern France. The Vatican rejected the offer, on the grounds that Innocent had died a few months earlier and that it did not want his financial links with William to become public knowledge.

Innocent's machinations are perhaps one of the earliest examples of the Cold War aphorism that 'the enemy of my enemy is my friend'. Despite his apparent record for doctrinal purity, Innocent, it now seems, was more an arch political strategist. In boosting William's fortunes to counter France, he ended up sacrificing James and Catholic England for good.

Was it an unintended consequence? Possibly. Innocent clearly was vulnerable to being exposed by William. He may therefore simply have done nothing to support James that could have risked that exposure. On the other hand, Louis was still a thorn in the side for the Vatican and the defeat of a potential ally was perhaps, all things considered, a price well worth paying. Innocent is known to have strongly disapproved of James's methods in restoring Catholicism to England and his support for Louis's disruptive conduct encouraged little sympathy for his plight. We shall probably never know, but what is certain is that our view of the Glorious Revolution has a permanently different angle to it now.

A Break in the Royal Chain? (2)

The best known of **George III's** personal secrets is his descent into madness, with his son, the future George IV, eventually assuming the throne as Regent in 1811 for the last nine years of the King's life. The less familiar skeleton in this royal closet is the likelihood that George III was a bigamist and that his secret wife gave birth to three children, who, on some interpretations of succession law, ought to be the rightful rulers of Britain.

The official version of history is that George married a German princess, Charlotte, two weeks before his coronation in 1761. She was his devoted Queen for almost the entire length of his 59-year reign (she died just two years before he did). It has long been rumoured, however, that he had secretly married a Wapping Quaker girl, Hannah Lightfoot, two years earlier. Furthermore, there were children of the marriage – supposedly two sons and a daughter – on some interpretations, the rightful successors to George and not the present royal line.

Without any evidence, it remained just a rumour. Tantalisingly, conspiracy theorists claimed that the royal archives had, in 1866, acquired the documentary proof that existed of the marriage and were holding it under wraps to prevent the British royal line from unravelling.

Over the last two centuries since the rumours started, investigators have created mountains of circumstantial evidence to try to prove the marriage. When Queen Victoria was under intense pressure during the bouts of unpopularity with the monarchy in the middle of her reign, the allegations were given new life by anti-monarchists to lay seeds of doubt in the public mind about her hereditary rights.

One particularly dedicated author, Mary Lucy Pendered, kept up the quest into the next century. After delving into the genealogies, she produced a book in 1939 asserting there were 17 families able to claim descent from George and Hannah, thus being the rightful heirs to the throne.

Modern Revelations

Interest was revived in 1997 when a researcher announced the discovery of the documents in the royal archives that purported to verify the story. They turned out to be signed witness statements confirming the marriage of George, then Prince of Wales, to Lightfoot in Kew chapel in April 1759, when he was just 21. Press coverage connected the discovery to claims that the eldest offspring, also named George, born before any of the King's children with Charlotte, was sent out to South Africa to avoid scandal. He was said to have adopted the name George Rex in coded acknowledgement of his true pedigree. A gravestone was uncovered by researchers showing he died in 1839.

Despite the finds, more traditionalist historians of the royal family continue to poor cold water on the story. Debunkers assert that they can trace George Rex to being, not George III's son, but the son of a humble trader, John Rex, a distiller from Whitechapel. Constitutional experts confidently pronounce that the present royal line is not threatened by the revelations as the marriage was not legal. Although solemnised in a formal ceremony and witnessed by others, it does not pass muster legally because the reigning King, George II, had not formally given his permission. On that technicality, therefore, the foundations of our current royal line apparently rest.

FIGURE OF FUN

George IV, when he succeeded in his own right in 1820, also suffered. As the debauched Prince of Wales, his early extravagances were extreme. By 1795, when he was just 33, he had accumulated a debt of £630,000 (approaching £50 million in modern values) which Parliament reluctantly partially settled. He came to be regarded by contemporaries, and history, simply as a licentious, self-indulgent buffoon. Wherever he went in public he faced abuse and catcalls from his subjects.

He was the most lampooned royal ever. So much so, and so corrosive it became to the institution of the monarchy, that a year later Prime Minister William Pitt secretly gave the most coruscating cartoonist of the day, James Gillray, £2,000 (some £150,000 today) not to abuse the royal family further.

As Prince Regent and later King, however, his foibles were of greater consequence. He had become addicted to laudanum – by the end he was imbibing up to 250 drops a day – and brandy, and was often delusional. He conversed with his Prime Minister, the war hero Duke of Wellington, under the impression that he taken part in Wellington's battles of Salamanca and Waterloo.

Mocked to the Last

When he died, even the austere *Times* gave a knock-down view, perhaps the least respectful commentary ever made by a bastion of the British establishment about its monarch: 'He led a course of life, the character of which rose little higher than animal indulgence . . . There never was an individual whose passing was less regretted by his fellow-creatures than this deceased King . . . If George IV ever had a friend the name of him never reached us.' It is difficult to imagine even a modern-day tabloid deigning to go so far.

His bulk – he had a 55-inch waist – was such that he had to be hoisted by winch onto his horse. *The Times* picturesquely lamented his 'uninterrupted inclination to corpulency'. It had been a trend of a lifetime. Only after his death did it become apparent just how far his self-indulgence had been at the expense of public business. His idleness had left 48,000 state papers waiting to be signed.

A further skeleton was only discovered after his death. He was found to have followed the curious practice of keeping a lock of hair from every one of his lovers. He placed it in its own envelope and labelled it with the woman's name. His staff found the collection of envelopes secreted away – all 7,100 of them.

She Was Amused

Victoria's personality has been cemented into the British mind as being dour and humourless. 'We are not amused' is most likely the only utterance most of us will associate with her (although late in life she denied to a relative she had ever said it). The reputation has been gradually unbundled in recent years. We now have a much more rounded picture of our longest reigning monarch, and a startling one at that which changes our perception of her, and her era.

New material that became available in the 1970s and 80s showed a vastly different portrait of the Queen to the one proffered by tradition. While she studiously maintained an appropriate decorum in public, the evidence shows a starkly different character behind the scenes.

Contrary to the received image of prudery, she was a highly sexed individual. (She did, after all, have nine children in 17 years, her first coming only 10 months after her marriage, and the second following just 11 months later.) The couple adorned their bedroom with nude statues and, according to one biographer, had a device that enabled them to lock the door without getting out of bed. In Prince Albert's bathroom, she had hung, in the words of one recent biographer, a 'startlingly sensual' painting of the mythical Queen of Lydia who kept Hercules as her personal slave. The symbolism would have been all too clear.

Far from setting the prudery agenda, she was enthralled by erotic art. She and Albert exchanged what has been described as 'awesome' amounts of nude sculpture as presents to each other. When a collection of similarly risqué statues were placed in the Crystal Palace for her ceremonial opening of the Great Exhibition in 1851, it was not her who objected but the country's bishops, who threatened to boycott the biggest national showcase of the century. Fig leaves were eventually rustled up to spare their blushes.

Victoria and Albert were also in the habit of sending nude paintings to each other. The story is told of the writer Compton Mackenzie who spotted an alluring nude portrait of the mythical figure Artemis in a Buckingham Palace corridor when he was there to be knighted in 1952. Wondering to himself what Victoria would have said to having such a painting hanging in the palace, he approached it to read an inscription that revealed it to be one of her wedding presents to Albert.

Tales of the Unexpected

Victoria had a passion for popular and more lowbrow entertainments. She loved freak shows, and the American showman P.T. Barnum would be summoned to perform when in the country. He arguably made his fortune from the royal patronage he could rely on. She made frequent visits to circuses and extravaganza shows when they arrived in London. She clearly had a passion for the exotic. She once replied to her Prime Minister, Lord Melbourne, when he asked her about her wishes for a pet, that she would like a monkey.

She was by no means a conformist. Despite the religious strictures of Victorian life, she and Albert never got into the habit of going to Church regularly on Sundays. It was an attitude that lasted throughout her life.

She is recorded as relishing whisky ('and not too weak') and the occasional betting spree on the horses. One photograph is described by a biographer as showing her, when she smiled, looking more like a jolly old barmaid than a Queen.

She was a strong believer in the spirit world and held seances after Albert's death to establish contact with him. A 14-year-old medium, Robert Lees, became her favourite when he claimed to have made contact with Albert – the first to do so – two years after Albert's death in 1861. The dead Prince Consort apparently passed a personal message, a pet name known only to Victoria, to Lees in front of two royal emissaries. Victoria later had him perform another seance at Windsor, and expressed herself convinced that contact had been made. He is said to have conducted six more seances over the years, each successful in reaching Albert.

In later life, she hid her frailties by a bizarre deception. Photographs of her as a proud matriarch surrounded by her grandchildren and holding the latest baby on her knee had to be artfully faked because she had lost almost all strength in her arms and could not support even a newborn baby. So she had a maid secrete herself underneath her broad, hooped skirt to hold the child in place.

A True Victorian

Victoria's father, **Edward, Duke of Kent**, was the most unlikely progenitor of Britain's most famous Queen. Fourth son of George III, and younger brother of George IV, he is surprisingly little known to history. But when one reads of his appalling character, perhaps it is not so odd the royal family have preferred to sweep him into history's dark corner. He lived unmarried with his French mistress for over 30 years. He only married at 50 when the problem arose that there was no legitimate heir to the throne in the generation after George III. As Governor in Gibraltar and Canada, he was a brutal disciplinarian. He was also an early socialist.

He had lived openly with Julie de St Laurent since meeting her in Canada in 1791. He was, ironically, the most settled domestically of all of George III's sons. He was sacked from two of his three overseas military postings for instilling mutinies caused by his stern approach to discipline. His first assignment to Gibraltar barely lasted a year before he had to be removed. He was shunted off to Canada where the same trend continued. When subalterns tried to escape to America, he took pleasure in inflicting cruelly heavy punishments. He sentenced one absconder to 999 lashes, watching and counting every single one.

He was back in Gibraltar in March 1802 where his pettiness for rules became legendary. He laid down in minutest detail the code of conduct controlling every aspect of his men's lives. His rule book on Gibraltar eventually filled 300 closely printed pages, and decreed everything from the length of soldiers' beards and whiskers to the regulations for carrying umbrellas by off-duty officers. He was finally removed yet again after he stopped Christmas Day privileges and his garrison revolted. He had three ringleaders shot and flogged a fourth to death.

He returned home to work with charities and took a deep interest in the social pioneering work of Robert Owen, one of Britain's early socialist thinkers. Declaring himself a devoted convert to Owen's ideas for alleviating what Edward himself called 'the evil of a depressed working class', he presided over Owen's meetings and pressed his cause in the higher reaches of the establishment, one of the earliest to do so.

Scramble for the Succession

When Edward's niece, Princess Charlotte, died in November 1817, leaving no royal heir for the next generation, there was a mad scramble amongst three of George III's sons to produce one. All were deep in debt and therefore had huge incentives to come up with the goods, and quickly. Edward's mistress was shuffled off to a nunnery and Edward was sent on a search of European princesses. Within six months, on 29 May 1818, he had married Victoria, a Princess of the German Saxe-Coburg dynasty. It was from her that, less than a year later on 24 May 1819, the future Queen Victoria was born. The British royal line was saved – just in time. Edward died eight months later. Many will have been very relieved indeed that he was not around to influence his daughter as she grew into the royal role now destined for her.

A Break in the Royal Chain? (3)

But was this last-minute salvation of the royal line all too good to be true? Research published in 1995 suggested that Edward may not have been Victoria's father after all, that she was in fact the offspring of an illicit affair between her mother and a courtier. If true, Victoria's legitimacy as Queen, and the royal line ever since, would be called into question. The true royal line would lie with present-day German princes. The evidence is quite compelling.

An analysis of Victoria's medical history discovered that although the royal family had for many generations been suffering from the genetic disease porphyria, the affliction that was responsible for the madness of George III, Victoria and none of her descendants had the illness. Odder still, Victoria did carry haemophilia, also a genetically inherited complaint. Using records in London's Royal Society of Medicine, the medical history of Victoria's royal ancestors was traced back for 17 generations. Not one instance of haemophilia was found, strongly suggesting that she must have acquired it from outside her supposed royal lineage. The only other route would have been a spontaneous genetic mutation in Victoria. Medical experts put the chances of that at 1 in 50,000.

The finger points to Irish-born Sir John Conroy, the comptroller of the royal household, with whom Victoria's mother is said to have had the affair. The Duke of Wellington wrote that Victoria herself discovered her mother and Conroy in 'some sort of intimate situation'. She would detest Conroy throughout the rest of his life. He was eased out of the court when she became Queen in 1837, and he died in 1854.

When the story broke in 1995, the present royal family adamantly refused requests for DNA testing, which would prove the issue one way or the other for certain.

MANAGED EXITS

George V, who reigned between 1910 and 1936, had a relatively uncontroversial life but, it emerged in the 1980s, he made up for it in the manner of his death. He died peacefully at the royal retreat at Sandringham in Norfolk just before midnight on 20/21 January 1936, and no one outside the inner circle had any inkling of anything untoward about the King's demise. It was not until 1986 that *The Times* revealed that the medical notes of Lord Dawson, the royal physician, indicated that his life had been ended 'prematurely' by fatal injections of morphine and cocaine. Part of the reason appeared to be simply to spare the dying monarch further pain. Controversially, the other important consideration was to ensure the death occurred early enough to allow the morning newspapers, in particular *The Times*, to be able to carry the news rather than, in Dawson's words, 'the less appropriate field of the evening journals'. Dawson revealed that he had told his wife to telephone *The Times* tipping them off to hold back publication that evening. The royal circle duly got the appropriate coverage they desired.

All in the Timing

Royal 'death management' was at the heart of another episode in 1972 according to author Michael Bloch who, while editing the private letters of the Duke and Duchess of Windsor, discovered evidence that the doctors treating the Duke, the abdicated **Edward VIII**, who lived in exile in Paris, were quietly urged to ensure that their patient did not expire during Queen Elizabeth's symbolic visit to him that May. The visit, seen as a public gesture of reconciliation within the royal family, was the first meeting of the former monarch with any of his successors since the abdication in 1936. According to Bloch, the letters showed that the British Government was concerned at the prospect of Edward's dénouement at an inconvenient moment. The British Embassy was said to have contacted the Duke's doctor telling him that it was in order for the Duke to die before the visit or afterwards, but not during it. At the time, he was dying of throat cancer and was too ill even to leave his bed for the Queen's visit.

Queen Elizabeth, the Duke of Edinburgh and Prince Charles duly met the Duchess for tea in a 40-minute visit on 18 May, and spent 15 minutes with the bedridden Duke. He died 10 days later. The Government denied the existence of any written evidence in the Embassy to support the claim.

ANTIPODEAN SECRET

In 1996, an Australian aboriginal woman from Darwin put forward a claim that she was **Edward VIII's** granddaughter. Barbara Chisholm spoke for the first time to the world's press to assert that her father had been the illegitimate offspring of a one-night fling when Edward, then Prince of Wales, paid a visit to Sydney in 1920 on a Royal Navy ship. The prince had a reputation for womanising and it is known he invited a woman, Mollie Little, back to the ship after the official reception at Government House. The episode is well documented as the Prince's escort was Earl Mountbatten who recorded it in his diary. The ship left the following day.

Chisholm, whose father had been born exactly nine months after the visit, willingly offered to take a DNA test to prove her case. Intriguingly, the royal family has never taken steps to refute the claim.

KING OF IRELAND?

Even though he may not have known it, **Edward VIII** remained legally King of Ireland right up until his death in 1972 because of a political game played by Irish leader Eamon de Valera that went chaotically wrong.

On Edward's abdication in 1936, de Valera refused to sign up to the Abdication Act passed by the Parliament in London which recited the assent of the dominions of Australia, Canada, New Zealand and

169

South Africa, who all had to pass an enabling law in their legislatures under the agreed principles of the empire at the time. De Valera made sure Ireland was excluded, and two days later passed his own Act purporting to set up a freer relationship with Britain by taking over the powers of the royal Governor General, but formally professing still to recognise the new King, George VI. That was his mistake.

Constitutional lawyers pointed out that the Act's recognition of the new monarch was invalid, as the Irish Parliament had not assented to Edward's abdication. They were legally stuck with him. Even Irish independence in 1949 may not have made any difference legally, as nothing in the independence arrangements mentioned the severing of loyalty to Edward, only of that to George VI. In strict legal eyes, then, Edward remained King of Ireland until his death.

I Remember Him Well

Walter Monckton, one of **Edward VIII's** closest friends and, as the royal household's legal adviser, guide to Edward through the abdication crisis, received a gift from him of an inscribed cigarette case to mark 20 years' close service. Edward had spelt his name wrongly.

Bowing to the Inevitable

Arch left-wing Labour politician John Prescott discovered in 1981 the royal family's (and it seems *every* royal family's) secret trick for securing apparent due deference from even the fiercest anti-royalist. As Member of Parliament for Hull, Prescott was required to be present when **Queen Elizabeth** opened the Humber Bridge. He told royal advisers that he adamantly refused to bow to the Queen when he was presented to her. On the day, and as the Queen approached him, Prescott was true to his word – until the Queen muttered something. Leaning forward in a reflex action to hear better, the Queen took his hand and smiled. The pose was as close enough to a bow to be taken for one. 'I was fooled,' Prescott later recalled.

He realised this trick was a trade secret amongst royals when speaking many years later to the Crown Prince of the Netherlands. When he began telling his story, the Crown Prince interrupted. 'Don't tell me, she muttered, you fell for it and leaned forward?' The only reply Prescott got when he asked how the Prince knew was a wink.

FAKING IT

During a royal tour of Canada in 1991, **Princess Diana** visited the state-of-the-art Ottawa Heart Institute to open a day-care wing. It was so ahead of the times that it emerged afterwards that it had had no actual patients on its books at the time of the visit. Managers bussed in eight former patients from a different part of the facility and planted them in beds to make them appear to be in residence. The Princess toured the wards, chatting to each 'patient' in turn. As soon as she had left, all the 'patients' got up, changed and left too.

The Princess was apparently unaware of the ruse, at least for 24 hours. The next day, the *Toronto Star*, the country's largest newspaper, splashed it across its pages.

FOREIGN FOLLIES

Foreign royalty also often failed to uphold the standards one might expect of their positions of leadership and social responsibility. So much so that when India was granted its independence in 1947, British officials of the Raj decided the better policy was to burn their archive of intelligence about the Maharajahs, the local princely caste who had provided much of the local rule of India under British auspices. Their antics were so extreme that its existence threatened many of them with blackmail.

An early **Nawab of Rampur** engaged in bets with other princes on who could deflower the most virgins in a year. The last **Maharajah of Kashmir** was blackmailed out of a fortune after being caught with a woman in a room at the Savoy Hotel by a man pretending to be her husband. The last **Nizam of Hyderabad,** who ruled from 1911 to 1948, was not only named as the richest man in the world in 1937 but was also an obsessed sex addict. A keen photographer, he amassed a mountain of pornography by installing hidden cameras in his guests' rooms in his six palaces. He was believed to have fathered over 100 illegitimate sons by 86 mistresses. This has led to a spectacularly complex 60-year legal battle, which remains unresolved, over ownership of his fortune and jewels. The number of claimants had, as of 2008, swollen to some 470 sons, daughters and grandchildren. Perhaps the worst was the **Maharajah of Alwar** who used boys from his villages as live bait in his tiger shoots, reassuring their parents that he had never missed a tiger before. He refused British plans to build a road into and through his state from Delhi because it would disrupt his gaming. His proclivities became so extreme that in 1933 the British had to force him into exile for the last four years of his life. The last straw was a fraught polo match after which the Maharajah took out his frustration at losing on his polo pony. He poured petrol over it and set it alight. The **Maharajah of Kapurthala** believed himself to the reincarnation of Louis XIV. He employed a French architect and historical advisers to build himself a complete replica of Louis's Palace of Versailles in his capital in the northern Punjab, which earned the nickname the 'Paris of the Punjab'. Completed in 1908, it had taken eight years to build and covered 200 acres. For over 40 years, the Maharajah held court there. He decreed that only French was to be spoken and all the servants were decked out in 17th-century-style uniforms. Perhaps mercifully for him he died just a year after the absorption of his princely state into independent India. (The palace remains to this day, and is now a school.)

LOOKING FOR CIVILISATION

The founder of modern Russia, **Peter the Great**, has an undoubtedly deserved reputation for leadership, industry and vision. In the space of a generation in the late 17th century, he turned the backward and notoriously barbarous province of Muscovy into a great power. He did it through opening up his lands to the culture and technical knowledge of the West, and personally fostered a blossoming of learning and innovation. Despite a relatively short reign – he ruled as sole Tsar for just 29 years from 1696 to 1725 – Russia was fundamentally transformed. The most celebrated feature of the project was how it all began: the 25-year-old ruler's 18-month 'Grand Embassy' tour of European centres of trade and industry in 1697–8. He travelled incognito and famously disguised himself as a labourer to take menial jobs in Dutch dockyards to learn the secrets of shipbuilding.

But the bringer of modernisation to Russia left a distinctly uncivilised trail behind him, particularly in England where his stay between January and May 1698 goes down as possibly the most anarchic state visit of all time. The gory details were covered up by an embarrassed Government so as not to destroy relations with the fledgling superpower.

Peter and his substantial entourage were loaned lodgings at a villa, Sayes Court, in Deptford, then a country retreat east of London. Chosen for being conveniently near the dockyards, it had been loaned to the Government by diarist John Evelyn who had spent 45 years painstakingly laying out the gardens, perfecting a bowling green, designing pathways and ornamental attractions. It was his pride and joy; quite literally a house fit for a King – but, unfortunately as it turned out, not a King like Peter.

Anarchy Reigns

The events that ensued caused Evelyn deeply to regret his generosity. Fortunately for history, he recorded all the details of what transpired. If he had known of Peter's exploits earlier on the tour, he might well have had second thoughts. A plaque in the royal park in Brussels

173

today marks the spot where he stopped to be violently sick after one of his many spectacular drinking bouts.

In the four months of the visit, the Tsar and his entourage systematically wrecked the home. Evelyn got anxious warnings of the destruction being wreaked, but the true calamity only became apparent when he returned there after Peter's departure. He called Sir Christopher Wren in to draw up an inventory and an estimate of the cost. Wren found the floors and carpets so stained and smeared with ink and grease that the whole house had to be re-floored. Tiles had been prised off walls and door locks pulled apart, no doubt all in the cause of investigation. All the paintwork was filthy dirty and over 300 glass windowpanes were broken. Every chair in the house – and there had been over 50 – had simply disappeared, probably into the stove. Feather quilts and sheets were ripped and over 20 paintings were torn – the evidence suggested that they had been used for target practice.

Outside the carnage was impressive. The lawn had been turned into mud 'as if regiments of soldiers in iron shoes had drilled on it'. The magnificent hedge, stretching in its full glory, 400ft in length, nine-feet high and five-feet thick, had been flattened – by having wheelbarrows rammed through it. It seems that the Russians had found some wheelbarrows which were unheard of back home, and had devised an entertaining sport consisting of one man, usually Peter, sitting in one and having an aide career him through the gardens.

Wren's estimate came to £350 (and nine pence), equating to something in the order of £50,000 in current values, which the Government hastily coughed up to prevent any undesirable publicity. A heavy sigh of relief must have greeted the news in early May that Peter was off. He didn't get a second invitation.

6

Science – New Discoveries

The unfolding of science is inevitably complex, and to non-scientists, inevitably more so. History simplifies the telling, but how we remember some of the most famous is often at variance with reality.

AN OVERRATED CARTOONIST

Mention **Leonardo da Vinci** in a scientific context, and the imagery immediately conjured up is of history's most far-seeing, inventive seer, supposedly designing some of the modern world's mechanical devices in the late 15th and early 16th centuries, 400 years before their time – the helicopter, tank, diving suit, parachute, hang glider and even the clockwork car. Surprisingly, this is an image that has only been cultivated since the 19th century. It is particularly beloved of a strand of history telling that revels in the mystique of the 'man out of his time'; that sees achievements out of kilter with the period.

Leonardo is famed for his notebooks – he is now thought to have left some 12–14,000 pages of jottings, of which only 7,000 have so far been deciphered – and in particular his illustrations of machines far removed from his 16th-century surroundings. Add the mystery of the mirror writing and history has given us a tantalising figure of intrigue. (More mundanely, it is now strongly believed that Leonardo may simply have been dyslexic: reverse right-to-left writing is a common trait of left-handed sufferers.)

For an icon of scientific achievement, Leonardo's output was rather modest. In his life, he made no actual scientific breakthrough, discovered no scientific law, and never made any of his devices work in practice. One revisionist, reviewing a 2006 exhibition at London's Victoria and Albert Museum dedicated to celebrating Leonardo's 'scientific genius' observed that his drawings appeared more the doodling musings of a science fiction fantasist than a working engineering genius.

Meeting a Modern Need

History's temptation has been to see Leonardo as the visionary who inspired modern inventions. In fact, there can be little substance to this since, as da Vinci experts point out, many of his notebooks never saw the light of day until the late 19th century (and two did not turn up until 1965), well after work on many of the inventions he depicted, such as flying machines and the car, was under way. He also copied from other sources. Experts now know of drawings of a parachute made 40 years before da Vinci by an unknown engineer from Siena.

Leonardo had great insight and imagination – no doubt about it – but as for being an accomplished technical inventor ahead of his time, there is possibly rather more a sense of the modern mind's eager interpretations of the sketchings, laced with a heavy dose of wish fulfilment.

He Never Saw an Apple Fall

Isaac Newton is renowned for being the scientist who set out in one grand scheme the mechanical laws of nature. Rigidly rational and logical, his theorems revolutionised the way humans understood the world around them and laid the foundations of physics as a distinct discipline of science. His portrayal of the relationship between mass, weight, inertia, force and gravity gave a fresh and coherent vision of the world that saw every facet of mechanical behaviour capable of being explained mathematically and according to a single theory. Newton 'mechanised' the world. Gone were the ancient Greek ideas of bodies possessing their own inner motivating spirits, or their actions being the result of higher gods playing games. Everything could now be explained (and predicted) by strict mathematical principles.

Surprising, then, that Newton was also a strong believer in the occult, mysticism and the powers of alchemy. Not the Newton we have come to know and admire. The buried side of Newton emerged in a 1997 biography, provocatively entitled *Issac Newton: The Last Sorcerer*, which claimed that Newton invented the tale of the apple falling from the tree in 1665 to cover up an uncomfortable reality that he had actually derived the concept of gravity from his experiments in the darker arts. Support for the theory is felt to come from the fact that he used his pretty niece, who was his literary agent and general promoter of his interests, to spread the story among her wide, and socially well-connected, coterie of besotted admirers. When he published the theory formally in his great work *Principia Mathematica* in 1687, the seeds of the myth had been well planted and became the word of history.

Inspiration from the Dark Arts

According to the new explanation, Newton first observed the attraction and repulsion of forces, key to his central theory of gravity, in the chemical reactions he created. Some materials attracted each other; some repelled. It got him thinking about the same phenomena he daily witnessed on earth, and in the heavens – observing a passing comet is known to have inspired him immensely. The variety of alchemical reactions he experimented with, and the mix and range of observations that these would have provided to an avid observer of detail, perhaps, on reflection, offer a rather more plausible set of circumstances to account for a scientist arriving at a grand theory than a sudden spark of inspiration from a single event, emotively attractive though the historic tale might be.

Practising alchemy was a risky business in 17th-century England –

177

the period was the peak of the witch-finding craze – so there is good reason for creating a cover story. Newton was obsessed with magic, and was known to be a hearty consumer of treatises smuggled in from the Continent. The general promise of alchemy, with its prospect of the elixir of life, the explanation of everything, clearly convinced him that it held the grand unifying theory of creation that he was searching for. He is known to have built a furnace in his rooms at Cambridge, and associates report that when he left the university, he deliberately burned many of his notes. He still left more than two million words on the subject amongst his papers, a facet of his life historians have tended to erase from their depictions of him for not fitting with the image of the rational science Newton has come to represent.

Believing There's Something More

Further remarkable revelations surfaced in 2003 when Canadian researcher Stephen Snobelen of the University of King's in Halifax, Nova Scotia, announced the discovery in an Israeli archive of a cache of Newton's religious writings. Among them was evidence that Newton spent more than 50 years (and 4,500 pages) trying to decode the Bible which he believed contained the secrets of God's laws for the universe. While history fails to show any link between these musings and the eventual laws Newton came up with, the find did divulge one bizarre final piece of deduction that no one had expected: a handwritten scrap of paper that calculated from the decoding that the end of the world would come in 2060. It was yet a further astonishing perspective on a figure who, up until now, has been portrayed as the arch rationalist and demystifier of Nature. It seems that Newton was far from the clinically materialist thinker history has painted him to be.

CHASING THE HAIR OF THE DOG

Long before his career focused on architecture, the young **Christopher Wren** was a true polymath – he was a gifted astronomer (his first academic position was as Professor of Astronomy at London's Gresham College in 1657 when just 24), a ground-breaking mathematician, designer of sundials and intricate contraptions including a 'pneumatic engine' and a machine that wrote in the dark, developer of a new language for the deaf and dumb, and a pioneering biologist. As a student at Oxford, he undertook some of the first experiments in anaesthesia, showing how dogs could be put to sleep for operations by intravenous injection of opium in 1656. He also carried out other experiments on live dogs, described by one modern account as being of 'a spectacularly cruel nature'. He wrote to an acquaintance with seeming pride, 'I injected wine and ale into . . . a living dog, by a vein, in good quantities, till he became extremely drunk.' In the course of one attempt, Wren had to chase the stupefied animal around the garden for half an hour to wear off the effects and prevent it from succumbing to alcohol poisoning.

When Wren was struggling to secure funds from the Government to complete St Paul's Cathedral, he got himself elected as Member of Parliament and engineered the tripling of London's tax on coal, so raising the money that allowed him to carry on.

BEHOLDEN TO THE GENES

Charles Darwin comes down to us as the founder of the theory of evolution by natural selection ('the survival of the fittest'). What tends to be left out of the story is the debt Charles had to his grandfather, Erasmus Darwin, a remarkable polymath in his own right, who himself first published the principle of evolution 40 years before his grandson formulated the concept in the form we now know it, and 65 years before he published it in the book for which history now remembers (only) him.

Erasmus was drawn into evolution through his dabbling in botany and plant classification – he helped to translate into English the work of the Swedish pioneer in the field, Linnaeus. He was fascinated by the varieties of living creatures and he set about classifying all the natural world into Linnean classes, orders and species. This led him also to reflect upon the connections between them. In 1794, 15 years before young Charles was born, he published his ideas in a controversial book *Zoonomia* that sought to categorise all of nature, but speculate too on how nature's wide diversity had come about.

Erasmus wrote cryptically, not least because in the late 18th century to challenge the primacy of God's place in the make-up of life was heresy, and liable to the firm sanctions of the law. He risked transportation to Australia. So Erasmus talked of the metamorphosis of tadpoles into frogs – he avoided courting controversy by shunning the more provocative characterisations associated with the later Darwin's *On the Origin of Species* which in the popular mind centred on whether Man was descended from apes, which may be the reason why his ideas did not become more prominent.

Modern assessments of his working notes show that he was clearly well aware of natural selection as being the mechanism for change and diversification. He wrote that 'the strongest and most active animal should propagate the species, which should thence become improved'. That is the essence of Darwinism, two generations before Charles. What Erasmus did not have was the well-thought through scientific proof; that was to be Charles's seminal contribution.

Charles Pays Homage

When, in July 1837, Charles first began to set down his initial thoughts as he ploughed through the specimens he had brought back from his voyage on the *Beagle*, he started his first notebook. He inscribed on the title page, in bold letters, one word – *Zoonomia*. It clearly showed that he considered himself simply following on from his grandfather's speculations.

Charles had never known his grandfather in life (Erasmus had died seven years before Charles was born), but he read Erasmus's book while studying at university, shortly before his five-year voyage. So it was – consciously or not – a deeply formative influence which guided his exploration. According to one biographer, Charles attempted late in life to acknowledge the debt by writing a biography of his grand-father, which included generous tributes to his influence on Charles's thinking. However, Darwin's daughter Henrietta, by one account a 'fussy' protector of the family's reputation, was keen to protect his, by then uncontested, position as the 'father of evolution'. She edited the manuscript and deleted most of his accolades to Erasmus. The historical narrative was thus settled, and Charles was to be portrayed as *the* progenitor of the theory.

Big Brain, Little Man

Universally regarded as the cleverest man of the 20th century, **Albert Einstein** – a byword for braininess in common parlance – was actually a slow starter in academia. He failed his first entrance exam (to the Swiss Federal Institute of Technology in Zurich as a 16-year-old). It may not have surprised him. The schoolmaster at his previous school in Munich had (now infamously) pronounced to young Albert that he 'would never amount to anything'. He passed on the second attempt. After graduation, he failed again – in his endeavour to do what he thirsted to do, teach. So he ended up taking a low-grade clerical post ('technical expert, third class') in the Swiss Patent Office in Berne. It was from that role that he produced his sensational paper five years later in 1905 outlining the revolutionary theory of relativity. Still, recognition failed to come his way. Few understood the significance of his ideas. When he applied two years later for a post at the university in Berne, he was rejected. It was to be another year before he was granted a minor teaching post, and 1909 – already now aged 30 – before he won appointment as a professor at Zurich. By 1913, though, he was being ranked amongst the most famous scientists in the world and within eight years was a Nobel Prize winner.

Life was far from straightforward even from then on. After fleeing Nazi Germany in 1932, he spent all his remaining years at Princeton University in the United States. When he died in 1955, the trustees of the 'world's most famous scientist' were keen to preserve an unblemished image. They set up a protective barrier around Einstein's reputation. They even took Einstein's eldest son to court in 1958 to stop him publishing a family memoir. It was to take 40 years, after they themselves had died, for a more rounded picture of the great intellect to surface.

The Weary of Relativity

In 1993, a different image of the man emerged from biographical research among these previously restricted private papers. From this, we get a grittier and less wholesome story. Already known to be a classic absent-minded eccentric, Einstein is seen also as an appallingly selfish husband. His (second) wife, Elsa, faced a constant struggle to live with him. The insomnia he often suffered was dealt with by him practising throughout the night on his violin, and in the kitchen because he felt the loud echo from the tiles gave him better acoustics. No thought for Elsa trying to sleep. He was also extremely dirty, and according to accounts Elsa suffered great distress trying to make him wash regularly. Lack of hygiene seemed appealing to him. A friend, citing his philandering, noted that 'the commoner and sweatier and smellier' his women were, the better. Amazingly, letters released in 2006 suggested that he had 10 mistresses.

He had already strayed during his first marriage when he began his affair with Elsa, his cousin. Einstein wrote to his wife, Mileva, with whom he had had three children, letting her know he would from now on sleep apart from her. She was instructed to serve his meals in his room in future and not to speak until spoken to. She had a mental breakdown as a result, and never recovered. His younger son also developed mental illness and entered a psychiatric clinic. Einstein effectively disowned him, and never visited. There are unproven assertions that his first child, an illegitimate daughter, born before he and Mileva married, was also dumped into adoption in Belgrade, the capital of Mileva's native Serbia, and all future contact severed. There might, thus, be a branch of the Einsteins still living there – no one knows.

Although he had a series of affairs with rich women, he turned increasingly misogynistic down the years. His granddaughter, speaking in 1993 when the revelations hit the world's press, acknowledged 'he was a male chauvinist pig'.

Living in Another World

Einstein's cleverness, which the world remembers, also came with a classic eccentricity, which accounts tend to underplay as it contrasts with the image of a mind that was in absolute control of the world around him. Einstein was incredibly forgetful. He once used a $1,500 grant cheque as a casual bookmark, and then lost the book.

FINDERS KEEPERS

The race for scientific discovery is full of tales of skulduggery, tricks and outright deception. History has tended to brush them under the carpet when settling the reputations of the famous.

Making a Name for Oneself

Louis Pasteur, who pioneered the creation of vaccines against a number of killer diseases, is now known to have stolen the credit for one of them from a rival. He had become famous in France in the 1860s for discovering the microbe that was killing silkworms and devastating the nation's silk industry, and he would in 1885 develop the first vaccine against rabies. In between, in 1881, he was in a battle to find a vaccine for anthrax, which was raging in an epidemic in sheep. The French Government was pressurising many scientists and there was great kudos to be gained for the successful finder. Pasteur's own vaccine was not ready. His method worked with weakened bacteria. A rival in Pasteur's research school, Jean-Joseph-Henry Toussaint, had developed a different method that killed the bacteria but left the immunising agent effective. In the key experiment, Pasteur secretly used Toussaint's method and, with Pasteur's sense of the dramatic, he invited press, officials and fellow scientists to witness the unveiling of the results. It worked triumphantly. Pasteur took full credit for the breakthrough and never mentioned he had borrowed Toussaint's method. He got elected to the Académie Française the same year and became installed as national hero. By 1888 he had his own Institute. It was only in 1998 that an academic historian from Princeton University established beyond doubt that Pasteur had, in fact, used his rival's method without letting on to anyone, before or after.

Dot Con

Samuel Morse, whose name is synonymous with the telegraphic code that for a century and a half was the basis for long-distance communications, twice effectively purloined other people's ideas and called them his own. Giving credit where it was due was not part of his style. Commonly cited as the inventor of the telegraph – he certainly obtained the patent for it – he actually borrowed heavily from the pioneering work of fellow American scientist Joseph Henry who in 1831, over a decade before Morse, built the first electromagnet which was to become the basis for generating signals for telegraphy. Henry believed in the common use of inventions, and did not patent his devices. Morse took the work and in the later 1830s commercially exploited it with the American Government. When the authorities recognised its potential, he slapped his own patent on it in 1840, from which he went on to make a fortune. He never acknowledged Henry's contribution.

Morse did not even invent the code that bears his name. That was the work of another collaborator, Alfred Vail. Morse's original idea was a complicated system based on semaphore principles of words being made up of individual four-digit codes. A massive dictionary was required with each word separately identified. It was Vail who came up with the idea of each letter having its simple dot and dash combination, but as before, Morse was the one who patented the solution and Vail's inspiration – and name – dropped out of history.

Digging Out a Reputation

Sir Richard Owen, one of the Victorian era's greatest scientific figures, founder of London's Natural History Museum and credited with being the creator of the science of palaeontology – the study of prehistoric life from fossils – snatched the idea of dinosaurs roaming the early Earth from a rival. The rival, an eccentric Sussex doctor, Gideon Mantell, had been digging up and analysing large fossil bones since 1817, and had theorised about there being a long extinct race of animal forebears in the 1820s. He was first to name the iguanodon in 1825, and by the 1830s was acknowledged as the leader in the new field. He created the vision of giant beasts roaming the Earth 15 years before Owen's contribution, genuinely pioneering, which was to coin the name 'dinosaur', from the Greek words meaning 'terrible lizard'.

It was Owen, though, who used the hard work and individual discoveries of Mantell (Owen never dirtied his own hands in actual excavations) to produce the coherent theory of a prehistoric world and it was his social connections which enabled him to claim far more credit for himself and ease Mantell out of posterity. As he rose up the scientific social ladder – eventually being given the task to create and run the Natural History Museum – he was able to prevent Mantell from getting recognised.

Owen's character has been described by biographers as 'deceitful and odious', 'addicted to controversy and driven by arrogance and jealousy' and possessing 'almost fanatical egoism with a callous delight for savaging his critics'. He is said to have prevented the Royal Society from honouring Mantell when alive, and when Mantell died in 1852, with Owen at the peak of his fame, an unsigned obituary appeared in the London press, universally attributed to Owen, which pointedly downgraded his achievements and ranked him as no more that a mediocre scientist. Owen had been in the supreme position to whitewash Mantell from the record. His vindictive streak of character impelled him to do so, and he did it. Owen became the golden boy of the new science; Mantell dropped out of sight.

Metric-kery

The creator of **metric measurement** may not be widely known by name, but Pierre-François-André Méchain's work, along with his equally resplendently named compatriot Jean-Baptiste-Joseph Delambre, between 1792 and 1799, is responsible for setting the precise measure of the metre on which the modern system is based. But according to an account published in 2002, the figures that he produced to create the original metre were falsified. The whole metric system was inaugurated on the basis of an error, and remains so today.

Méchain and Delambre had been tasked by the revolutionary French Government to devise a new system of measurement to replace the old style associated with the recently defunct monarchy. The new unit would be one ten-millionth of the distance between the North Pole and the Equator. The pair were required to work out what precisely that measure was. They spent seven years measuring to the closest detail ever attempted, the meridian line across France. From this, they could calculate the size of the earth and hence the fraction which would represent the exact length of the new metre. According to the history of the project published in 2002, Méchain discovered well into the project that he had committed an error in measurement in the early years. Unable to face retracing his steps and starting again, he covered up the error and carried on. It resulted in the overall calculation of the metre being out – not by much, just 0.2mm – but when the exercise is all about an absolute definition . . .

More than two centuries after the prestigious French Academy of Sciences had unveiled the platinum bar – a fraction shorter than it ought to be – as 'the' metre, the universal standard, Delambre's journals were rediscovered. They were astonishingly candid: 'I deposit these notes here *to justify my choice of which version of Méchain's data to publish*. Because I have not told the public what it does not need to know. I have suppressed all those details which might diminish its confidence in such an important mission . . . I have carefully silenced anything which might alter in the least the good reputation which Monsieur Méchain rightly enjoyed.' (Emphasis added.)

186

Today, for greater consistency (since metal obviously expands and contracts with temperature variations), the metre is formally measured not by Méchain and Delambre's platinum bar but by the distance light travels in a vacuum in one 299,792,458th of a second – but that length of time was only chosen in order to fit with the original bar. So the whole metric system of distance measurement remains based on a covered up error by a panicked scientist.

7

Reputations – The Unexpected

The gap between our settled picture of history and the actual reality can be extraordinarily large. In this chapter, we explore some of our cultural compass points that could be assumed to be well defined, understood and accepted. Except, on closer inspection, we find a whole lot's been left out.

PAPAL BULL

As head of the worldwide Catholic Church, the **Pope** occupies one of the most influential (and historic) positions on Earth. The present incumbent traces a direct line of succession back to St Peter, disciple of Jesus. Despite the supreme spirituality that has come to be the essence of the modern papacy, history has not always produced Holy Fathers that can be said to have completely adhered to the Church's expectations. Some, in fact, have shown a spectacular worldliness. Unsurprisingly, their feats do not feature prominently in the mainstream accounts of the Church's history.

Pope **John XII,** who ruled from 955 to 964, had many extraordinary claims to notoriety. To start with, he was just 18 when he assumed the papal throne. His claim to it lay in *realpolitik,* not religion. His father was the princely ruler of Rome and a year earlier, on his deathbed, he had got the city nobles to swear they would elect him Pope when the current one died. John went on to steal most of the papal treasury to fund a gambling obsession, held power over Rome not by spiritual command but through a gang of hired thugs, held hugely debauched orgies in the Vatican and once toasted the Devil before the high altar in St Peter's during a drinking binge. He had a sexual appetite grossly out of line with the head of the Church. Critical observers compared the goings on inside the Vatican as akin to a brothel. His end was outstandingly appropriate. One history of the papacy records that 'no Pope ever went to God in a more embarrassing position'. He was caught having sex with his latest mistress by the woman's husband, who beat the Pope with a hammer. Three days later, he died.

Benedict IX, was holds the unique record of being Pope three times (from 1032 to 1044, 1045 and again between 1047 and 1048), was only 12 when elected through the bribery of his father. The main 12 years of his reign were spent 'in utterly dissolute fashion'. He was thrown out of the Vatican by Rome's citizens on account of his corruption, from which he managed to recover and restore himself to the throne. In 1045, he sold the papacy to his godfather who temporarily ruled as Pope Gregory VI.

Gregory IX ruined the finances of the papacy to such an extent that when his successor, Innocent IV came to the throne in 1243 after a prolonged interregnum – it had taken two years to elect a new Pope – he had had to hide in a corner of the Lateran Palace during his accession ceremony to escape a mob of creditors seeking settlement of their long outstanding bills.

Indulging to Extremes

Sixtus IV, Pope between 1471 and 1484 and remembered by history for building the Sistine Chapel in the Vatican, one of the world's greatest cultural possessions, is less remembered by history for the way he raised some of the funds. He licensed Rome's brothels, which brought in 30,000 ducats a year. Taking a worldly view of the strictures of the Church, any priest who married (which was against canon law) or had mistresses (strict celibacy was central to the Church's teaching), he taxed rather than sacked. It was a far more beneficial approach all round. He decreed a papal monopoly over all grain sold in Rome, and invented offices and titles simply for selling. Sixtus used to say that he only needed a pen and ink to raise any sum he needed. He was responsible for the money-raising scam that would leave the biggest legacy for the Church. He vastly extended the selling of indulgences. From 1476, not only could living people buy them to expiate their own sins, they could buy them for the souls of relations who had already gone to purgatory. It was to lead to Luther's Protestant revolt of the next century.

The extent of Sixtus's nepotism was astonishing even for the time. Three of his six nephews were made cardinals, one of them becoming a Pope. To one, he gave not the usual single bishopric but four, including the major cities of Seville, Valencia and Florence, from which the young man plundered 200,000 gold florins, and died inside two years from the over-debauched lifestyle at just 28.

The inaptly named **Innocent VIII**, who followed Sixtus maintained the habit. According to one biographer, 'neither his personality nor his record justified his elevation'. He was the first Pope to openly acknowledge he had illegitimate children by mistresses. As the price for betrothing his son to the daughter of the famed Lorenzo de' Medici, he made Lorenzo's 13-year-old son a cardinal.

The Best of the Worst

The pinnacle of papal mischief came with the next incumbent. Rodrigo Borgia fathered several illegitimate children – sources vary as to whether it was four, five or seven – before becoming Pope **Alexander VI** in 1492. (His final tally, including during his papacy, was 10.) He was reputed to have committed his first murder when he was 12 years old. He bribed his way to election, giving four mule-loads of silver to his closest rival to persuade him to stand aside and, still one vote short, relied on a 96-year-old senile cardinal to swing the decision. When in office, he appointed 47 friends and associates as cardinals, including five of his own family.

While Pope, he was a keen organiser of orgies in the Vatican. At one banquet, a prize was offered to the man who could copulate the most times. He is said to have had an incestuous affair with his celebrated daughter, Lucrecia Borgia. If true, and the sources are not certain, one history described him as 'setting a record even for a Renaissance Pope to have had sex with three generations of women – his daughter, her mother and her grandmother. Borgia's other Party trick was to draw huge bribes from those wanting to be appointed cardinal, and then poison them to increase the turnover. Not only did he continue to extract a steady income, but the dead cardinals' assets were forfeited to the Church – and who was the Church, but the Pope? Borgia died unexpectedly in 1503, some say from poison by having mistakenly drunk from one of his brews prepared for an unwitting cardinal.

Madness Rules

The least explicable event in papal history was the trial conducted by **Stephen VI** in January 897 of one of his predecessors, Pope Formosus. Formosus was dead at the time. His body was exhumed, dressed in cardinal's robes and propped up in a chair for the duration of the proceedings. The so-called Cadaver Synod was played out in strict legal form, the body being interrogated as a witness. Not surprisingly, he was found guilty of the charges of conduct not befitting a canon and struck off the official list of Popes. Shortly after the trial, an earthquake hit Rome, which was seen as a divine sign, and in August of the same year Stephen himself was deposed.

Modern Foibles

In modern times, the Popes have conformed more to our expectations of religious piety. However, some practices may still surprise us. **Pius IX** (1846–78) was passionate about billiards and had two tables installed in the Vatican and his country retreat. He would spend most of his relaxation on the tables playing against his Swiss guards. **Pius XII** (1939–58) carried a flask of wine under his robes 'for medical reasons'. He had a phobia about flies as well and carried a swatting stick, also tucked into his belt underneath his robes. His successor **John XXIII** (1958–63) smoked a packet of cigarettes a day. For much of his adult life, **Paul VI** (1963–1978) wore a hair shirt beneath his formal robes studded with metal points that dug into his chest and often drew blood. **John Paul II** (1978–2005) a goalkeeper in his pre-Church youth, is supposed to have insisted that his inauguration ceremony be timed so as not to miss an important football match on television.

Correcting a 700-Year Error

Although many of these scandals are effectively overlooked, the Vatican does care about some issues surrounding its reputation. In 1975, a papal encyclical took the trouble 700 years after the event to remove one Holy Father from the official list of Popes because of an embarrassing detail about their life. Pope **Adrian (or Hadrian) V** ruled for just 45 days in the summer of 1276. But it was not for any fornicating or criminal activity that he was to be expunged from the records. It was that he had not been a bishop or a cardinal at the time of his election. On that spiritual technicality, he should never have become Pope. Some things *do* matter, even seven centuries on.

A BOOK TO LIVE BY?

The **Bible** itself obviously defies a strict historical approach to judging its social value. Long accepted as having been written many decades or even centuries after the events it describes, historical truth is not the yardstick we use to draw from it what we do. But what *do* we take from the Bible? To most minds, the image that likely forms is one of a set of injunctions from a higher moral being, instructing us lesser mortals on how to conduct ourselves for the common good of all. The themes that come readily to the fore would be some comfortable and comforting familiars – peace, fellowship, social justice, honesty, tolerance: a loving and merciful God. These we would say are the essentials of the message of the Bible. A look at the dustier corners of the book, however, shows just how filtered that image is. Within the scriptures there are some surprisingly unsettling finds.

Love Not War?

There is, for example, the sanctioning of massive violence. Mosaic Law prescribes the death penalty for cursing one's parents (*Exodus 21.17, Leviticus 20.9*), adultery (*Leviticus 20.10, Deuteronomy 22.22–24*), rape (*Deuteronomy 22.25*), incest (*Leviticus 20.11–12*), homosexuality (*Leviticus 20.13*) and even working on the Sabbath (*Exodus 31.15 and 35.2*). (*Numbers 15.32–36* records the killing of a man for gathering sticks on the Sabbath.) Parents are permitted to kill a son who is 'stubborn and rebellious' (*Deuteronomy 21.18–21*) and a daughter who is not a virgin at marriage (*Deuteronomy 22.20–21*). The death penalty for murder is set down in at least six places, including *Genesis 9.6, Exodus 21.12* and *15* and *Leviticus 24.7*. Retaliation killing is permitted (*Leviticus 24.19–20, Numbers 35.26–27*) as well as the famed 'eye for an eye, tooth for a tooth' retribution – but less well-known is its continuation, 'hand for hand, foot for foot, burning for burning, wound for wound' (*Exodus 21.24–25*).

Injunctions on lesser forms of violence are also on the strict side. The famous rule of corporal punishment, 'He that spareth his rod, hateth his child' (*Proverbs 13.24*), is good for inducing wisdom ('Foolishness is bound in the heart of a child; but the rod of correction shall drive it far from him.' *Proverbs 22.15*) as well as salvation ('Thou shall beat him with the rod, and shall deliver his soul from hell' *Proverbs 23.14*). The penalty for an 'untoward mouth' is cutting out of the tongue (*Proverbs 10.31*).

Peace Be Amongst You?

Violence generally is not shied from as a central part of life. Joshua approves of the killing of Achan, a thief who has stolen 200 shekels of silver and 50 of gold, who is stoned and burned to death (*Joshua 7.21–25*) and he massacres the 12,000 inhabitants of the city of Ai in a single day (*Joshua 8.21–29*). Judah cuts off the thumbs and big toes of a captured King (*Judges 1.6–7*). More than once, God is recorded as actually being displeased with his people that they have not annihilated more cities (*Judges 2.1–2, I Samuel 15.9*). When David displeases the Lord, God strikes down his child who later dies (*II Samuel 12.15*).

193

An early King of Israel, Abimelech, kills 70 brothers to be King (*Judges 9.5*). Samson kills for even less – slaying 30 to satisfy his anger at not being able to work out a riddle that he had been set (*Judges 14.18–19*). As a military commander, Samson used an unusual method to destroy his enemies' crops. He tied firebrands to the tails of 300 foxes and let them loose amidst the cornfields, vineyards and olive groves (*Judges 15.4–6*).

Elisha has 42 little children killed because they taunted him over his baldness (*II Kings 2.23–24*). The forms of diplomacy practised by Jehu were hardly conducive to friendly relations. He kills the 70 sons of Ahab, a rival King, and sends their heads back home in baskets (*II Kings 10.6–11*). He also murders 42 visiting emissaries from another fellow royal, Ahaziah, King of Judah (*II Kings 10.13–14*). Converting unbelievers was clearly less exciting of fulfilling God's expectations. Jehu sends out invitations 'through all Israel' inviting suspected idolaters into a service worshipping Baal, the evil spirit. When the Party was under way, he massacred the lot (*II Kings 10.20–28*).

A Benevolent Father?
God's own desire for vengeance is given full vent in Isaiah's forecast of the nature of his punishment for unbelievers, 'their children will be dashed to pieces before their eyes, their houses shall be spoiled and their wives ravished' (*Isaiah 13.13–16*). The punishment of Samarians for rebelling against God would be that their infants 'shall be dashed in pieces, and their women with child shall be ripped up' (*Hosea 13.16*). In a lesser-known reversal of the famous 'they shall beat their swords into ploughshares' injunction, God calls directly for war: 'Prepare war, wake up the mighty men, let all the men of war draw near; / Beat your ploughshares into swords, and your pruning hooks into spears. Let the weak say, I am strong' (*Joel 3.9–10*).

Scriptural interpreters still muse over the true meaning of the infamous ending of the 137th Psalm, 'Blessed shall he be who takes your little ones and dashes them against the rocks.'

Choose Your Words Carefully

Words of Jesus also give rise to ambiguity. These are guaranteed not to be heard as frequently as the professions of harmony and universal love. 'Think not that I am come to send peace on earth; I come not to send peace, but a sword. / For I am come to set a man at variance against his father, and the daughter against her mother' (*Matthew 10.34–36*), and 'Suppose ye that I am come to give peace on earth? I tell you, Nay; but rather division' (*Luke 12.51*). As to their meaning, the preference is often simply not to mention their existence.

Other tenets of the Bible can also read unfamiliarly. A thief who cannot pay back the value of his haul is to be sold as a slave to raise the funds (*Exodus 22.3*). Everyone should sacrifice one's firstborn son (*Exodus 22.29*) and lepers should be severely ostracised (*Leviticus 13.45–46*). Women should not wear men's clothes, nor men women's (*Deuteronomy 22.5*).

Unexpected Acts

Some of the revered characters have aspects of their lives recorded in the Bible that we probably were not told about by our Sunday school teachers. Moses was a murderer (*Exodus 2.12*). Abraham committed adultery with his maid (*Genesis 16.4*). Samson consorted with a prostitute (*Judges 16.1*). A jealous Saul plotted against David by purporting to declare him his legal son and offer his daughter's hand for marriage. Instead of a dowry, he demanded David secure 100 Philistine foreskins, expecting David to be killed in the effort. David brought him back 200 (*I Samuel 18.25–27*). Despite the Biblical injunctions against witches and witchcraft, Saul consults the witch of Endor (*I Samuel 28.7*).

YOU THINK YOU KNOW . . .

A number of the familiars of the Bible we take for granted emerge as unfounded, or at best contradictory. There is no mention of an apple in the Garden of Eden, simply the 'fruit' of the forbidden tree (*Genesis*

3.6). Apple is likely to have come from an ambiguous translation by the 4th-century theologian and translator St Jerome, who used the Latin *malum* to describe the fruit. The word means evil, but can also be translated as apple.

Christmas Sleights

The timing of Jesus' birth is not agreed (it certainly was not 25 December – that was only settled by Church leaders in the 4th century; the winter timing has much to do with keeping in with the pagan end-of-year celebrations that had long preceded Christianity). As to the year, there is clear disagreement. Matthew dates it in the reign of King Herod, who died in 4BC. Luke places it at the time when the Roman Governor of Syria was Cyrenius, and according to Roman historians he did not start his rule until 6AD.

Of the birth itself, there is no agreement whether he was born in a manger (*Luke 2.7–16*) or a house (*Matthew 2.11*). Nowhere is there mention specifically of a stable. There is no indication of the time of day, or time of year. The only clue is in *Luke* that the birth happened while shepherds were 'keeping watch over their flock by night' (*Luke 2.8*) which adds to evidence that it was any time other than winter. Astronomical calculations in 1999, based on identifying the 'star in the east' that supposedly led the wise men to the birth, suggest it was most likely April.

The number of wise men is not mentioned, and their existence at all is only mentioned in one of the four Gospels, *Matthew*. (*Matthew 2.1* just mentions that 'there came wise men'.) History appears to have assumed three on account of the three different gifts of gold, frankincense and myrrh. They are not named either. (In 2004, the Synod of the Church of England decreed in new interpretative rules that they should be referred to in Church services only as 'the Magi'. The decision came as part of an effort to simplify language and call them 'wise men'. This was rejected, according to the Synod's 'revision committee', on the grounds that 'the visitors were not necessarily wise and not necessarily men'.) There is no mention of oxen, asses, sheep or in fact any other animals in the manger.

The Nativity itself is only mentioned by two Gospels (*Matthew* and *Luke*). The well-worn phrase 'Unto us a child is born' is likely to be assumed to be a record of Jesus' birth. Not so. It actually appears in the Old Testament (*Isaiah 9.6*) and is a prophecy of his arrival.

The 'Sermon on the Mount' is never referred to in these terms in the Bible. The feeding of the 'five thousand' is misconstrued. *Matthew 14.21* refers to the feeding of 'about five thousand men, beside women and children'.

On Jesus' crucifixion, the Bible makes no reference to him falling three times while carrying the cross. Only *John* (*19.17*) refers to Jesus actually carrying his own cross. All three other Gospels refer to it being carried for him by Simon (*Matthew 27.32*; *Mark 15.21*; *Luke 23.26*). The image of Jesus in a loincloth is a later elaboration. *Matthew* says he was stripped and his clothes shared amongst the executioners.

False Memories

Some things we think we know turn out not to be the case. Adam and Eve did not have two sons (Cain and Abel) but three (*Genesis 4.25*). It is, in fact, this third son, Seth, from whom Jesus is descended (*Luke 3.38*). The mark of Cain, often assumed to have been placed on him by God to identify him as a murderer, was the reverse. *Genesis 4.14–15* makes it clear that it was designed to protect him from being killed, one assumes to ensure his punishment of exile was prolonged as long as possible. The olive branch, signifying peace, derives from the dove that brought back to Noah the signal that the flood was over. *Genesis 8.11* is clear that it was an olive leaf, not an olive branch. Samson's hair was not cut by Delilah, but by an unnamed assistant (*Judges 16.19*). Jonah is only ever swallowed by 'a great fish' (*Jonah 1.17*), never a whale. The daughter of Herodias who asked Herod for, and was given, the head of John the Baptist, is never named as Salome (*Matthew 14.3–11*).

Common phrases we associate with the Bible are also figments of imagination. Jesus' oft-assumed sentiment that 'It is more blessed to give than to receive' does not appear in the Sermon on the Mount (or anywhere else in the scriptures). Likewise, the injunction to 'Go forth and multiply' actually appears as 'Be fruitful, and multiply' (*Genesis*

197

9.1). It's not quite 'Those who live by the sword, shall die by the sword'. *Matthew 26.52* renders it as, 'All they that take the sword shall perish with the sword.' And it is not 'Money is the root of all evil' but 'The love of money . . . ' (*I Timothy 6.10*). Pride does not go before a fall, but, as in *Proverbs 16.18*, 'Pride goeth before destruction, and a haughty spirit before a fall.' 'The lamb will lie down with the lion' appears nowhere. *Isaiah 11.6–7* actually says, 'The wolf also shall dwell with the lamb, and the leopard shall lie down with the kid, and the calf and the young lion and the fatling together.'

Perhaps after all this, we will have second thoughts on the term 'gospel truth'.

If It's Good Enough for Him . . .

The poet **John Milton**, who strongly believed in the utility of lying to anyone when it was to his advantage, once wrote out every reference from the Old Testament where it appeared that God approved lying.

SAINTS ALIVE!

Our own familiar patron saints are not entirely what one might assume when we scratch beneath the surface. England's **St George** was a 3rd-century Palestinian or Turkish soldier (his cult was brought back to England by the Crusaders). He never set foot in England, and did not become our patron saint until Edward III's time in 1344.

Scotland's **St Andrew** was also a Palestinian, from Galilee, the fisherman disciple of Jesus from original biblical times. He ended his life martyred in Patras, Greece, according to one account after a woman he had converted then refused sex with her husband. The husband happened to be the Roman Pro-Consul, who ordered his execution. His link with Scotland is said to come from the missionary work of 4th-century abbot, St Rule of Patras, who had a dream in which an angel told him to take Andrew's remains 'to the end of the earth'. For St Rule, that turned out to be Scotland and he supposedly travelled with the Saint's relics to deposit them on the present site of St Andrew's in Fife.

Wales's **St David**, the only one of the four to actually be a national of the country of which they are the patron saint, was a 6th-century monk conceived as the result of a rape by a Welsh warrior chieftain of the pious St Non. He is supposed to have eaten nothing but bread, salt and leeks, which is why the leek became the national symbol. That other national symbol, the daffodil, may derive from the similarity of his name in Welsh (Dafydd).

Ireland's **St Patrick** was not Irish, but Welsh. His British name was not Patrick but Succat, and he was not the first Christian missionary to Ireland. In 432, he took over the work of the first bishop of Ireland, St Palladius, who had started the Church there at least two years earlier. He had first reached Ireland as a 16-year-old, captured as a slave by Irish pirates. He was being forced to work herding sheep and pigs when he had his first religious visions, which some historians have suggested were caused by mental illness.

DON'T BE MY VALENTINE

Probably the only other saint that modern folk think they know about (leaving St Nicholas/Santa Claus aside, whom we have already dealt with in Chapter One) is **St Valentine**, the patron saint of lovers. The connection, however, is far from the straightforward one that might be assumed. The 'celebration' of St Valentine on 14 February has nothing to do with the memory of a particular saint. It is the date that is significant. It marks the eve of the ancient Roman festival of Lupercalia, which was the culmination of a series of winter festivals. It was celebrated all over Europe, paid homage to Februa, the Roman goddess of marriage, childbirth and sexuality, and marked the onset of spring and fertility. It prompted a riotous outpouring of mate-seeking among the males of any community. On the night before the festival, that is, on the 14th, young men would draw lots for the favours of the local women. On the following day, the festival would end in drunken orgies and licentiousness. The Church hierarchy, desperate to control this, wanted to move away from the pagan origins, so searched to substitute a recognised Christian figure to replace Februa. Their choice was limited; they had to pick one of the Saints who had been martyred on that date. None were women. There were two candidates, both called Valentine and both men – one a Roman priest and the other a bishop from Umbria – and it is not clear which one formally got the nod. Awkwardly for the Church, then, they had to change the gender of the symbolic figurehead of a festival that was all about fertility and childbirth from a woman to a man. No matter, if it quietened the ardour coursing through youthful veins.

So in future as you exchange your Valentines, the secret truth to be remembered is that the whole event has its origins not really in fostering love and togetherness, but in the Church's effort to dampen down the spirit of young love.

John of Arc?

Research published in 1981 in the *British Journal of Sexual Medicine* cast a new light on the reputation of French heroine **Joan of Arc** who led the resistance to the English occupation of France in the early 15th century. It suggested she might actually have been a man.

Religious scholars have long tussled with the theological awkwardness created by St Joan's decision to adopt male dress, which strictly was against the injunctions of the Bible. They cite exceptions endorsed by Church theologians that permitted the practice in extreme necessity – and leading the fight against the English invader counted as that – but then get on to stickier ground in trying to deal with her reluctance, throughout her trial, to shed her male clothing. No compelling necessity applied then, unless 'Joan' had something intensely personal to hide.

American biologist Robert Greenblatt's analysis of accounts of

Joan's physical appearance led him to conclude that 'she' was a man suffering from the rare condition of testicular feminisation. This disorder gives a genetically male person female characteristics. Testicles are not apparent, being retained inside the body. The person does not menstruate, and has no pubic hair.

These features would explain the accounts that have survived of those who documented observations of Joan in the flesh. She was said to have a womanly appearance, but insist on wearing male attire. Two midwives are said to have examined her shortly before her execution and reported their observation that she did not appear to have reached puberty (presumably her lack of pubic hair). She was actually 19 at the time. Other eyewitnesses recorded that Joan was never seen to menstruate.

Such reports would theoretically all be consistent with the condition Greenblatt advances.

EMPRESS-IVE BONEY

Greenblatt returned to the pages of the *Journal* in 1983 with research into another historical giant. He concluded that in the last decade of his life **Napoleon** was turning into a woman. He was showing symptoms of Zollinger-Ellison syndrome, caused by the malfunction of his endocrine glands giving him a hormonal imbalance. This would explain the Emperor's increasing pudginess, difficulty in sleeping and the curious yellowing of his skin that those around him reported. According to one account of the autopsy done after his death in 1821 in exile on St Helena, Napoleon had 'a chest that many a woman would envy'.

Napoleon officially died of stomach cancer. The intriguing aspect of this new diagnosis was that the Zollinger-Ellison condition, which was first identified only in 1955, also causes tumours and ulcers in the stomach, so for doctors of the day it would have been an entirely reasonable deduction that their patient was simply suffering from cancer.

LEGENDARY LOOKS

Through 2,000 years of history, **Cleopatra** has been almost universally portrayed as one of the great beauties not just of her age, but of all time. With the help of the Greek writers, then Shakespeare, and finally Hollywood she is an iconic figure of attraction that snared both Caesar and Mark Antony. Recently discovered evidence suggests, however, that she was far from being a beauty. (And she was not even Egyptian either, but actually Macedonian.) A 2,000-year-old coin that had languished in an obscure collection in a museum in Newcastle-upon-Tyne was identified in 2007 to be a silver denarius coin from 32BC, two years before she died at the age of 39, depicting Cleopatra, one of the very few representations known to exist of her. And it was not flattering. It showed a distinctly plain and homely face with a sharp nose, pointed chin, thin lips and a large mouth.

Director of the museum, Lindsay Allason-Jones, pointed out that Roman accounts of Cleopatra had referred to her intelligence, charisma and the seductive qualities of her voice, but none ever make mention of her facial appearance. It seems that literary licence and perhaps a certain required deduction, cast her image for the history books. (After all, the logic likely went, she must have had something going for her to produce one of the greatest love affairs of all time, until one discovers – from the reverse side of the same coin – that Antony was no great looker either. He is depicted with a hooked nose, bulging eyes and an extraordinarily thick neck. Together they would seem in reality to have been a right pair).

A PASSION TO RECORD

Samuel Pepys is England's most celebrated diarist of the 17th century – although it may come as a surprise, in view of its reputation, that his diary lasts only nine years, between 1660 and 1669. He recorded more in his journal than usually gets passed on in modern memoirs.

He was an avid consumer of pornography, and recorded every act of masturbation by a special symbol. In the words of the *Dictionary of National Biography*, he 'relentlessly chronicled' his multiple illicit affairs, also denoting each sexual congress with another symbol.

Much was written down in a shorthand code, freely mixed with foreign languages for the more risqué content. The code was not deciphered until 1825 when about half of the 3,000 pages was published. It had taken a Cambridge undergraduate more than three years, working 12 to 14 hours a day. Most of the text emerged in a larger edition in 1899, but the complete unexpurgated text did not see the light of day until as late as 1983.

An Open Secret

Lewis Carroll, famed for his fanciful and innocently engaging mid-Victorian creations, *Alice's Adventures in Wonderland* and *Through the Looking Glass*, troubles modern observers because of his passion for photographing naked prepubescent girls. He is estimated to have maintained the friendship of some 200–300 young girls. He kept a horde of toys in his college room (he was an Oxford lecturer all his life) to entertain them privately there, and he also would take them on seaside holidays. His habit of photographing them began in 1856, a decade before his trip with 10-year-old Alice and two other girls (an 8- and a 13-year-old) on the river that inspired his famous work. At first, his pictures showed children posing in alluring rags. One exists of Alice herself. He always insisted on the purity of his motives, and astonishingly kept parents informed when he moved to nude photography in 1867. 'Children who know me regard dress as a matter of indifference,' he wrote to one mother.

The Unobservant Scout

Robert Baden-Powell, founder of the Scouts movement, incorpo-rated the swastika into the design of the Scouts' 'Thanks Badge' long before it was adopted by the Nazis. It is an ancient Sanskrit symbol from South Asia denoting good luck. It became popular among nationalist movements in Europe shortly before the First World War, and one of the first uses came in Hitler's native Austria as early as 1907. It was adopted by the Scouts from about 1912. Despite the rise of Hitler's Nazis and their use of the swastika, Baden-Powell insisted on keeping it as part of the Scout symbolism until as late as 1935 when Scouts were starting to be mistaken for supporters of Hitler and getting attacked by anti-Fascists. Baden-Powell was unambiguous about where he stood. He called Hitler's blueprint for world domination, *Mein Kampf,* 'a wonderful book'.

Is Anybody There?

By most accounts the greatest inventor of the 20th century, **Thomas Edison,** who died with over 1,000 patents to his name, might be imagined to be one of the more rationally minded people in history. In fact, he had a bizarre belief in what really made human intelligence tick. He theorised that human brain cells consisted of millions of sub-microscopic beings, actual miniscule entities which he likened to tiny human beings. He called them 'the little peoples'. He described them in his *Diary and Sundry Observations* as being frantically busy under-taking tasks inside the human mind given them by 'master entities'. At the time of his death, Edison was working on a machine designed to communicate with these 'little peoples', and on another to make contact with and record messages from the spirit world.

MONKEYING AROUND

The standard story of the celebrated 1925 Scopes monkey trial in the rural backwoods of America is that it pitched a highly principled, diligent and innocent small-town biology teacher, **John Scopes**, against the might of the State of Tennessee which had just banned the teaching of Darwin's theory of evolution. That is how history tells the bare bones. In fact, it was all a put-up job. The town fathers of Dayton, Tennessee, got together when they saw there was a huge commercial and publicity windfall to be won by hosting what would be a circus event. Their town was languishing, business falling away and townsfolk leaving (the population had fallen from 3,000 in the 1890s to under 1,800 at the time of the trial). It needed attention from the wider world. The trial was to put it on the map forever.

They had noted the declared intentions of the American Civil Liberties Union to challenge the Tennessee law in a test case, and spotted a once-in-a-generation opportunity to cash in. They roped in John T. Scopes, who was not even the school's regular biology teacher, but a temporary stand-in – he actually taught physics, maths and football. Fortunately, he was able to confirm that he had once used in class a biology primer that contained the offending sentiments. He also agreed to their proposition to be the front man for the trial. He fitted the bill perfectly – young, unattached with no family responsibilities to put at risk and, with no intention of staying permanently in Dayton, having nothing to lose from what one account calls 'as a summertime caper'.

The town announced the prosecution within days. The urgency had nothing to do with the supposed seriousness of the offence. It was rather that a lot of other small Tennessee towns had the same idea and were lining themselves up for the task.

In the event, 200 journalists from across America, and from as far away as Britain, descended on the town to cover the trial when it opened in July. Newsreel cameramen joined them, along with, in the words of a local history, 'a fair of lemonade and hotdog stands, banners and monkey pennants, caged apes, hawkers of religious tracts and biology texts, Holy Rollers and evangelists'. Dayton was the centre of the world for the fortnight of trial action, it made a mint in the short term, and got itself firmly into the history books forever – although, to Dayton's mercy, not quite in the way that they often recall it.

Upstanding Image

Perhaps the most iconic American painting of all time is **Grant Wood's** *American Gothic* – the depiction of a gaunt-faced farmer and daughter, their elongated images accentuated by the farmer clutching a thin, long pitchfork, standing in from of a Gothic-style house which is taken to be their farmstead. The picture, finished in 1930 as the Great Depression was deepening, is seen as a totem for the hard-working stoicism, purity and rectitude of heartland America. Wood had posed his subjects in front of the house, which he had discovered in the small town of Eldon in his native Iowa. He was entranced by its homely image. Only later did he learn it was a brothel.

On the Wagon

Another American icon, second man on the Moon, **Buzz Aldrin,** admitted in 1976, seven years after his historic voyage, that he had been an alcoholic for several years *before* the Apollo 11 mission. He had stopped drinking just two days before the flight took off. He resumed it shortly after returning. He has now become a famed reformer and publicist for alcohol recovery programmes since the mid-1980s.

OLD ROLLER

The most iconic of **Rolls-Royce**'s advertising slogans, from the 1950s – 'At 60mph, the loudest noise in the new Rolls-Royce comes from the electric clock' – was in fact copied from a trade journal's review. David Ogilvy, the advertising guru who penned it, had seen a 1907 review in *Autocar* appraising the new Silver Ghost. The writer had told his readers fifty years before, 'At whatever speed the car is driven, the auditory nerves when driving are troubled by no fuller sound than emanates from the eight-day clock.' Admittedly, Ogilvy earned his crust, and a whole lot more fame, with his slicker rendition.

FASTER, HIGHER, STRONGER – AND FIRST

The politically acceptable story of the revival of the Olympic Games in the late 19th century, through the tireless efforts of French aristocrat **Baron Pierre de Coubertin**, has always been that it was motivated by the desire to unite an increasingly fractured world under the banner of common humanity and friendly competition. The theme still runs strongly today as the hallmark of the Olympic movement. The obvious harking back to the ancient Greek games added further association with imagery of returning to classical norms of civilisation. The truth was far from this, but is rarely known.

De Coubertin's motivation came from witnessing the growing importance of sport in English public schools in the last quarter of the 19th century. (He is said to have become besotted with the concept after reading *Tom Brown's Schooldays*.) In 1883, he started a series of tours of England specifically to examine the effects, visiting Harrow, Eton and Rugby as well as Oxford and Cambridge universities. He came every year up to 1887, his longest foray coming in 1886 when he spent the entire summer hopping round a myriad of establishments. He is known to have been to Charterhouse, Marlborough, Toynbee Hall, Wellington, Westminster, Winchester –

all bastions of the flourishing 'muscular Christianity' movement that hit late-Victorian Britain and which emphasised the value of sporting endeavour in learning obeisance to rules, sportsmanship, honesty and fair play, as well as collective commitment to a cause. The sentiments ingrained on the playing field would serve to spur the British Empire on to its apogee of moral righteousness and superiority over competitors, actual or potential.

De Coubertin absorbed all this with gusto. He contrasted the strikingly robust approach to raising future English generations with the flaccid defeatism prevailing in France following its crushing defeat in 1871 by Bismarck's ascendant – and now unified – Germany. He said he saw about him in his native country not 'truly noble men' as he had seen in England but dandies and idlers 'imprisoned in the ruins of the past'. He became a passionate advocate of strengthening France's national fibre, through strenuous physical education, which, he admiringly stressed, produced 'firm wills and right hearts at the same time as robust bodies'.

English Inspiration, Greek Vindication

De Coubertin himself admitted to arriving at his plan by succumbing to a vision – in all places, at the tomb of Thomas Arnold, author of *Tom Brown*, at Rugby school in 1886. This would impel his mission to deliver Arnold's concept of 'athletic education' in France. He became convinced that this reinvigoration of the national sinews would be the means by which France would 're-bronze' itself.

Competing with other nations was not primarily about promoting international harmony and brotherhood. De Coubertin's writings make it clear that competition was to be for honing and improving French strength. 'It would be necessary to organise contacts between our young French athleticism and the nations which had preceded us in the way of muscular culture.'

As the first modern Games passed off in Athens in 1896 in a blaze of celebratory glory and success, de Coubertin wrote a commentary that he must have come to regret for its openness in musing on the effect the Games might have on Greek 'vigour'. He wondered aloud

208

that 'when one realises the influence that the practice of physical exercise may have on the future of a country and on the force of the whole race, one is tempted to wonder whether Greece is not likely to date a whole new era from the year 1896. It would be curious indeed if athletics were to become one of the factors in the Eastern Question. Who can tell whether, by bringing a notable increase in vigour to the inhabitants of the country, it may not hasten the solution of this thorny problem?'

An Unwelcome Answer

Arguably it did. Greece had been at odds with Turkey for centuries, but particularly in recent decades over the pain of Crete which, although geographically closer to Greece and largely inhabited by Greeks, was held by Turkey under an international peace settlement of some 20 years before. Within 10 months of the Athens Games (and three months of de Coubertin's commentary), Crete broke out in nationalist insurrection which led just after the first anniversary of the first modern Games to all-out war between ancient rivals Greece and Turkey. That lasted until September 1897. It took another year to settle Crete's future under Greece.

Although by the time of the Games, their purpose had been presentationally purified to better reflect the spirit of internationalism, which officially underpins the modern Olympic movement, de Coubertin could hardly have been surprised by this violent postscript to the first experiment. Greek 're-bronzing' may well have been stirred by the patriotic fervour induced by the Games. If it was, de Coubertin had got exactly what he had been looking for when first dreaming of the national benefits of 'athletic education'.

Running Rings Around History

The branding of the movement as a recreation of the ancient Greek model was also often overplayed. There is frequently confusion about the origin of the five-ring Olympic symbol which many believed was drawn from the original games on account of the discovery at Delphi, the home of the original games, of a five-ring carving on a rock face.

209

In the 1950s, two visiting archaeologists mistook it for an ancient inscription and the legend began. They gushingly wrote how 'in the stadium at Delphi, there is a stone altar on which is carved five rings . . . the circles form a link between [the] ancient and modern Olympics. . . . The interlocking circles [which are] definitely connected with the ancient games are considered by three experts to be 3,000 years old.'

It later emerged that the rings had been etched there by Nazi filmmaker Leni Riefenstahl while filming background scenes for her infamous documentary of the 1936 Berlin Games. It even took in the International Olympic Committee. An official guide as late as 1980 claimed the ring symbol dated back to the original Greek games. It was, in fact, a logo created by de Coubertin for a planned world Olympic congress in 1914, which never took place because of the First World War. It signified nothing more than the completion of five modern Olympiads. It was first flown as the official flag of the Olympics when the Games resumed in 1920 in Amsterdam.

ASHES TO ASHES

Cricket's iconic trophy, the '**Ashes**' may have an even more unusual pedigree than is commonly thought. A story surfaced in 1982 that suggested that the small terracotta urn now contained something rather different to its original contents. As every English schoolboy knows, it had been presented to England captain Ivo Bligh in 1883 after England's victory in the Test series in Australia, revenging the 'death of English cricket' inflicted by the touring colonials in England the previous year. Bligh, who later acceded to his title as the 8th Earl of Darnley, had his stately home at Cobham Hall, near Gravesend in Kent and for almost 45 years until his death in 1927, the Ashes simply stood on his mantelpiece at the hall.

In the summer of 1982, *The Cricketer* magazine published a letter casting doubt on whether the contents of the urn, which is now safely behind glass at Lord's, are what they purport to be. The letter writer, publican John Newton-Isaac, told of a conversation with Cobham Hall's aged butler in the 1950s. According to him, a new young housemaid had one day engaged him in conversation, during which she remarked, 'You know that old urn-vase thing that stands on the mantelpiece in his Lordship's room? Well, I knocked it over this morning and it was all full of old ash stuff, so I gave it a jolly good clean out and polish before putting it back!'

Clearly expecting to be complimented for her diligence, the unsuspecting girl got the sharp end of the appalled servant's temper and he quickly grabbed a handful of wood ash from the hearth, refilled the urn and put it back on the shelf. Neither Lord Darnley nor any of his family were ever told of the incident.

Sometimes, It Is Only After Death That the Truth Dawns . . .

Jim Fixx, the New Yorker who made millions from pioneering America's and the world's jogging craze as the way to a healthy and long life, collapsed and died of a massive heart attack while out on his morning run in 1984, at the age of just 52.

At Christmas 1982, the **Great Lyndoe** died. He had done the weekly astrology feature in the *Sunday People* newspaper continuously since 1933. Perhaps his powers only declined towards the end, but his editors may have been reassessing his career after discovering that two days before his death he rang up the news desk to ask them to send him fresh supplies of copy paper.

8

Arts – Unvarnished Truths

Contrary to our usual image of the artistic genius as a blessed and carefree individual who enjoys a miraculous talent that the rest of us mortals can only envy, the lot of most of history's wunderkinds has often been very much the opposite – lives blighted by torment, psychoses and sickness. The link between creativity and affliction, both physical and mental, is surprisingly common. Indeed, some medics subscribe to the notion that it is the body's physiological response to adversity that hones the very senses and talents that some of the world's finest artistic exponents have possessed. Far from an unadulterated blessing, genius has usually come with a heavy price.

BAD TO VERSE

In 2001, social anthropologist Daniel Nettle, author of a study into the connection between mental instability and **poetic genius**, concluded that 'to be a poet in Britain in the 18th century was to run the risk of manic depression 10 to 30 times the national average, suicide five times the national average, and incarceration in the madhouse at least 20 times the national average.'

ALL-CONSUMING

John Keats, one of the most accomplished poets of the 19th century, suffered from consumption – the term used then for what we now know as tuberculosis – at the same time as he produced some of his greatest works (he died aged only 25). There is some evidence that because of its fever-inducing effects that increase the body's metabolism, it can enhance the senses and fire the imagination.

UNKNOWN ENDEAVOUR

Emily Dickinson, one of America's foremost poets of the 19th century, pursued a bizarre adult life, for most of it confining herself to living in a single room in her Massachusetts mansion. Analysts believe she suffered a deeply psychotic episode, possibly due to a thwarted love affair in her youth, or the onset of agoraphobia. She hardly left her room from the early 1860s, when she was just passed 30, and from around 1867 refused to see any visitors in person. She would talk to them as they stood on the other side of the closed bedroom door.

The effects were devastating to her as a living individual, but spurred an intensity of verse which today is recognised as some of the most powerfully emotional writing ever produced. One critic has called her output 'perhaps the finest by a woman in the English language'. Of the 1,775 poems that she wrote, only seven were published in her lifetime. She would write them, sew them together into little books and put them away in a box. Hundreds of them. Even her sister, who lived in the same house all her life, never knew. It was only when Emily died in 1886 at the age of 56 that she found them, 60 volumes worth, the product of a lifetime's self-agony.

AN EYE FOR IT

Harvard neurosurgeons announced in 2005 that they had found evidence that the secret of Dutch master painter **Rembrandt** was that he was afflicted with a lazy eye, which meant that he saw a three-dimensional world as flat which helped him to recreate what he saw on canvas. Known as stereo-blindness, it was spotted by analysing 36 Rembrandt self-portraits: in all but one there was the telltale sign – his right eye looking straight ahead and his left pointing away from his nose.

SUFFERING FOR ONE'S ART

The *Journal of Medical Biography* reported in 2004 that **Michelangelo** showed every sign of suffering from Asperger's syndrome, a mild form of autism, which affects a person's ability to interact socially and communicate. Sufferers, however, often show unusual creative talents. Michelangelo is known to have been a loner, had no ability to show emotion, and was obsessed with routine and in controlling every aspect of his life and business

This was followed later in 2005 by an analysis from a world expert in Asperger's that many other creative geniuses likewise were afflicted. Professor Michael Fitzgerald of Ireland's premier university, Trinity College, Dublin, identified similar traits in iconic literary and artistic characters pointing to the syndrome being an important driver of genius.

The classic elements of autism, as described by the doctor who first identified the condition in 1943, are 'a profound withdrawal from contact with people, an obsessive desire for the preservation of sameness, and a skilful relation to objects'. Obsession with patterns and details and poor physical motor skills are frequent signs. Among those who are now thought to have derived their talent partly from being autistic or having Asperger's are:

Fairy-tale writer **Hans Christian Andersen**, was renowned for his hypersensitivity (he stuffed newspapers up his shirt front because of self-consciousness about his sunken chest) and an obsession with being on time. When travelling by train, he would regularly arrive at stations hours before the departure to make sure he was not late. His acute fear of uncertainty is a classic symptom. He always carried a length of rope when staying in a hotel in case there was a fire, and always turned back twice after leaving a room just to make sure all the candles were properly out. He found it difficult to socialise. Charles Dickens said of him after he had visited that 'a little of Andersen's company went a long way'.

Irish legend **Jonathan Swift,** author of *Gulliver's Travels*, was notoriously tactless in personal interactions, 'never smiled and almost never laughed'. It is said he once went an entire year without speaking to another person. He 'hated mankind' according to one biographer, especially Scots, women and children. Women, he once wrote, 'were a sort of species hardly a degree above a monkey'. He once declared that no woman was really worth giving up the middle of one's bed for. He eventually went senile (but who would have noticed?) and was probably seriously mentally disturbed when he produced *Gulliver's Travels*, his most famous work with its surreal worlds, at the age of 59.

Lewis Carroll (Charles Lutwidge Dodgson), who created his own surreal world in *Alice in Wonderland*, kept meticulous records of the meals he served to guests so he never repeated them. He, too, was socially reserved. Mark Twain described him as the shyest full-grown man he had ever encountered. He preferred not be noticed; one of the reasons that he wrote his most popular works under a pseudonym. He refused a request to sit for a *Vanity Fair* caricature, one of the marks of success in his day, because 'nothing would be more unpleasant for me than to have my face known to strangers'.

Social Misfits

W.B. Yeats was a loner at school and had great difficulties with one-on-one relationships. 'I have no instinct for the personal,' he once said of himself. His social aloofness combined with a vivid imagination is a classic combination of an autistic. He also exhibited the classic repetitive body movements. He would compose his poetry while walking the streets of Dublin. While doing so, he would swing his arms around violently, on one occasion attracting the unwelcome attention of a passing policeman.

Scientists in the 1990s have come to believe that both **Isaac Newton** and **Albert Einstein** suffered from Asperger's, which may have accounted for their ability to conceptualise the universe in an entirely different way. Both showed classic signs – obsessive interests, an inability to communicate with others easily and difficulty in maintaining social relationships. Newton often became so engrossed in work that he forgot to eat, and was infamously argumentative. Einstein always preferred being left alone to having company. We see his appalling family relations in chapter six.

Mozart's prodigious memory is a classic symptom of Asperger's. He was able to write out from memory a complete score that he had heard just once. Dr Benjamin Simkin, a specialist at the respected Los Angeles Cedars-Sinai Medical Center, published research in the *British Medical Journal* in 1992 concluding that Mozart probably also suffered from Tourette's syndrome, which classically shows symptoms of hyperactivity, restlessness and – notoriously – uncontrollable bad language.

The affliction has been graphically summed up as 'an incontinence of the emotions', and that description fits Mozart neatly. He was well known for his obnoxious behaviour, for which, as with all geniuses, a broad toleration tended to be given. Until these findings, historians had accounted for his style as being akin to the toxic brew enjoyed by modern rock and sports stars – fame, money, youth and excess. But the new assessment, based on an analysis of the composer's letters, suggested the behaviour was more physiological and deep-rooted than someone simply enjoying the laxity of an indulgent gallery. It may even have contributed to his creativity.

The letters revealed a fixation with obscenities, and how Mozart delighted in reciting vulgar rhymes to his orchestras. Some of his operatic compositions contained expletives in the scores, which had to be cleaned up by his wife before going off to the publisher. One, which was rendered in final form as 'let us be happy', was originally written by Mozart as 'lick my arse, quickly, quickly'. The research enabled an intriguing link to be drawn between the bouts of crudities and Mozart's creative drive. One peak, in 1791, came just at the time he was completing two major operatic works and his *Requiem*.

The other symptom of the syndrome, constant restlessness, was also characteristic of Mozart's behaviour. People close to Mozart recorded how his body seemed 'perpetually in motion'. He would 'play incessantly with his hands or tap restlessly on the floor with his feet'. Even when doing his morning ablutions, 'he walked up and down . . . never standing still'. He would often make 'extraordinary grimaces with his mouth'.

All compelling evidence in the eyes of experts that we may have to acknowledge that the talent producing some of the most sublime artistic creations ever, drew its strength from one of the human body's strangest and least endearing maladies.

OUT OF ADVERSITY . . .

Beethoven is now believed to have suffered from Asperger's – as well as a variety of maladies including chronic colic and diarrhoea in his late teens, and the increasing problems with his hearing that started when he was 27, and continued to deteriorate unremittingly over the next 20 years until he was completely deaf. He is also now suspected of having an immunopathic disease which caused violent swings of emotions. Together with the characteristic traits of Asperger's – he was famously unkempt and clumsy – and the excessive drinking – he is now thought to have died from kidney and liver failure complicated by his habit – this panoply of miserable complaints produced a personality that was universally documented as being gloomy, anti-social and difficult to get on with.

Not of This World

He was ill at ease when with others and 'held the world to be detestable'. He showed obsessive behavioural traits. He would make his coffee in the mornings with exactly the same number of beans each time, counting then individually. He was prone to flying into a rage at the smallest provocation, and was notoriously bad tempered with his house staff, throwing food back at them if it was not to his liking, and accusing almost everyone he came into contact with of trying to cheat him out of money.

In fact, the reverse was true. It seems he cheated most of his music publishers. Letters he wrote to them show that at one point he was composing three pieces, but promising them to five different publishers under agreements he had reached. In the event he finished just one, and he sold that to a different publisher entirely. He resolved his outstanding commitment to the others by his usual ploy of starting up furious, accusatory arguments alleging that he had been tricked by them. He allowed the dispute to reach such a pitch that publishers usually preferred to drop the argument before he did.

He was often seen wandering down the lanes near his house, composing by waving his arms and accompanied by a loud 'barking', a style which is said to have frightened the cows. In 1820, seven years before his early death at 56, he was mistaken for a tramp, arrested and put in the cells. He had to be rescued by friends.

He lived in self-imposed squalor, his rooms and clothes were untidy, his financial affairs a mess, his moods unpredictable, and the patience of his friends and staff sorely and perpetually tested.

At the Heart of the Problem

He was more and more beset with physical ailments. While these could not have helped his social affability, new evidence in 1996 suggested that they may have helped the composing. Some of his tunes, doctors now believe, Beethoven got from his increasingly bad heart. A Bonn University professor announced that his analyses of Beethoven's scores suggested that as he became increasingly deaf and his heart increasingly erratic, the unusual rhythms gave him new

218

inspirations for tunes. Professor Berndt Luderitz pointed to an 1809 piano sonata *Les Adieux*, which has an unusual stop-start tempo. The off beats may have been echoing a heart playing up. Professor Luderitz noted key passages in the opera *Fidelio* that have 'heart-like' rhythms, and the famous Third Symphony, the *Eroica*, which contains unusual phases which are curiously off beat or irregular. 'If you were running up a hill with a heart problem, this is the kind of thing you might be listening to in your mind's eye.'

The findings were received with little contention from other musicologists. 'When you are deaf, your heart is the one thing you will listen to,' said one. Another pointed out that many composers had used their hearts as prompts, and before metronomes, as beat measurers. Beethoven may have been a classic example of the artistic paradox – that the freshness of achievement can often only come from an amalgam of personal troubles. For Beethoven, this bizarre combination of misery and disorder produced some of the greatest music that has ever been written.

A Light-Fingered Composer

That last sentiment has, however, become more complicated in recent years. In the same year as the research into Beethoven's heart revealed a previously unknown inner inspiration, another musicologist published evidence suggesting a rather less benign explanation for where he might have got some of his tunes from. This strongly indicated that Beethoven may have been plagiarising lesser-known composers.

John Eliot Gardiner, a concert conductor, director of the French Orchestre Révolutionnaire et Romantique and who had recorded a complete set of Beethoven's work, claimed that Beethoven borrowed some of his most famed passages – including the iconic four-note opening of his Fifth Symphony – from obscure Revolutionary French composers.

Beethoven would have been familiar with the music emerging from the new revolutionary France of the 1790s as he lived just over the border in Bonn. The most surprising of the findings was the discovery that the start of Beethoven's *Fifth* – Fate knocking at the door – which has become almost the signature motif of the composer, was actually a straight copy of a tune in the work *Dithyrambique* by Claude Joseph Rouget de Lisle, the composer of the *Marseillaise*, the French national anthem. The last movement of Beethoven's famous *Pastoral Symphony*, one of the most evocative musical depictions of a country landscape, was copied from *Hymn to Agriculture* by the little-known French composer Lefèvre. The stirring last movement of his *Seventh*, again one of his best remembered, appears to have been culled from a work originally written by Belgian composer François Gossec. Many of Beethoven's piano sonatas appear to be very similar to the lesser-known Italian pioneer of piano composition, Muzio Clementi.

Despite the gravity of the claims, most music historians came out in broad support of Gardiner's conclusions. The editor of the musical bible, the *Grove Dictionary of Music*, offered the view that Beethoven would have been 'just like other composers' if he had indeed succumbed to picking up ideas from others. Clearly no great harm done in the eyes of the experts, but it may make the average listener now think a little longer about the originality of Beethoven's achievements when they next tune in.

ADDICTED TO DEATH

Gustav Mahler suffered from bouts of severe depression and had a morbid obsession with death throughout his life. He wrote his first funeral march at the age of six.

SILENT PARTNERS

Peter Tchaikovsky's life was moulded by his depression. He said he was 'haunted by an indefinable terror'. He is said to have produced his best works in 1877, when he was 37 – his *Symphony No 4* and his opera

Eugene Onegin – when under psychological stress and his marriage in crisis. He had married a besotted student from his music conservatory but realised within a month it was a disastrous match. He ran away after three months, and spent the rest of his life trying to get out of the commitment. He tried to commit suicide by standing in the ice-cold waters of the Moscow river all night. He merely caught pneumonia, and survived. He professed to her to have committed adultery (which he had not) to try to get a divorce, but she would not agree. When he learned of her adultery four years into the marriage, he hesitated to sue for divorce for fear she would expose his own secret – homosexuality. He eventually supported her until his death in 1893.

At the same time as the fateful marriage, Tchaikovsky started the other main relationship in his life. He benefited from the attention and money of a wealthy patron who was equally besotted, but with his music, not him personally. She paid him 6,000 roubles a year salary, giving him his independence. Bizarrely, she insisted that the pair never meet and they communicated entirely by letter – they exchanged more than 1,000 of them over 13 years until shortly before his death.

WAVING, NOT DROWNING

Composer **Robert Schumann** died aged only 46 incarcerated in a Bonn mental asylum for his last two and a half years, after a lifetime of recurring depression. He voluntarily committed himself after unsuccessfully trying to commit suicide. He had begun to suffer hallucinations and had longed feared the onset of madness. His aim in going into the asylum was to seek help to recover. He believed that as a willing patient, it would be easy to leave when he felt ready. Modern reviews of the treatment regime in the asylum suggest that his time there further contributed to the downward spiral, rather than helped. He was deprived of his books and writing materials, his diet was enlarged with huge meals, then followed by laxatives and diuretics. When he repeatedly asked to leave, the pleas were ignored. A modern assessment by mental health specialists in 2001 concluded that he was probably not mad when he died. He may have suffered the nightmare fate of the sane person – realising you are the only normal person in the madhouse.

DRIVEN TO THE EDGE

Exponents in other artistic fields also seem to have been driven by extreme physical or mental afflictions.

Philosopher **Immanuel Kant**, according to modern medical interpretations, showed behaviours that were symptomatic of mild schizophrenia.

Charles Dickens was a frenetic and tireless worker. He was always writing, often with more than one book under way at a time. According to one psychiatric study, he never stopped because when he did he always fell into a deep depression.

French master **Honoré de Balzac** was similarly affected by morose depression. His bizarre way of dealing with it was to deliberately run up huge debts, which forced him to write furiously to pay them off. He added to his despair by drinking copious amounts of strong black coffee to keep him going. He would drink up to 50 cups a day, and eventually died of caffeine poisoning. He had had an inauspicious start to life. He was sent away to boarding school by his parents, who then never visit him, between the ages of 8 and 15.

Robert Louis Stevenson owed his masterpiece, *The Strange Case of Dr Jekyll and Mr Hyde,* to a cocaine-fuelled night in 1886 when he dreamt the bizarre mind-bending plot.

An Avoidable Tragedy
Vincent Van Gogh famously severed his own ear, supposedly in a fit of depression and psychological despair, on Christmas Eve, 1888. He committed himself into an asylum where a diagnosis of epilepsy was

made. He was allowed to continue painting, but attendants noted his practice of drinking his turpentine and trying to eat his paints. Within 18 months he had committed suicide. He was only 37, and just beginning to produce the paintings he would become famous for.

Early medical historians endorsed the analysis of epilepsy, pointing to the sharp colours of Van Gogh's style, which is said to be typical of sufferers from temporal lobe variant of the condition. More recently, others have disputed this, pointing to a no less debilitating cause and one that could explain his ear mutilation. Research published in 1990 on the centenary of his death and based on scrutinising the 796 letters Van Gogh wrote in his last six years, as his medical condition deteriorated, suggested he suffered from Menière's disease, a complaint caused by the excess and painful build-up of fluid in the inner ear. The affliction causes buzzing and ringing in the ears, vertigo and nausea, effects that must have been deeply depressing. He complains in his letters of hearing strange noises and having violent attacks of vertigo that often lasted for days. It looks more likely that it was this reaching an intolerable level that caused his infamous self-mutilation.

The misdiagnosis may have condemned Van Gogh to his early demise. The complaint is easily treatable. It had first been identified by a French physician 30 years before, but word had not reached the remote southern Provence when Van Gogh sought help. The mistake may have affected more than one life, as well as depriving art of Van Gogh's future output. Less well known about the family is that Van Gogh's youngest sister, Willemina, spent the last half of her life in a mental institution. She was committed in 1902, more than a decade after her brother's death, with unclear problems. The association with her more famous brother may have tainted her case and condemned her to a diagnosis that saw her incarcerated away until her own death in 1941.

Seeing Things Differently

The radical change in artistic style of **Pablo Picasso** in mid-life has been identified by neurologists as likely to stem from a rare form of migraine. Picasso's early style was quite normal. His depictions of people were normal. Then, around 1937 when he was in his mid-50s, Picasso's work took a dramatic shift and he began producing his now more famous modernist portraits. These strangely disfigured faces, with eyes and ears lopsided and mouths misshapen, resemble looking at a face in a broken mirror. In 2000, Professor Michel Ferrari from the Dutch University of Leiden reported that such visual distortions were recognisably the same as those recorded by patients of his suffering from this rare migraine complaint. The illness causes 'vertical splitting' to sufferers' perception of their surroundings. Ferrari added that in rare cases, the symptoms can occur without the telltale headache that would signal the sufferer having a migraine. This would explain why there are no references in Picasso's life to him suffering from migraine-type headaches. According to Ferrari, the spells can last up to an hour. They are less disabling than a full-blown migraine, but 'could have inspired Picasso, as they show a very different way of seeing the world'.

The World is Too Much

Early 20th-century French writer **Marcel Proust** must rank amongst the strangest of artists to be conditioned by their health problems. He achieved world fame through just one book – but what an effort: *Remembrance of Things Past* ran to 13 volumes and appeared over a period of 14 years, half of them being published after he had died in 1922. The most introspective work in literary history, Proust wrote it from a combination of extreme medical and psychological factors. He was an acute asthmatic (although some medics believe many of his attacks were psychosomatic), and his allergy to flowers, dust, perfume and smoke, as well as the cold and damp, made contact with the outside world perilous to his psyche as well as his physical condition. He was sensitive to noise too, and he could only work in utter silence.

His mother was a dedicated carer, and her death in 1905 when he was 34 deprived him of his only anchor to the outside world. Losing her prompted him to withdraw completely. He shut himself up in a cork-walled, soundproofed room in his apartment in the Boulevard

Haussmann in central Paris and devoted the last 17 years of his troubled life to digging up his past, and having nothing to do with the rest of humanity.

His attacks were less severe at night, so he turned his life utterly around. He only worked during the hours of darkness, and went to bed around eight in the morning, fully clothed and often with gloves on to protect against cold, and with his windows tightly shuttered to prevent any light coming in.

Other hidden secrets lay behind the success of many another renowned figure.

A Secret Locked Away

The American short-story writer **O. Henry** was inspired into authorship by being jailed for over three years in Ohio from 1898 for embezzlement. The 36-year-old bank clerk had 14 stories published under various pseudonyms while inside. A friend forwarded the stories to publishers so that nobody would know of his imprisonment. He never told his 11-year-old daughter the truth about his incarceration, only that he had been 'away on business'. He ended up writing over 250 short stories, and became one of the foremost exponents of the genre, particularly noted for ending many of his tales with an unexpected twist.

The Borrower

J.R.R. Tolkien, creator of *Lord of the Rings*, always liked to portray the inspiration for his story as coming from the obscure myths and legends of long-lost Celtic, Norse and Icelandic cultures. It certainly lent additional cerebral cachet to the publishing sensation of the mid-1950s, already noteworthy because of its unusual source – Tolkien was a 62-year-old Professor of English at Oxford University where he had been closeted since 1925. It was this other worldliness that helped propel *Lord of the Rings* into a completely different category of literature to the usual adventure fare. Or was it?

Controversy broke out in the usually languid world of Tolkien-ologists in 1981 when two respected literary critics published their analysis which maintained that, far from these esoteric origins, Tolkien's sources seemed much closer to home, and far less obscure. They claimed to see evidence that Tolkien in fact drew his inspiration from modern, stirring *Boy's Own* style stories, which would have been the staple fare of anyone growing up in Edwardian culture at the start of the 20th century, as Tolkien did.

Closer to Home

Challenging the accepted wisdom of Tolkien's work, critics Robert Giddings and Elizabeth Holland suggested that the themes were more strongly derivative from rollicking tales like *King Solomon's Mines*, *The Thirty-Nine Steps* and *Wind in the Willows*. 'Like all great writers, Tolkien was a tremendous plagiarist,' Giddings told an astonished literary world. 'The plots of the *Rings* weren't conjured out of northern mists.' He pointed to the almost identical theme of the opening of *Lord of the Rings* and *The Thirty-Nine Steps* – both involve discovery by the main character of a secret that has significance for the whole world, the ransacking of their homes by mysterious enemies looking for it, the characters fleeing, and the start of the adventure. Giddings even pointed to the clues Tolkien may have laid to pay secret tribute to his inspirers. The place where Frodo stops for his meal is called Buckland. *The Thirty-Nine Steps* was authored by John Buchan. Giddings strongly believed that Tolkien – a philologist and crossword fanatic – deliberately left such markers as an extra for sleuths to spot. Giddings claimed the clues were 'literally on every page'.

The mines in Tolkien's tale are at Moria. In the Bible, King Solomon built his temple at . . . Moriah. An identical motif occurs in both Tolkien and *King Solomon's Mines* where a strange wanderer appears to the travelling group, who seems to know all about their mission and later reveals himself as a King. The map of Middle Earth – which the authors pointed out was simply 'Mediterranean' translated back from Latin, and which has similarities to the real Mediterranean coastline from Turkey to Egypt – drew inspiration from the famous map in *Wind in the Willows*. Through the Shire in Tolkien runs the river Withywindle. 'Withy' means 'willow', 'wind' is 'wind' and 'le' French for 'the'. Also, *Wind in the Willows* has 'Pan Island'. In Tolkien, there is Girdley Island – 'girdle' is a Scots form for 'pan'.

The esteemed followers of Tolkien were outraged at the slights being cast on their hero. Perhaps within their ire there was more than a tinge of guilt. Their enjoyment of the spectacular adventure yarn, with its respectability buttressed by its rarefied origins, had been shown to be no more elevated than that of the masses.

ELEMENTARY

Another famed author who may have overly borrowed from others appears to be **Sir Arthur Conan Doyle**, according to fresh evidence that emerged in 1993 when academics published the definitive collection of Sherlock Holmes stories along with their origins. Investigative work worthy of the great detective himself had brought to light evidence of striking similarities between the storylines of some of the early tales and news stories appearing in the popular low-brow magazines of the day which traded on sensation, such as *Titbits* and *Answers*. At the time, Conan Doyle was rushing the stories out, sometimes at the rate of one a week, so it does not seem improbable that he was scouting very hard for eye-catching ideas.

Other early stories appear to be 'lifts' from two earlier highly successful crime writers, Edgar Allan Poe, the best-selling American whose stories appeared in the 1830s and 1840s and Emile Gaboriau, the pioneer of French detective fiction who flourished from the 1860s to 1880s. The first Sherlock Holmes stories appeared in the late 1880s. According to new evidence, Conan Doyle's early efforts were not just inspired by these contemporaries, but at times were 'copied so faithfully that he appeared to be quoting from them'.

IRRESISTIBLE

Novelist **Anthony Burgess** (author of amongst other works, *A Clockwork Orange,* the controversial 1962 portrayal of a violent future society in Britain) was also a prodigious book reviewer for the *Yorkshire Post.* As well as writing under his own name, he produced two novels under a pseudonym, Joseph Kell. When one of them was sent to him unwittingly by his editor to review, he shamelessly gave it a raving write-up. When he was found out, he was fired as the paper's reviewer.

SLEIGHTS OF HAND AND EYE

Some of the **greatest painters in history** may have used a technical cheat to aid their artistic creations. The claim, first made in January 2000, comes not from a dusty academic, but from one of the world's greatest living artists, British-born David Hockney, adding, in critics' eyes, weighty substance to the theory.

Hockney claimed to have discerned the method from explanations contained in the archives of the great art galleries. He maintains that the sudden 'golden age' outpouring of fantastically realistic paintings in the 15th and 16th centuries was due to the use of the pinhole 'camera obscura' which relied on the invention of quality glass lenses. It worked by mounting the lens in front of a pinhole in a canvas strung across a studio, and providing a light source behind the lens.

Any image nearby was projected through the pinhole onto the wall (or another canvas) on the other side of the room. Hockney theorised that artists used the outline projection to give them a headstart in composing their pictures. It explains the major advances in proportion, perspective and realism in detail that great artists like Leonardo da Vinci, Caravaggio, Vermeer, Holbein and van Eyck achieved. It came relatively suddenly because it needed good lenses. The birth of the Venetian glass industry at that time provided the best lenses since Roman times.

This trick of the trade was hinted at, according to Hockney, by **Caravaggio**'s preference for working in a dark cellar. 'I believe he would pose his models at one end of the cellar and then put his lens, which he would carry around with him in a bag, in the middle of the room on a stand and drape a curtain wall around it. The tableau is projected through the lens to where he stands with his brush and canvas, when he quickly sketches guidelines which he can then fill in while the models take a break.' Everyone kept quiet about the technique as such projectioning was close to magic and heresy. So models and assistants were only too willing to keep the process under wraps. And the artists themselves, glorying in public esteem – and riches – would hardly want to give away such a valuable trade secret.

Evidence Mounts

In 2001, a new biography of **Vermeer** appeared to support the theory. It had always been a mystery why X-rays of Vermeer's paintings showed no evidence of 'underdrawing' – most artists would make a dark outline sketch of their subject first to give basic shape to the composition first, before overpainting with the final detail. Vermeer never did. How did he manage to get a finished picture of perfect shape and proportion without the guideline underneath? The camera obscura offers the answer. He already had the image projected temporarily on his canvas.

His biographer also pointed to the unprecedented achievement of light effects, which seem too subtle for an unaided eye and hand. Even more convincingly, by taking photographs of the room scenes he painted and comparing them with Vermeer's productions, they are shown to be perfectly accurate representations to the minutest degree of proportion and measurement, something almost impossible to achieve by recreating a scene only by unaided human eyesight. It is the most compelling evidence that one of the most famous painters hid from the world an important aspect of his creative process. And, it seems, many others used the same assistance.

The theory has not gone uncontested, and furious rows have ensued in the usually restrained world of classical art criticism in the years since. The claims do not take away the talent the great masters all clearly possessed. But they do reveal that they had a telling secret they did not want their patrons to know of. It would certainly have reduced the rewards they were able to garner from their apparent genius skill. They had genius, indeed. But it now seems it was not quite the complete genius that their paymasters thought they were paying for.

HORSE PLAY

Britain's most famous animal artist, **George Stubbs**, celebrated for the perfection of his paintings of horses in the 18th century, achieved his objective through rather less subtle methods, far removed from the rural idyll and cultured style conveyed by his pictures. At a deserted farmhouse in Lincolnshire, he dissected the dead bodies of real horses to understand their anatomy and use as models. Bodies would be kept for weeks in the studio. He would bleed his specimens to death after which he pumped into their veins a solution that hardened the body so it retained its shape. He then hung the carcasses upright from metal hooks to provide a lifelike pose.

MIXING IT

Michelangelo, who is now accepted as having been homosexual, often used male models to sit for his sculptures of women. When he accepted the commission to produce Lorenzo de' Medici's tomb in Florence, the reclining female nude 'Dawn' gracing the piece exhibited all the telltale signs. One critic described the lass's legs as 'not disgracing a rugby fly-half', and her breasts being 'more like plumber's plungers'.

FORGING A CAREER

Spanish artistic legend **Salvador Dali** was one of the 20th century's most recognisable painters. Like him or loathe him, he produced works that took the surrealist school of art to its height of popular fame. He is remembered for dream-like portrayals of melting watches and bizarre depictions of animals. He was eccentric in his physical style too – he sported a long, thin waxed and flamboyantly up-turned moustache – and dressed like a circus ringmaster. He achieved worldwide fame for his pushing of the boundaries of modern art.

After his death at the age of 84 in 1989, it also became clear that the mock charlatanism he liked to exude was actually all too close to the bone. Dali's life was exposed as one based more on making ready money than the pursuit of artistic achievement. The arrest of his former business manager in 1999 revealed the astonishing depths of Dali's insatiable thirst for riches. Not for nothing did his disillusioned friend and founder of Surrealism, André Breton, point out that his name was an anagram of 'Avida ('greedy') Dollars'. It transpired that in his later years, Dali would regularly sign thousands of blank canvases so that others could print fake Dalis for sale on the world market. He became the most faked artist in history. Victims are estimated to have lost £2 billion over the years in discovering they had a product of the Dali fraud factory. Police found 10,000 fake lithographs when they raided the gallery of Dali's former business manager in the 1999 operation. He then told investigators that Dali signed, in all, some 350,000 blank sheets. He once did 1,800 in a single hour. The manager was convicted in 2004 of the minor offence of retouching one of Dali's works and, under Spanish law, 'damaging the rights of the author'. No one, however, has ever been prosecuted for the mass deception that still today haunts the art world whenever a Dali comes up for sale. Perhaps for the very solid reason that the main culprit is very truly dead.

Team Effort

Italy's foremost expert on **Leonardo da Vinci** announced to the world's press in June 1999 that he had found 'hitherto unknown proof' that the great artist had probably not personally painted *The Last Supper*, one of the works which has become an iconic representation of the great man's output.

Professor Carlo Pedretti said that he had uncovered the evidence in a 16th-century book that had lain unread in the British Library for centuries. The 1538 volume by artist Giovanni Lomazzo recorded da Vinci himself confirming that he had only 'directed' the work and that the actual painting had been done by two master assistants he had hired. He even named them, Marco da Oggiono and Giovanni Antonio Boltraffio. The fresco in a Milan convent was commissioned in 1494 and painted between 1495 and 1498. Pedretti pointed to the plausibility of the new evidence. The commission came at the same time as the increasingly over-tasked artist is known to have set up a school for apprentice artists and masters. The two master assistants are known to have been recruited by da Vinci for his school.

Little evidence exists to document the actual period of the painting. All the records of the Santa Maria delle Grazie convent itself relating to the project have been lost. No one therefore has known how far Leonardo himself got out the paintbrush for this commission. It would be natural for history to emphasise his attribution because it was he whom his Milanese patron, Duke Ludovico Sforza, commissioned. One only needs to accept that the social kudos in 'having a Leonardo' would have played a central part in the Duke's original request, to appreciate that no one – the Duke, the convent or Leonardo himself – would have any inclination to play up the realities of it being a team effort, even if assistants did most or all of the work. Even in those days, brand was everything for a rich patron.

Looked at this way, the new discovery appears even more likely to be true. Years after the event, Leonardo is recorded divulging what really happened. Why would he want to downgrade his involvement if it was not, in fact, true?

BACH FROM THE DEAD

It will be surprising to learn that far from enjoying unbroken fame, **Johann Sebastian Bach**, today one of the mainstays of the Western music canon, was all but forgotten for 80 years after his death in 1750, and only 'recovered' his fame at the start of the 20th century. While he achieved a wide reputation during his life, it quickly evaporated after his death, largely because his composition style (Church and choral) was outmoded in contrast to the exuberance being developed by the then modern composers such as Beethoven, Mozart and Schubert. Even his sons regarded his output as outdated and lost many of his scores in the years after his death.

It was not until Mendelssohn resurrected his *St Matthew Passion* in 1829 that Bach's name returned to popular appreciation. It was still a slow recovery, his definitive collection of works not being published until 1900. It was only six years after his long-lost grave had been relocated in Leipzig. So while aficionados today may believe that Bach has been around continually for 300 years, the truth is very different. His pedigree is really little more than a century old.

STRINGING THE AUDIENCE ALONG

Niccolò Paganini was such a freakily accomplished violinist that many practitioners even today find his routines impossible because of their physical demands, which require abnormally long reaches for the fingers. It is believed his unusually large span – 18 inches – was due to his suffering from Ehlers-Danlos syndrome, or 'India rubber skin', a genetic condition that produces unnaturally flexible joints. An observer noted how 'his wrist was so loose that he could move and twist in all directions. Although his hand was not disproportional he could thus double its reach and play in the first three positions without shifting'.

He was also a consummate showman, and not above canny tricks to increase his audiences' appreciation of his already fabulous skill. A favourite ruse was to deliberately put frayed strings on his violin. When they broke in the middle of a performance, he could show his versatility by completing the piece on the remaining string(s). He liked it best when just a single string remained. It looked spectacularly spontaneous, was guaranteed to provoke outbursts of admiring rapture . . . and was entirely pre-planned.

A LIFE OF TWO HALVES

Far from being the lifelong composer one would assume him to be from his modern portrayal, **Gioachino Rossini,** wrote 38 operas in the first 37 years of his life, and then wrote none in the remaining 39. He achieved worldwide fame in 1829 with his last one, *William Tell,* with its celebrated overture, and decided to call it a day, essentially to live the good life. At the time of his retirement, he was the most popular opera composer in history, and had the world at his feet. Quite why he gave it all up has mystified musical historians, who salivate at what might have come from him had he continued on his apparently effortless path. At the peak of his extraordinary

234

productivity, he had churned out 20 operas in just eight years, between 1815 and 1823.

But for nearly four decades, he elected for a life of seclusion, self-indulgent pleasure and gourmandising, mainly in Paris. It was a seemingly astonishing choice, one for which no one has ever managed to find any reason to explain it other than that, simply, he could. Perhaps one day a skeleton might just rattle.

A SECRET EVEN TO HIMSELF

It turns out that violin maker **Antonio Stradivari** (often better known by his Latinised style, Stradivarius), universally recognised as the master craftsman of the instrument and for creating violins that have never been bettered for their tone, may not have known himself how he had produced such perfect violins.

In 2001, a Texan university biochemist, who had devoted his life to trying to reveal Stradivari's secret, published his research which provided the astonishing prospect that, far from being a genius of insight, Stradivari had been just plain lucky.

Joseph Nagyvary studied the vibration properties of Stradivari violins in his laboratory, tried to recreate the maple and spruce concoction that Stradivari used, but failed to reproduce the same quality of sounds. He then discovered that the woods in original Stradivaris had been treated with borax, a preservative to prevent woodworm. Analysing the effect of the borax chemically, Nagyvary discovered that it bound the wood molecules together differently, producing the distinctive sound. He claimed proof of his theory by building a violin himself, which was treated in the same way, and having a concert violinist play both his instrument and a genuine Stradivari in the same recital, switching between the two. Expert listeners, including the violinist, claimed it was not possible to detect from the sounds produced which was the original.

Stradivari had faced a woodworm outbreak in his home city of

Cremona at the time he was producing his instruments. By the time he died, it was over and borax was no longer used to preserve the wood of violins. Nagyvary believed that no one realised the effect of the preservative on the sound properties, not even Stradivari, who at the time could not have known that his instruments would come to be seen centuries later as exceptional. When he died, the 'secret' died with him, a secret even he did not know he had.

Hidden Beliefs

Personal political views of great figures of art may not necessarily have played any significant role in influencing their work, but some recent revelations certainly may change our historical perception of them.

Dictating Ideas

Dramatist and essayist **George Bernard Shaw** has long lodged in our memories as one of the 20th century's most playful iconoclasts. His favourite pastimes were challenging authority and convention, and expounding the causes of social justice and egalitarian (i.e. socialist) democracy. In the First World War he wrote a celebrated pamphlet against the perils of militarism. A less well-known side of him, however, saw him endorse many of the brutal philosophies of the totalitarian dictators.

He was an enthusiast for eugenics – the theory of selective breeding. As early as 1933, as Hitler was winning power in Germany, Shaw was writing in the preface to his play *On the Rocks* that the mentally disabled and those 'of incorrigible social incompatibility' should be 'exterminated'. It was Stalin, though, that Shaw saw as the perfect embodiment of the modern leader. He had travelled to meet Stalin in 1931 and lauded the regime. He called the Soviet Union 'the most fortunate country on earth', and even nominated Stalin for the Nobel Peace Prize. (Stalin did not return the compliment – he regarded Shaw as an 'awful' man.) In October 1939, shortly after the outbreak of war, Shaw published an article that praised the skill by which Hitler had undone the peace settlement after the First World War, and called for an urgent negotiated settlement. As late as 1942, he was eulogising over Hitler's achievement in taking 'the courage of his convictions to a sublime height'.

Although not anti-Semitic, Shaw defended Germany's racial policies on the grounds that any country had the right to decide that Jews were, in his words, 'unfit to enjoy the privilege' of living there. He wrote in 1938 to socialist colleague Beatrice Webb that the Jewish question should be tackled by 'admitting the right of the State to make eugenic experiments by weeding out any strains they think undesirable'.

Duly Noted

As a commentator of influence, Shaw's early wartime utterances over Hitler undoubtedly caused the authorities unease. But he faded – he was in his mid-80s – and as Britain endured the Blitz, people made up their own minds about the Nazis. Had the German invasion come, he would have had his reward of sorts. When, after the war, the Allies discovered in the papers of SS Chief Heinrich Himmler the 'Special Search List', the compilation of 2,300 prominent people in Britain whom the Nazis would round up after a successful invasion, while many famous figures of the literary/political set were there (including Aldous Huxley, J.B. Priestley, Virginia Woolf, C.P. Snow, Noel Coward, Bertrand Russell, Harold Laski and not forgetting Beatrice Webb), Shaw's name was conspicuously absent.

A LOOK INTO THE FUTURE

We associate **H.G. Wells** with some of the most famous and mind-expanding science fiction of the early 20th century. *The First Men in the Moon, The Time Machine, The Invisible Man* and *The War of the Worlds* remain among the path-breaking works of English literature. To most, Wells stirred imaginations with such effect because his depictions of the possibilities of science seemed all too plausible. He is remembered as a far-seeing visionary on the technology front. It is fortunate that few picked up on his equally adventurous social views. His prognostications here were rather less heartening.

Like Shaw, he was an advocate of eugenics and population 'management'. His picture of the desirable future path of mankind was far from endearing. He first published his version of social utopia in 1901, having already achieved huge success with his fiction with eight novels, including all those mentioned earlier. He was thus someone whose writings people noticed. *Anticipations* was his first foray into non-fiction forecasting of what the world should ideally be like. He foresaw an end to the feckless, unguided democratic way of life. In its place – and he thought it would come within the next decade – Man's future rested on the emergence of 'an unprecedented sort of people' who, through social engineering (and more brutal methods) would create a homogenous society based on 'an ethical system which . . . will be shaped primarily to favour the procreation of what is fine and efficient . . . in humanity'. It would involve checking the growth of lesser types: 'the method that must in some cases be called in to the help of man is death.'

The World is Not a Charity

For anyone on the wrong side of Wells's vision, the prospects were full of foreboding. 'For a multitude of contemptible and silly creatures, fear-driven and helpless and useless . . . feeble, ugly, inefficient, born of unrestrained lusts and increasing and multiplying through sheer incontinence and stupidity, the men of the New Republic will have little pity and less benevolence.' It was clear who he had in mind. 'And for the rest – those swarms of black and brown and yellow people who do not come into the needs of efficiency? Well, the world is not a charitable institution and I take it they will have to go.'

And the method by which it could happen was clear too: 'This thing, this euthanasia of the weak and sensual is possible. I have little or no doubt that in the future it will be planned and achieved.' Some might be allowed to live, but 'only on sufferance, out of pity and patience, and on the understanding that they do not propagate; and I do not foresee any reason to suppose that [the New Republic's leaders] will hesitate to kill when that sufferance is abused.'

Anticipations was regarded by Wells as his 'first line of battleships' in the coming social struggle. That it received little attention among reviewers fortuitously allowed his ideas to fade into the background of Wells's reputation as the horrors of totalitarian regimes became clearer as the century wore on. They are now virtually forgotten amid the glowing legacy Wells enjoys as a creative visionary. When he died in 1946, his obituary in *The Times* ignored this darker side completely. It opined that 'his name and fame will live, no doubt, as a great public figure of his time, as an educational force . . . There was also a fundamental humanity'. His standing in history was thus set.

TRUE TO HIS WORD

The apogee of a poet's career in Britain is to be appointed Poet Laureate. **William Wordsworth** held the coveted honour for seven years between 1843 and his death in 1850. He initially declined the offer on account of his age (he was 73), and only relented when the Prime Minister Sir Robert Peel pressed, telling him it was Queen Victoria's personal wish and that nothing would be expected of him. Wordsworth took him and the Queen at their word. He refused the usual obligations of the post to write at the royal command for state occasions and, for the entire time of his laureateship, he did not produce a single piece of poetry.

MUM'S THE WORD

Author **Enid Blyton** penned some of the most popular children's stories of all time. She was a true literary phenomenon, writing over

600 books in all (at her peak, pushing out 59 titles in a single year). Generations of young Britons grew up between the Second World War and the 1960s with the exploits of *Noddy* and her *Famous Five* and *Secret Seven* series. For a writer apparently so adept in knowing how to interest and excite children, revelations 20 years after her death in 1968 put a surprisingly different slant on her character.

Her younger daughter, Imogen, published a memoir in 1989 of life with her mother that showed in contrast to expectation a very distant and unloving relationship. One review summed her up as '[coming] across . . . as ruthless, almost to the point of sadism'. She largely ignored her own two children and refused to read to them (bizarre for an author of children's books). The children were kept separate from Blyton's working life, never allowed to go into her workroom, and by this account emotionally starved. A literary critic concluded at the time of the revelations that this behaviour explains much about her stories. They were designed to do to young readers what she did to her offspring – 'to keep them imprisoned in a world of false childish emotions, away from . . . social and psychological realities' – a rather harsh and different appraisal to the warm and innocent image accepted over the decades and still likely to be the impression most have today.

BEHIND THE MAGIC

Walt Disney is another figure whom mainstream cultural memory defines in unambiguous terms. His name and work are the very epitome of sugar-coated, perfected innocence. The Disney brand is the byword for wholesome, spirit-raising adventure. Yet revelations 30 years after his death – a 1993 biography came labelled with the subtitle *'Hollywood's Dark Prince'* – has put a different gloss on cinema's archetypal maestro of fun.

Walt Disney was a deeply troubled individual, disturbed since his own childhood by an abusive father and later suspicions as to whether he had, in fact, been adopted. (In 1917, when he was 16 and wanted to enlist in the Army as America entered the First World War, he was told by his family that no birth certificate for him existed.) He never resolved these doubts, and they stirred a theme that would appear frequently in his most famous cartoons – the lost or parentless child motif crops up countless times, in *Snow White*, *Pinocchio*, *Bambi*, *Dumbo*, *Peter Pan*, *Lady and the Tramp* and *101 Dalmatians* to name a few.

A Cold Heart

Disney's personal anxieties also produced a cold-blooded attitude to others that was in stark contrast to the warm and cosy image publicly projected by his corporate persona. Behind the scenes at the magic factory, he ruled his studio with an authoritarian streak that was extreme even by Hollywood standards. His workers were forbidden to smoke or drink, and a peculiar prejudice forbade any employee from sporting facial hair. When some of his team produced a risqué cartoon involving Mickey and Minnie Mouse for a private showing to Disney to celebrate his birthday, he responded by instantly sacking all those responsible, and then left the room without another word. He was ruthlessly parsimonious in giving credit to his talented teams of cartoonists, cultivating an image that it was Disney alone who was responsible for all creative output. (He was, according to co-workers, in fact an indifferent artist.) When there were rumours after his death in 1966 that he intended to have his body cryogenically frozen, the joke ran round the studio that it was Disney's attempt to make himself a warmer human being.

He was always on the edge mentally, and had at least one breakdown. He was a heavy drinker and a favourite breakfast was doughnuts soaked in whisky. He was also an FBI informer. It seems he hoped the Feds could help track down the truth about his parentage. In return, he undertook to inform on Hollywood trade union activists and suspected Communists. After the Second World War, at the height of the McCarthy anti-Communist crusade, he enthusiastically testified to McCarthy's Un-American Activities Committee where he named some of his former animators as Communists, and accused them of fomenting strikes to disrupt Hollywood. The Committee described him for the record as 'a good witness'.

WHAT WOULD HOLMES HAVE THOUGHT?

Sir Arthur Conan Doyle, creator of Sherlock Holmes, may have amazed the reading public with his intensely rational approach to solving crime mysteries, but he had another deep passion which casts a very different slant on his attitude to life – he passionately believed in spiritualism, and once published photographs in the same magazine that had published his Holmes stories supporting the now infamous Cottingley Fairies hoax, in which two Bradford schoolgirls claimed to have photographed fairies in their back garden. He later followed this up in 1922 with a bizarre book, *The Coming of the Fairies*, in which he aimed to prove their existence.

He claimed there could be as many fairies as there were members of the human race. As well as a giving a spirited defence of the Cottingley girls' claims, Conan Doyle listed a multitude of other sightings of elves and goblins. These include the testimony of one correspondent who claimed them to be 'about 2 feet 6 inches to 3 feet in height, and dressed in duffle brown clothes'. Another witness had detailed a personal encounter in which they 'saw amid the obscure light and misty moonbeams what appeared to be a small Army of indistinct figures – very small, clad in gossamer garments. They appeared to be perfectly happy, scampering and tripping along the road'. Such evidence – and he quoted page after page of it – he declared demonstrated that there was 'a good deal of evidence which cannot easily be brushed aside as to the existence of these little creatures'. He then advanced the case for believing them not only to exist but to be bountiful throughout the world.

The fact that they could be photographed meant that they 'must of

242

necessity be physical'. Fairies were forms of existence 'whose bodies are of that rare tenuity and subtlety from our point of view that they lie beyond the range of our normal senses' using 'bodies of a density that we should describe, in non-technical language, as of a lighter than gaseous nature'. He then concluded with a worldwide gazetteer of the different types of fairy tribes inhabiting the globe, with their distinct characteristics, from the 'vivacious, rollicking, orange-and-purple or scarlet-and-gold manikins who dance among the vineyards of Sicily' to the 'lovely white-and-gold species' of California and the 'rich medley of gorgeously gleaming colours, almost barbaric in their intensity and profusion' to be found in India.

Wishful Thinking

Quite what possessed Conan Doyle to plunge so uncritically into this manic world of make-believe is difficult to say. He *was* a committed spiritualist – he joined the newly created Society for Psychical Research in 1883 when just 34. (His wife was an even more committed believer, claiming to be a conduit for messages from the afterlife of characters going as far back as Arabian scribes from 3000BC.) Like many others, these sentiments found new strength in the years just after the Great War, as survivors of the bloodletting sought to discover fresh perspectives on the human condition. Conan Doyle had lost a son and was desperate to establish contact with him in the afterlife through mediums. But the fairies episode was a sad extreme that attracted hostile views from some of his erstwhile literary admirers. Some observers of the Cottingley Fairies affair (which was only confirmed as a hoax in 1981) also suggest that Conan Doyle's avid advocacy of the girls' case contributed to them persisting in their claims longer than they might. They could hardly have expected to attract such a high-profile supporter. Confessing to trickery became all the more difficult when one of the nation's most famous personalities was arguing your case so strongly.

A PLOT THAT GOT OUT OF HAND

The most famous event in the life of **Agatha Christie** was her mysterious disappearance in 1926 when, for 11 days, the nation was held in a grip of intrigue about what had happened to the rising star crime novelist. (She was 36 and had just published her sixth book.) The discovery of her in a hotel in Harrogate, nearly 200 miles away from her Berkshire home, was always afterwards explained to be the result of her suffering temporary amnesia from a car accident. She maintained that she had had no idea who she was until hotel guests recognised her from the newspaper coverage and contacted the police. For the rest of her life, the accepted story was one of misfortune and ill luck. The truth, however, was actually very different.

Years of sleuthing by author Jared Cade produced in 1998, more than 20 years after Christie's death, the real explanation that turns out to have been every bit as calculated and cold-blooded as one of Christie's own ingenious plots.

Spoiling the Weekend

Her disappearance, far from an accident, was a deliberate trick to spite her husband Archie, whom, she had just found out, was being unfaithful. On the evening of Friday 3 December, knowing that he intended to spend the weekend with his mistress, Christie elaborately contrived to abandon her car in an isolated beauty spot near Guildford, leaving it dramatically hanging over the edge of a chalk pit as if the outcome of a mishap. She added a hint of mystery by leaving her fur coat in the vehicle. It was a cold night, so when the car was discovered the following morning, police inferred that the coat could not have been left there willingly.

Archie Christie duly had his weekend ruined as police probed the circumstances of his wife's departure and state of mind. It was known that the marriage was strained, and as the hours turned to days, Archie's anxiety grew that he may have pushed her to suicide. As the police investigated the car further, suspicions took an even more sinister turn. The car had been left in neutral, with the brakes off and

244

there had been no sign of skid marks on the gentle slope leading down to the edge. When police questioned the family's servants and established that the pair had had a major argument on the morning of the disappearance, they began to wonder whether they might be dealing with a domestic murder.

The Plan Misfires

All the while, Christie, with the help of her best friend, Nan Watts (who would be the one eventually to reveal the truth 70 years later), had made her way to Harrogate to sit out the escapade while her errant husband stewed. Nan had planned in advance that Christie should claim amnesia at the end of the episode to avoid awkward explanations. Agatha had written a letter to Archie's brother, deliberately sent to his work address in order to delay receipt by a few days, saying she was going to a Yorkshire spa. This she hoped would lead to her 'being found' in a few days – after sufficient discomfort to her husband. She had not counted, however, on the rabid press interest that made her front-page news for most of the next few days. What had been intended as a private quarrel had turned into a public cause célèbre. She therefore decided to keep her head down assuming she would be quickly located.

In the end, it would be 11 days before she was tracked down – for some reason, never explained, the letter to Archie's brother had not led to police picking up the trail to Harrogate – and it took the eagle eyes of two hotel guests to solve the mystery and make the first report to the local force. Christie appeared totally unsurprised when her husband confronted her, along with the Berkshire police, in the hotel lounge. The couple quietly had dinner where Agatha told her husband of the whole scheme. She was genuinely shocked and dismayed at the publicity that had occurred. This put a new gloss on the affair. It would ensure that her image would now be severely dented if the truth emerged. As Archie Christie, too, faced social ruin if the real story came out, the two settled on the mutually protecting accident and amnesia tale. Thus Christie's disappearance was explained, and a 70-year myth was born that successfully preserved reputations from a domestic tiff that had got out of control. The pair would divorce just over a year later (Archie married his mistress within three weeks of the split), and Agatha would enjoy an unblemished career until her death almost 50 years later. She would take her secret to the grave.

HIGHS AND LOWS

It is a commonplace observation that we know so little about the real life of **William Shakespeare.** Age-old and very familiar controversies will continue about whether he authored the plays that have come down to us in his name, or whether he was in fact a stooge for Christopher Marlowe, the true author, who needed cover to enable him to keep publishing in England after being exiled to the Continent for his own safety after his Government spying career had been exposed; whether he was gay; what he did in the 'lost' years between 1585 (when his twin children are recorded in the baptismal register) and 1592 (when he is first mentioned as a playwright in London), seven years for which no records exist; how he managed to get enough money by 1597 to buy a tenth share in the Globe Theatre and the second largest house in Stratford, all by the time he was just 33 – perhaps, it is thought, by being a surreptitious tutor to a wealthy Catholic family which would have put him at huge risk of persecution in this era of religious intolerance. All these will hang around the Shakespeare industry for a long time to come. Less familiar perspectives on his life do, however, from time to time emerge which give us a different view on what spurred his creative energies.

Smoked Out

In March 2001, South African researchers from the Transvaal Museum in Pretoria published the results of their analysis of clay pipes found in Shakespeare's home in Stratford-upon-Avon. They contained residues of cocaine, hallucinogenics and compounds created by burning cannabis. It raised the prospect that the Bard may have been fuelled by mind-bending drugs.

The discovery of cocaine was viewed as highly intriguing as it was the earliest known evidence of its use in Europe. It had been thought that it wasn't used in Europe until the 1860s. None of the pipes were definitely known to have belonged to Shakespeare, but the traces found in 24 fragments suggested that the smoking of substances other than tobacco was much more widespread than previously thought. Literary sleuths were quick to see references in Shakespeare's writings as supporting the thesis that he might have experimented in drugs to help his wordsmithing. They pointed to *Sonnet 27* in which Shakespeare refers to 'a journey in his head' and in *Sonnet 76* where he talks of the 'invention of a noted weed' and 'compounds strange'. Other mentions occur. Othello talks of 'thou weed who art so lovely fair and smell'st so sweet that the senses ache at thee'. And in *The Taming of the Shrew,* Vincentio calls over to a character, 'Come hither, crack-hemp.' Critics maintained it was all circumstantial. But with Shakespeare, much is, and always will be.

Bard to Worse

A new biography, also in 2001, painted an even less admiring portrait of him. Professor Katherine Duncan-Jones, an Oxford academic, presented the results of her research into Shakespeare's management of his financial affairs, and a very seedy picture it was. Instead of a popular and lauded hero of the people, he emerges as an elitist skinflint. Duncan-Jones described him as a tax dodger, hoarder, snob and a Scrooge willing to pursue the smallest debt through the courts. 'We all want to believe he was a nice chap,' she told reviewers, but 'frankly, I don't think the evidence supports that.' She referred to her examination of the archives as 'a grim experience'.

She cited records in the London borough of Southwark and the City of London showing Shakespeare to have failed to pay his parish dues. He appears to have managed to spend 25 years in London but never get his name down in the parish records, even though at times it was compulsory to register. In 1599, at a time of local famine, he was listed by a court in his Stratford home as hoarding malt and corn, a nasty anti-social deed in stricken times, and hopes for later profit-making could be the only explanation. Evidence from the will of a poor local farm worker that asked for monies owed to him by Shakespeare's wife to be paid to the poor of the parish could, Duncan-Jones interpreted, mean only one thing – that Shakespeare kept his own wife so short of cash that she had had to resort to borrowing, despite his own fame and wealth.

His elitism showed through when he gave his support to a rich Stratford landowner trying to enclose local common land that summarily ended the rights of the town's farmers to graze their livestock. Despite appeals to change his mind, he refused. 'This is one of the best-documented episodes in his life, and it is not a pretty tale,' said Duncan-Jones. 'He certainly wasn't anxious to please posterity.'

THE REAL TRAMP

The greatest comic genius of the silent movie era, **Charlie Chaplin**, gained rightful accolades for his performances on screen. The playful, innocent little tramp was cinema's first celluloid 'character'. It cast the mould in which history sees him to this day. However, in his personal life, Chaplin cut a distinctly different figure.

Within five years of arriving in Hollywood, having established his fame, his alter ego was also apparent. His love life was on the cutting edge of acceptability. He was, in the word of one 1997 biographical review, 'a sexually rapacious, mendacious and generally deplorable human being'.

Beginning in 1913 at Mack Sennett's Keystone Studios as a 24-year-old on a one-year contract at $150 a week, Chaplin shot to fame filming 34 comedy shorts the following year. By the end of 1915, his salary was $1,250 a week, at the time one of the highest in the world, and by following year he was commanding $10,000 a week (around $200,000 in modern values). In 1918 he married the first of his four wives, Mildred Harris, a 17-year-old actress. (He had been 'seeing her' since they had first met when she was just 14.) It lasted barely two years.

Continuing Scandal

He then married Lillita ('Lita') Grey, just 16, in 1924. He had first noticed her when she was only six. By the time she was 12 she was a starlet at Chaplin's studio and he first had sex with her when she was just 15, technically a statutory rape under California law. According to Lita, after bouts of energetic sex, Chaplin would set her school homework assignments. He was forced to marry her when she became pregnant the following year, and as they travelled home from their wedding in Mexico, he suggested she commit suicide by throwing herself off the train.

He divorced her two years later. During that time, according to divorce papers filed in court, he had had five mistresses. As part of the divorce settlement, he had to pay her $625,000 (about $7m today) to stop her naming them in public.

A third marriage, to Paulette Goddard, formally lasted seven years. He had met her in 1930 when she was 20, but only married her, in great secrecy, in 1936. He broke it off in 1942 and the next year married Oona, daughter of playwright Eugene O'Neill. She was just 17; by then, he was 54. She bore him eight children. By any measure today, Chaplin would have qualified as a paedophile.

The Great Dictator

Chaplin had other quirks that contrasted with his public happy-go-lucky demeanour. According to the comprehensive biography by Kenneth Lynn (1997), Chaplin could not bear to have other actors in his films be shown in close-up, and hated giving credits to others. He insisted on being the first guest to be invited and announced at any important Hollywood Party. He was also capricious if things went wrong on set. He once ordered a pet cat that had scratched him during a take to be killed and stuffed so it would not cause trouble in the re-shoot.

THE DREAM FACTORY?
NIGHTMARES ONLY

The excesses of Hollywood's stars and starlets have often been successfully covered up by their successful PR handlers so their charge's image remains a polished one for the fans. Sometimes, details slip out . . .

Money, Money, Money

Demi Moore quickly acquired from insiders the nickname of 'Gimme Moore' after her excessive foibles became too much even for an industry used to pampering huge egos. When promoting *Ghost*, the hit that gave her her big break in 1990, she insisted on being accompanied by an entourage of six, costing $10,000 a day. The team essential to her capacity to undertake her duties comprised a bodyguard, a masseuse, a hairdresser, a make-up artist, a wardrobe assistant and a personal assistant. When she arrived at a film festival in France she allegedly changed her suite of rooms because the colour of the décor did not match her clothes.

Rent-a-Crowd

At the other end of the scale, **Sir Richard Attenborough**, when directing his phenomenally successful 1982 film *Gandhi*, which grossed over $50m at box offices in the US alone, paid each extra in the epic funeral scene a fee of 40p. Mind you, there were 94,560 of them. Oddly, there were a further 300,000 volunteers who received nothing.

Persuasion

Director **Norman Taurog** only managed to get Jackie Cooper, his 10-year-old lead, to cry in the 1931 children's film *Skippy* by telling him that he would have his dog shot. He even got a security guard to take the pet away, telling the boy, 'The policeman's got your dog . . . and he's going to kill it because you won't cry.' A gunshot was heard, and Taurog told Cooper, 'He shot him because the dog distracts you.' At

250

this point, Cooper burst into tears and Taurog got his take. It also propelled Cooper to the youngest Oscar nomination for the next 40 years (Taurog got the Director's award). Amazing to think that Cooper was Taurog's own nephew.

Otto Preminger achieved the same effect among a group of child actors by telling them all that their mothers did not want them any more and that they had gone away forever. In *The Birds*, **Alfred Hitchcock** achieved the dramatic scene of the attack on the leading character by tying several live seagulls to Tippi Hedren's clothes with elastic bands and filmed them trying to escape. One nearly gouged out Hedren's eye. The scene had a permanent effect on Hedren, who fell out with Hitchcock over his methods. He threatened to ruin her career by holding her under contract but not using her. 'And he did,' she told an interviewer, reflecting on the episode 40 years later. **Orson Welles** got his celebrated drunk scene in *Citizen Kane* by keeping Joseph Cotton up the whole night before the shoot to get him disoriented.

Demanding Stars

MGM specified in its contract with **Joan Crawford** what time she had to be in bed. **Buster Keaton**'s trademark poker face in the 1920s was a contractual condition. MGM forbade him from smiling on screen. **Maurice Chevalier**'s contract with Paramount would be nullified if he ever lost his French accent.

Stars also managed to impose their idiosyncratic wishes. Silent-era star **Clara Bow** had written into her contract that no one within hearing distance on set could utter an expletive. 007 actor **Roger Moore** had a clause in every contract providing for a supply of hand-rolled Cuban cigars. Cricket fanatic **Trevor Howard**'s contracts exempted him from working on days when England were playing a Test match. **Steve McQueen** required his films to include shots of him naked to the waist. **Goldie Hawn** insisted in a contract that her bottom be prominently filmed during her performances.

Thirties' glamour star **Claudette Colbert** was a renowned beauty, but insisted on being photographed only on her left side. Studios had to build their sets with entrances specifically positioned to allow her

251

foible to be respected. **Marlene Dietrich** engineered her seductive sunken-cheeked look by having all her back teeth removed. **Carole Lombard**'s image was of an angel, but according to those who had experienced working with her, she 'swore like a sailor'. She was also so shy that she refused to walk anywhere in the studio without a publicist or secretary at her side. Despite the saccharine persona that **Julie Andrews** presents on screen, the inside story from her co-star of *The Sound of Music*, Christopher Plummer, was that working with her was 'like being hit over the head with a Valentine's card'. Film critic Leslie Halliwell once described her as 'like a nun with a switchblade'. When she played opposite Rock Hudson in 1970, 15 years before he died of AIDS and when his homosexuality was still a secret known only to the industry, she kept taunting him in public, 'Remember, *I'm* the leading lady.' **Robert Redford** would book whole rows of seats on aircraft when he travelled so he could avoid having to talk to other passengers.

Edward G. Robinson, who cornered the Hollywood market in the 1930s and 40s as the archetypal gangster hard man, reacted so strongly to loud noises in his debut 1931 film that thrust him to stardom that every time he had to fire a gun on-set, his eyes instinctively screwed up into a squint. After many failed takes, the practice began of taping his eyes open in order to keep a fixed face when he pulled the trigger.

Getting a Few Words in

Hollywood's obsession with keeping up with trends came under most pressure with the introduction of 'talkies' in the late 1920s. The sneakiest of ruses were used to cash in. **Gary Cooper** had just completed a silent picture, *The Shopworn Angel*, in 1927 as *The Jazz Singer*, the first talkie, was being released. **Paramount** instructed director Richard Wallace to add two lines of dialogue – fortunately, there was a wedding scene at the very end of the film. So Cooper and co-star Nancy Carroll say 'I do' to each other. 'On those four words,' Cooper later told an interviewer, 'the film was released as a talkie.'

252

Spending Wisely

Cooper himself was not beneath trickery. When filling up his car at petrol stations, he would invariably pay by cheque. Ecstatic pump attendants would seize the signed chit and declare they would frame it rather than cash it. Asked once how many of his cheques were ever presented for paying, Cooper slyly replied, 'About one in ten.'

A Fine Mess

Silent-era star **Stan Laurel** married eight times. Only four women were involved – two he married three times each.

Index